07/ 03N

D0859691

THINGS THAT COUNT

THINGS THAT COUNT

Essays Moral and Theological

GILBERT MEILAENDER

ISI BOOKS

Wilmington, Delaware

2000

Cataloging-in-Publication Data

Gilbert Meilaender, 1946—
 Things that count / by Gilbert
 Meilaender. —1st ed. —Wilmington, DE:
 ISI Books, 1999.

  p. cm.

 ISBN 1-882926-36-6
  1. Christian ethics. 2. Social ethics.
 I. Title

BJ1251 .M45 1999   00-64353
241—dc21   CIP

BOOK DESIGN BY MARJA WALKER

Published in the United States by:

ISI Books
P.O. Box 4431
Wilmington, DE 19807-0431
www.isibooks.org

Printed in Canada

CONTENTS

TO JUDY

Placetne, magistra?

PREFACE

The essays collected in this volume, written over a span of some fifteen years, are about "things that count" in life. Although the earliest was written in 1985, and although some are considerably more technical than others, they do, I think, have a certain coherence. And if they are not about everything that counts in life, they are, nonetheless, about much that is important. The essays are "moral and theological" in character. They focus, that is, on how we ought to live and who we ought to be, and they take up such questions, though not exclusively, from within the perspective of Christian belief.

The essays focus far more on the personal than on the political. They treat, in particular, the marriage and family bonds, and our sense of being located in particular communities. This should not be taken to imply that the political does not "count." On the contrary, it counts enormously. But it counts not in the way classical thinkers tended to suppose, as the arena for human fulfillment, but in the way Augustine supposes, as the arena that provides an ordered peace within which to pursue the rest of life. Hence, the essays in Parts I and

II reflect, from various angles, on the meaning of our sexuality, the bond of a man and a woman in marriage, the bond between parents and children, and some of the stresses and strains to which these bonds are subjected in our society. Likewise, the essays in Part III reflect upon some elements in everyday life, which also has its stresses and strains, joys and sorrows. The essays seek to learn from pain, to affirm the beauties of life, and to renounce even those beauties when and if they come between us and God.

Among the things that count in life are books! Not just books, of course, but their authors and those authors' ideas. The essays in Part IV are reviews, some of them quite long, of books, some of them quite long. At many points along the way, they take us back to themes from the earlier essays in Parts I-III: the limits of the political, the nature of the parent-child bond, the place of suffering in life, the power of possessions. The books discussed here are not all alike. Some are theological; others are not. A few of them are already important books; one has been for centuries. A few of them will never be important; one of them should not be. But all invite us to think, from one angle or another, about what counts in life.

Inevitably, readers will find some repetition scattered throughout the essays. We repeat what we know and care about, and some persisting interests of my own—in the thought of C. S. Lewis, in the place of everyday experience in the moral life, in the difference religion makes, in the meaning of friendship, in the limits of politics, in the fragile bond of the family—will crop up at various points along the way. This, I take it, shows simply that there has, in fact, been a single, somewhat coherent, mind at work in the essays—written, though they were, for quite different audiences at quite different times. And the themes treated here are, indeed, things that count. As Socrates says in the *Republic,* "we are discussing no trivial subject, but how one ought to live."

CREDITS

Although many of them have here been revised, the chapters in this volume have appeared previously in the publications listed below. Acknowledgment is made for permission to reprint them.

Chapter 1 appeared as "Men and Women—Can We Be Friends?" in *First Things*, No. 34 (June/July 1993).

Chapter 2 appeared in *Theology Today*, 50 (January 1994).

Chapter 3 appeared in *First Things*, No. 24 (June/July 1992).

Chapter 4 appeared as "The First of Institutions" in *Pro Ecclesia*, 4 (Fall 1997).

Chapter 5 appeared in *First Things*, No. 16 (October 1991).

Chapter 6 appeared in *The 9 Lives of Population Control*, ed. Michael Cromartie (Eerdmans, 1995).

Chapter 7 appeared as "Begetting and Cloning" in *First Things*, No. 74 (June/July 1997).

Chapter 8 appeared as "Abortion's Impact on Parenthood" in *The Lutheran Forum*, 23 (Advent 1989).

Chapter 9 appeared in *First Things*, No. 85 (August/September 1998).

Chapter 10 appeared in *First Things*, No. 47 (November 1994).

Chapter 11 appeared in *First Things*, No. 72 (April 1997).

Chapter 12 appeared in *The Preferential Option for the Poor*, ed. Richard John Neuhaus (Eerdmans, 1988).

Chapter 13 appeared as "Recovering Christendom," in *First Things*, No. 77 (November 1997).

Chapter 14 appeared in *First Things*, No. 54 (June/July 1995).

Chapter 15 appeared in *Religious Studies Review*, 16 (July 1990).

Chapter 16 appeared as "The Conditions and Limits of Tolerance," in *The Christian Century* (April 15, 1998).

Chapter 17 appeared in *First Things*, No. 5 (August, September 1990).

Chapter 18 appeared as "Professing Business: John Paul meets John Wesley," in *The Christian Century* (December 4, 1996).

Chapter 19 appeared as "One Soul in Bodies Twain: The Lure of Friendship," in *The Christian Century* (November 3, 1993).

Chapter 20 appeared without title in *Religious Studies Review*, 12 (January 1986).

Chapter 21 appeared in *The Christian Century* (May 16-23, 1990).

Chapter 22 appeared in *The Cresset* (October 1985).

Chapter 23 appeared in *The Cresset* (Christmas/Epiphany 1996-97).

PART 1

Men and Women

1

FRIENDSHIP BETWEEN MEN AND WOMEN

In Xenophon's *Oeconomicus*, Socrates and Critobulus are discussing household management, in which the wife plays a major role. The exchange goes this way:

> "Anyhow, Critobulus, you should tell us the truth, for we are all friends here. Is there anyone to whom you commit more affairs of importance than you commit to your wife?"
> "There is not."
> "Is there anyone with whom you talk less?"
> "There are few or none, I confess."[1]

Friendship between husband and wife is, of course, only one possible kind of friendship between the sexes, though an important one. But most classical thinkers (with the important exception of Epicurus) were inclined to think friendship between men and women impossible.

No doubt this can be accounted for in part, perhaps a large part, by social and cultural circumstances—differences in education, a public life from which most women were excluded, constant warfare that drew men away from home. In my own view, these circumstances have changed considerably, but not everyone agrees. Thus, for example, Mary Hunt, author of *Fierce Tenderness: A Feminist Theology of Friendship*, says: "Economic, political, psychological, and other differences between the genders result in the fact that women find it difficult to be friends with men and vice versa."[2] Though I think Hunt is somewhat mistaken about the reasons, it is true that the relation between the sexes is in our society a tense and often anxious one. It still makes sense to ask the classical question: Is friendship possible between men and women? Or, more modestly put, are there reasons why friendships between men and women may be more difficult to sustain than same-sex friendships?

FRIENDSHIP AND EROS

When we ask this question, the first problem that comes to mind is the one raised by Harry Burns in the 1989 movie *When Harry Met Sally*. In the opening scene, as he and Sally are driving together from Chicago to New York, Harry says: "Men and women can't be friends—because the sex part always gets in the way." Harry has a point—indeed, an important point. And, though I do not think that this is finally the deepest issue that confronts us here, I shall devote a good bit of attention to it.

Aristotle, whose two books on friendship in the *Nicomachean Ethics* are recognized almost universally as the most important pieces of writing on the subject, tends to agree with Harry. Aristotle recognizes, of course, that there is a kind of friendship between husband and wife, but it is one example of what he calls friendship between unequals. In such bonds the equality that friendship always requires can be present only if it is "proportionate" rather than "strict"—only, that is, if "the better and the more useful partner...[receives] more affection than he gives."[3] Still, of the three types of friendship that Aristotle discusses—based respectively on advantage, pleasure, or character—the highest, based on character, can exist even between unequals as long as the right proportion is present. And Aristotle seems to think that, given the necessary proportionate equality, such a character friendship is possible between husband and wife (cf. VIII, 12).

More generally, however, Aristotle suggests that a relation grounded in erotic love will not be the highest form of friendship. (When he takes up the question, he has in mind, it would seem, pederastic relationships, but this does not affect his view of the relation between *eros* and *philia*.) He distinguishes a bond like friendship, grounded in a trait of character and involving choice, from a bond grounded in an emotion (VIII, 5). And, while there can be friendship between lover and beloved, it will not be the highest form of friendship. It will be a friendship grounded not in character but in pleasure—and it is, therefore, likely to fade. "Still," Aristotle grants, noting how one sort of love may grow from another, "many do remain friends if, through familiarity, they have come to love each other's character, [discovering that] their characters are alike" (VIII, 4).

It is important to note that *eros* and *philia* are indeed different forms of love, even if they may sometimes go together. In *The Four Loves*, while making a somewhat different point, C. S. Lewis suggests the following thought experiment:

> Suppose you are fortunate enough to have "fallen in love with" and married your Friend. And now suppose it possible that you

were offered the choice of two futures: "*Either* you two will cease to be lovers but remain forever joint seekers of the same God, the same beauty, the same truth, *or else*, losing all that, you will retain as long as you live the raptures and ardors, all the wonder and wild desire of Eros. Choose which you please."[4]

In recognizing the reality and difficulty of the choice we discern the difference between the loves. That difference Lewis captures nicely in a sentence: "Lovers are normally face to face, absorbed in each other; Friends, side by side, absorbed in some common interest" (p. 91). Friends, therefore, are happy to welcome a new friend who shares their common interest, but *eros* is a jealous love that must exclude third parties.

Lewis believes that friendship and erotic love may go together, but in many respects he agrees with Harry and with Aristotle that the combination is an unstable one. He suggests that friendship between a man and a woman is likely to slip over into *eros* unless either they are physically unattractive to each other or at least one of them already loves another. If neither of these is the case, friendship is "almost certain" to become *eros* "sooner or later" (p. 99). This is not far from Harry's view of the matter. Having asserted that "men and women can't be friends—because the sex part always gets in the way," Harry adds a corollary when he and Sally meet again five years later: "unless both are involved with other people." But then, in one of his characteristically convoluted pieces of reasoning, he adds: "But that doesn't work. The person you're involved with can't understand why you need to be friends with the other person. She figures you must be secretly interested in the other person—which you probably are. Which brings us back to the first rule." A little more optimistic than Harry, Lewis suggests that lovers who are also friends may learn to share their friendship with others, though not, of course, their *eros*. Still, that does not address Harry's chief concern: the instability of friendships with members of the opposite sex when those friendships are not shared with one's beloved.

We ought not, I think, deny that friendships between men and women—friendships that are not also marked by erotic love—are possible. We ought not, that is, let a theory lead us to deny the reality we see around us, and we do sometimes see or experience such friendships. Nor need we express the view shared by Harry and Lewis quite as crassly as did Nietzsche: "Women can enter into a friendship with a man perfectly well; but in order to maintain it the aid of a little physical antipathy is perhaps required."[5] Nor, surely, need we hold, as my students occasionally have, that friendship between men and women is possible only if at least one of the friends is a homosexual (a view that will make same-sex friendships difficult for those who are homosexual, unless, of course, their experience of *eros* is in no way jealous or exclusive). At the same time, however, there is no reason to deny some truth to Harry's claim, even without the additional support of Aristotle and Lewis, for our experience also suggests that there is something to it.

The difficulties of combining *eros* and *philia* are the stuff of our daily life. Equalizing the relation of the sexes, bringing women into the academy and the workplace, has not made these difficulties disappear. Indeed, in certain respects they may have been exacerbated. Men and women are radically uncertain about how they are to meet in such shared worlds. Friendship requires an easy spontaneity, a willingness to say what one thinks, talk with few holds barred and few matters off limits—precisely the sort of thing that some will find difficult on occasion to distinguish from sexual harassment.

I have discovered that college students often wish to argue that Harry is wrong, that there need be no obstacle to friendship between the sexes. That may be, however, because they have great difficulty managing erotic attachments (which are quite a different thing from sexual encounters). Fearful of the kind of commitment *eros* asks of us—fearful of being drawn toward one who is completely other than the self but to whom the most complete self-giving is called for and before whom one therefore becomes vulnerable—they take refuge in groups of friends, hoping thereby to achieve what parents of forty years ago saw as the advantage of group dating: the domestication of *eros*. But *eros* is a wild and unruly deity, unlikely, I think, to be tamed so easily.

It is wiser to grant the point. Friendship between men and women will almost always have to face certain difficulties that will not be present in same-sex friendships. There will almost always be what J. B. Priestley calls "a faint undercurrent of excitement not present when only one sex is involved."[6] This may even give to the friendship a tone not easily gotten any other way. Thus, as Priestley again puts it: "Probably there is no talk between men and women better that that between a pair who are not in love, but who yet *might* fall in love, who know one another well but are yet aware of the fact that each has further reserves yet to be explored" (p. 59). Priestley offered this opinion in a little book titled *Talking: An Essay*, published in 1926 as one of several volumes in "The Pleasures of Life Series." But he might well have been describing what many viewers found appealing in *When Harry Met Sally*. In

one scene, Harry and his friend Jess are talking while hitting some
balls in a batting cage:

> Jess: "You enjoy being with her?"
> Harry: "Yeah."
> Jess: "You find her attractive?"
> Harry: "Yeah."
> Jess: "And you're not sleeping with her?"
> Harry: "I can just be myself, 'cause I'm not trying to get her
> into bed."

And yet, of course, not too much later comes the party at which
Harry and Sally dance together—and recognize the presence of
Priestley's "faint undercurrent," which we call *eros*. This is, let us
face it, a problem for friendships between men and women, even if
it may also be enriching. *Eros* always threatens; for, unlike friendship, *eros* is a love that is jealous and cannot be shared.

If we grant this, we may not agree with Mary Hunt, whom I
quoted earlier. She ascribes the difficulties facing friendship
between men and women to "economic, political, psychological,
and other differences"—unwilling, almost, to admit the power and
presence of erotic attraction between men and women in life.
When we consider the problems that men and women face in
forming friendships, we ignore *eros* at our peril.

THE SIGNIFICANCE OF SEXUAL DIFFERENCE

These problems go deeper, however, than the presence of erotic
attraction alone. They involve the very nature of the bond of friendship. The friend is, in Aristotle's influential formulation, "another

self" (IX, 4). At several points, Aristotle considers whether friend-ship is more probable among those who are like or unlike each other. And, although he notes defenders of each view, he holds that friendship "implies some similarity" and that in the highest form of friendship "the partners are like one another" (VIII, 3). In arguing that a person of good character should not—and ultimately cannot—remain friends with someone who becomes evil, Aristotle again appeals to the notion that "like is the friend of like" (IX, 3).

Anyone who reads Aristotle's discussion of the friend as another self is likely to find it puzzling in certain respects. It grows out of a peculiar treatment of self-love (IX, 4) as the basis of friendship, of love for the friend as an extension of the friendly feelings one has for oneself. And there are, in fact, aspects of his discussion that I would not claim to understand fully. What he has in mind, however, in depicting the friend as an alter ego is some-thing *we* might discuss in terms of the social origins of the self. The friend is the mirror in which I come to know and understand myself. I have no way to look directly at myself and must come to see myself as I am reflected by others—and especially, perhaps, by close friends. In the friend I find that other self in whom I come to know myself. That is why friendship "implies some similarity" and why, at least in the most important kinds of friendship, "the part-ners are like one another."

Friends wish, Aristotle says, to pursue together activities they enjoy. "That is why some friends drink together or play dice together, while others go in for sports together and hunt together, or join in the study of philosophy: whatever each group of people loves most in life, in that activity they spend their days together" (IX, 12). I myself think that Aristotle is largely correct here. We want in the friend someone who cares about the things we care about; yet we want the friend to be "another" who cares about these things, another with whom we can share them and with whom we come to know ourselves (and our concerns) better. The friend must be "another," but not entirely "an-other." Perhaps we do not, therefore, seek from the friend quite that sense of otherness that the opposite sex provides.

This takes us beyond the issue of erotic attraction alone—into much deeper, perhaps unanswerable, questions about what it means to be male or female. I do not know precisely how we can make up our minds about these questions today; we have a hard enough time just discussing them openly and honestly. A child of either sex begins in a kind of symbiotic union with its mother, without any strong sense of differentiation between self and mother. But as that sense of self begins to form, it develops differently for males and females. In attaining a sense of the self as separate and individuated, we take somewhat different courses. Thus, psychologist Lillian Rubin argues, boys must repress their emotional identification with their mother, while girls, though repressing any erotic attachment, can leave the larger emotional identification with the mother (and, more generally, other women) intact.[7] The process of becoming a self involves identification with those who can be for us "another self" without being completely "an-other"—those, as it happens, who share our sex.

This does not, in my view, mean that friendship between men and women is impossible. It does mean, though, that J. B. Priestley was right to say of their "talk": "It will be different from the talk of persons of the same sex." These differences are the stuff of bestsellers. Thus, for example, Deborah Tannen, who teaches linguistics at Georgetown University, could write a best-seller titled *You Just Don't Understand: Women and Men in Conversation*. Full of illustrations in which one often sees oneself, Tannen's book suggests that for men life is "a struggle to preserve independence," while for women it is "a struggle to preserve intimacy" and maintain connection.[8] The sort of problem this creates is illustrated clearly in a story Tannen recounts:

> Eve had a lump removed from her breast. Shortly after the operation, talking to her sister, she said that she found it upsetting to have been cut into, and that looking at the stitches was distressing because they left a seam that had changed the contour of her breast. Her sister said, "I know. When I had my operation I felt the same way." Eve made the same observation to her friend Karen, who said, "I know. It's like your body has been violated." But when she told her husband, Mark, how she felt, he said, "You can have plastic surgery to cover up the scar and restore the shape of the breast."
>
> Where she felt the need for understanding and sharing, he discerned a problem to be solved.

If this can sometimes be disconcerting, we need not be too serious. And these differences have provided the occasion for much humor. Dave Barry, the columnist, can title a column "Listen up, jerks! Share innermost feelings with her"—and most of us are likely to read it.[9] "We have some good friends," Barry writes,

> Buzz and Libby, whom we see about twice a year. When we get together, Beth and Libby always wind up in a conversation, lasting several days, during which they discuss virtually every significant event that has occurred in their lives and the lives of those they care about, sharing their innermost feel-

ings, analyzing and probing, inevitably coming to a deeper understanding of each other, and a strengthening of a cherished friendship. Whereas Buzz and I watch the play-offs.

This is not to say Buzz and I don't share our feelings. Sometimes we get quite emotional.

"That's not a FOUL?" one of us will say.

Or: "You're telling me THAT'S NOT A FOUL???"

I don't mean to suggest that all we talk about is sports. We also discuss, openly and without shame, what kind of pizza we need to order. We have a fine time together, but we don't have heavy conversations, and sometimes, after the visit is over, I'm surprised to learn—from Beth, who learned from Libby—that there has recently been some new wrinkle in Buzz's life, such as that he now has an artificial leg.

Our world is full of attempts, not always terribly humorous, to remove such differences from life. In Tannen's words, "Sensitivity training judges men by women's standards, trying to get them to talk more like women. Assertiveness training judges women by men's standards and tries to get them to talk more like men" (p. 297). Better, perhaps, she suggests, is to learn to understand and accept each other.

In this effort, I have found Priestley's old essay quite helpful. If talk between men and women is different from talk between persons of the same sex, it will not give the same kind of pleasure. But it may, Priestley suggests, compensate in other ways, and he suggests a kind of threefold movement in our friendships. The first condition of such talk is, he says, "that sex must be relegated to the background.... The man and the woman must be present as individualities, any difference between them being strictly personal and not a sexual difference. They will then discover, if they did not know it before, how alike the sexes are, once their talk has dug below the level of polite chatter and they are regarding the world and their experience together and not merely flirting" (p. 57). That is, to revert to the terms I drew from Aristotle, they must find in the friend another self, another individuality, but one whose otherness is not so overwhelming as to threaten to engulf or invade their selfhood. No doubt this is not always possible, for reasons we noted earlier when considering the impact of *eros* on friendship. But when, for whatever reason, "passion is stilled," men and women may meet as individuals who care about the same things or seek the same truth.

There may, however, be something dissatisfying about the suggestion that a crucial aspect of our person—our sexuality—must, as it were, be bracketed for such friendship to be possible. And this *would* be unsatisfactory, I think, were no more to be said. Priestley goes on, though, to suggest that friendship between men and women can go beyond the play of individual personalities. "Secure in this discovery" of how alike they are, men and women "will then go forward and make another one, for at some point they must inevitably discover how unlike the sexes are.... This double play, first of personality and then of sex, is what gives intelligent talk between men and women its curious piquancy." (57ff.).

In this second movement, when individual personality no longer brackets sexuality, Priestley ultimately discerns something more fundamental still—a third factor, which goes beyond the level of individual identity to a difference between the sexes. "Men frequently complain," he writes, "that women's conversation is too personal." And, even writing in an age that knew not Carol Gilligan, Priestley finds some truth in this judgment:

[Women] remain more personal in their interests and less concerned with abstractions than men on the same level of intelligence and culture. While you are briskly and happily
generalizing, making judgments on this and that, and forget-
ting for the time being yourself and all your concerns, they are
brooding over the particular and personal application and are
wondering what hidden motive, what secret desire, what sti-
fled memory of joy or hurt, are there prompting your
thought. But this habit of mind in women does not spoil talk;
on the contrary it improves it, restoring the balance.... It is
the habit of men to be overconfident in their impartiality, to
believe that they are godlike intellects, detached from desires
and hopes and fears and disturbing memories, generalizing
and delivering judgment in a serene midair. To be reminded of
what lies beyond, now and then, will do them more good
than harm. This is what the modern psychologist does, but
too often he shatters the illusion of impersonal judgment with
a kick and a triumphant bray, like the ass he so frequently is,
whereas a woman does it, and has done it these many centuries, with one waggle of her little forefinger and one gleam
of her eyes, like the wise and witty and tender companion she
is. Here, then, is a third kind of play you may have in talk
between the sexes, the duel and duet of impersonal and personal interests, making in the end for balance and sanity and,
in the progress of the talk, adding to its piquancy (p. 63ff.).

In this sense, friendship between the sexes may take us not out of
ourselves but beyond ourselves—may make us more whole, more
balanced and sane, than we could otherwise be.

FRIENDSHIP AND MARRIAGE

Indeed, I myself think that this is one of the purposes of friendship. By such teleological language I mean: one of the purposes God has in giving us friends. We are being prepared ultimately for that vast friendship which is heaven, in which we truly are taken beyond ourselves and in which all share the love of God. Something like this understanding of friendship, though without the strong theological overtone I have just given it, can be found in Katherine Paterson's *Bridge to Terabithia*—a book about, among other things, friendship, and a book that it would be misleading to describe simply as a children's book.[10]

The friendship in the book is between a boy and a girl, Jess and Leslie, though they are a little too young for *eros* yet for it to have an overt impact on their relationship. In different ways they are both outsiders in the world of their peers at school, and that very fact draws them together. They create—largely at the instigation of Leslie—a "secret country" named Terabithia, in which they are king and queen. This country—a piece of ground on the other side of the creek, to which they swing across on a rope—is, in Leslie's words, "so secret that we would never tell anyone in the whole world about it" (p. 38). And, at least at first, it must be that way. Were no friendships of theirs to be special and particular, were they to have no secret country that others did not share, they would never come to know themselves as fully as they do. Thus, for example, Jess finds that his friendship with Leslie opens up new worlds for him. "For the first time in his life he got up every morning with something to look forward to. Leslie was more than his friend. She was his other, more exciting self—his way to Terabithia and all the worlds beyond" (p. 46).

Jess says that Leslie is his way not only to Terabithia but also to "all the worlds beyond," but he learns that truth only slowly and with great bitterness. When the creek is swollen from a storm and Jess is gone, Leslie still tries to cross to Terabithia on the rope. It breaks, she falls onto the rocks and is killed. Grief-stricken and alone, without his alter ego, Jess can barely come to terms with what has happened. But he does, finally, and in doing so learns something about the purpose of all friendship.

> It was Leslie who had taken him from the cow pasture into Terabithia and turned him into a king. He had thought that was it. Wasn't a king the best you could be? Now it occurred to him that perhaps Terabithia was like a castle where you came to be knighted. After you stayed for a while and grew strong you had to move on. For hadn't Leslie, even in Terabithia, tried to push back the walls of his mind and make him see beyond to the shining world—huge and terrible and beautiful and very fragile? (p. 126)

To learn to see beyond our own secret countries—to what is at the same time both terrible and beautiful—is, from the perspective of Christian faith, the purpose of friendship. And to the degree that friendship, not only with those of our own sex but with those of the opposite sex, may more fully enable such vision, we have every reason to attempt it, despite its inherent difficulties.

We should not, therefore, underestimate the importance of the most obvious location for friendship between men and women: the bond of marriage. There are many differences between our world and that shared by Socrates and Critobulus. By no means least of

them is the formative influence of Christian culture, with its exaltation of marriage as the highest of personal bonds. To be sure,
precisely because the husband or wife as a friend is not only
"another self" but as fully "an-other" as we can experience,
friendship in marriage cannot be presumed. If there is any truth in
Lillian Rubin's analysis, each spouse may fear the otherness of the
partner and the loss of self that intimacy requires. The man fears
engulfment, "losing a part of himself that he's struggled to maintain over the years" (p. 24). The woman fears invasiveness that
threatens the boundary she has struggled to maintain between herself and others. Each is tempted to avoid such otherness, to settle
for a friend more like the self. But if we can overcome that temptation—in this case, perhaps, with the aid of *eros*—we may find a
bond that truly helps us see beyond ourselves, that makes us more
balanced and sane.

When Harry finally realizes that he loves Sally and wants to
marry her, he ticks off the reasons: the way she's cold when it's sev-
enty-one degrees outside; the way it takes her an hour-and-a-half
to order a sandwich; the way she crinkles up her nose when she
looks at him. All these might be the signs of an infatuated lover
looking at the beloved, not of a friend who stands beside the friend
and looks outward. But the last in Harry's litany of reasons is that
Sally is "the last person I want to talk to before I go to bed at
night." And J. B. Priestley—though worrying that spouses' lives
may be "so intertwined, that they are almost beyond talk as we
understand it"—has a view not unlike Harry's: "Talk demands
that people should begin, as it were, at least at some distance from
one another, that there should be some doors still to unlock.
Marriage is partly the unlocking of those doors, and it sets out on

its happiest and most prosperous voyages when it is launched on floods of talk" (p. 60).

In marriage, if we are patient and faithful, we may find that "balance and sanity" which friendship between men and women offers, and we may find it in a context where *eros* also may be fulfilled without becoming destructive. Against the view of Critobulus we may, therefore, set the wisdom of Ben Sira (40:23): "A friend or companion is always welcome, but better still to be husband and wife."

2

TOUCHED BY THE ETERNAL

No human being exists, or can exist, outside of or apart from relation to God. To try to think of human beings apart from the God-relation is, therefore, an exercise in metaphysical deception. To try to live as if that relation did not encompass us on every side is to fly in the face of reality, to live a lie.

This shared relation to God points to both the source and the goal of our life. As the source of our life, the Creator has bound us together, giving us what our purportedly postmodern world is increasingly reluctant to speak of—a universally shared human nature. Thus Augustine read the story of creation: "God created man as one individual.... God's intention was that in this way the unity of human society and the bonds of human sympathy be more emphatically brought home to man...."[1] As the source of our life, God has made us finite creatures, formed from the dust of the ground, occupying a limited time and space. As the goal of our life, God has made us for himself—free spirits who transcend any given time and space, because we are made to rest in him. This duality within our nature—our creation as both finite and free—locates one of the recurring issues for Christian reflection upon human nature.[2] But not the only one.

"The Dogma is the Drama," Dorothy Sayers once titled a short essay.[3] According to the church's dogmatic utterance, our Lord Jesus Christ, who is "begotten not made" and "of one Being with the Father," is also one who "for us and for our salvation came down from heaven, was incarnate by the Holy Spirit of the virgin Mary, and was made man." We cannot, therefore, ever fully comprehend the drama of human life apart from Jesus, in whom God takes our nature into his own life. And similarly, if we switch from that incarnational language to the equally dogmatic assertion that "on the third day he rose again in accordance with the scriptures," we will be driven to describe human nature and life not only in terms of this present evil age, but also of the age to come already present in the risen One. And again, we will be unable to express the full meaning of human life apart from its relation to the risen Christ, in whom that life is renewed.

Perhaps the oldest and most enduring problem for Christians seeking to talk about our shared human nature is finding a way to do justice to that nature as we know it without supposing that we can ever be whole or can flourish apart from the new life in Christ. Shall we pit created or unredeemed nature against the new life in Christ? Shall we suppose that created nature could, almost on its own, grow into what it is meant to be? Shall we suggest that our created nature is whole but incomplete, needing to be supplemented by the relation to God through Christ? Shall we argue that our created nature is always and continuously in need of transformation, as it is brought ever more fully into a right relation with God? Alternatives such as these have been the stuff of Christian ethics in the twentieth century—shaping discussion of the relation between *eros* and *agape* and, in a way that focuses more on structures and institutions, denoting different ways of relating Christ and culture.[4]

THE DISINTEGRATION OF A MARRIAGE

There are, then, two general issues that arise for Christians when they try to think of human beings always in relation to God. They must reflect upon our created nature in its freedom and finitude. And they must consider the relation of Christ to the moral life. I have no new insight to offer here on such general questions—and certainly no final word for what must continue to be an ongoing discussion among Christians. Instead, I will take a very narrow and particular road as my path into these large and persistent issues. For several years, in a course on moral problems, I have assigned John Updike's *Too Far To Go.*[5] A collection of short stories, the book chronicles the disintegration of the marriage of Richard and Joan Maple—and its end in divorce. The Maples prove unable to sustain their marriage through the whole of their lives; that is just too far to go.

The stories are told chiefly from Richard's point of view. I have never found it easy to like or even to sympathize with him, though at least some of my students react differently. That fidelity through time should be difficult for him is not surprising, since time itself always seems to be his enemy. Even quite early in their marriage, Richard begins to feel the pressure of sustaining commitment, and he finds the effort tiring. "Courting a wife takes tenfold the strength of winning an ignorant girl." Amid the mundane and deadening realities of daily life, he is one night "taken by surprise at a turning when at the meaningful hour of ten you come with a kiss of toothpaste to me moist and girlish and quick; the momentous moral of this story being, An expected gift is not worth giving." Richard evidently believes what the counselors who surround us on every hand say: We need change and variety if love is to survive. Indeed, he hypothesizes one day that "[r]omance is, simply, the strange, the untried"—a hypothesis likely to be devastating for the marriage vow.

The plumber comes one day—an old man working on pipes that his father had once installed in the Maples's house. He recommends a new pump with the assurance that it will "outlast your time here." And when he and Richard come out of the cellar into the sudden brightness of the day, "a blinding piece of sky slides into place above us, fitted with temporary, timeless clouds. All around us, we are outlasted." Yet Richard and Joan are unable to match the forces of nature, unable to make their love outlast pipes and pump.

As Richard rides the subway in Boston, getting the legal papers needed for the divorce, he reads a scholarly paper on the forces of nature. He reads of electromagnetic and gravitational forces, of strong and weak forces, and he thinks of life. "In life there are four forces: love, habit, time, and boredom. Love and habit at short range are immensely powerful, but time, lacking a minus charge, accumulates inexorably, and with its brother boredom levels all."

I have described this as the story of the disintegration of a marriage. That is, however, my description, not the author's. When Richard and Joan finally consummate their divorce in court, Updike creates a wedding tableau. Richard and Joan are each in turn asked by the judge whether they believe that their marriage has suffered irretrievable breakdown. Each in turn answers, "I do." And then, the divorce final, Richard remembers to do what he had, in fact, forgotten at their wedding: he kisses Joan. The scene has about it an air of triumph and completion, not failure or disintegration, and there are plenty of indications that Updike would have us read it this way. When Richard finally moves out of the house and takes an apartment in Boston, he one day discovers that the previous tenants of the apartment have scratched their names into the glass of a window, together with the vow: "With this ring I thee wed." And when Richard and Joan are having one of their giddy yet agonizing conversations after the separation, each seemingly happy, each communicating with words and gestures that years have made familiar, Richard reflects on one of Joan's gestures. "The motion was eager, shy, exquisite, diffident, trusting: he saw all its meanings and knew that she would never stop gesturing within him, never; though a decree come between them, even death, her gestures would endure, cut into glass." And, again, the suggestion seems to be that this is a marriage that succeeds even in separation and divorce.

EMBRACING TIME

In his foreword to the collection of Maples stories, Updike himself reflects on their meaning. "That a marriage ends is less than ideal; but all things end under heaven, and if temporality is held to be invalidating, then nothing real succeeds." When assigning these stories, I have regularly required that students write a short paper reflecting on this passage in the foreword. They are to consider whether the passage really captures the point of the stories. (And it need not, of course, since an author may not always know best what his stories mean.) They are also to evaluate the judgment Updike offers—that, because we are temporal beings, failure to sustain a commitment need not be "invalidating" and, even, that this marriage (as something "real" and not merely "ideal") succeeds.

Students, of course, have many different views. Some—a good number—will, in fact, agree with Updike. They will argue both that the stories support the claim in the foreword and that, in fact, his claim articulates the truth about human life. Nothing lasts, time and boredom do level all. Even if there is something sad in this, it is an accurate picture of human nature. They may also argue that this marriage has, in fact, been successful. Precisely because Richard and Joan have left their mark on each other, because Joan will never stop gesturing within Richard, they have achieved something. A number of students will take a different approach. They will not concede that this marriage should be termed a success, filled as it is with duplicity and selfishness. Nevertheless, these students also are reluctant to deny Updike his point. They hope they might one day do better than Richard and Joan, but they are reluctant to call the Maples's marriage a failure, since they agree that "all things end under heaven." Some marriages end in the death of a spouse, others in divorce, but all end. The difference seems less important than the commonality. One cannot equate a broken promise with failure, since temporality and change are the stuff of human nature and life.

Very few students flatly disagree with Updike's claim, though some will. But such an argument can be made—and should be. "Commitment," Margaret Farley writes, "is our way of trying to give a future to a present love."[6] Certainly commitment is not absent from the Maples's marriage, but commitment always involves our understanding of time, since it is an attempt to bind present and future together. And, Farley writes, "it is not immediately obvious whether commitment is, therefore, a way of resisting time (of making love endure in spite of time, as if there were no time) or embracing time (giving love a history by giving it a future)."[7] Updike's statement in the foreword seems to suggest that commitment could only be a way of resisting time, of acting as if there were no time. And that, he implies, would be to miss the texture of reality, which is incorrigibly temporal.

No doubt we can understand this and may ourselves have sometimes felt this way. There is, indeed, a sense in which commitment seems profoundly *un*natural to us. Thus, Denis de Rougemont could write that "men and women as they are now must look upon fidelity as the least of natural virtues.... In their eyes and as they put it, faithful marriage can only exist as the result of an inhuman effort."[8] To press this point too far, however, would be to suppose that human nature could be adequately described by reference to temporality alone; it would miss what Reinhold Niebuhr rightly termed "the basic paradox of human existence: man's involvement in finiteness and his transcendence over it."[9] For we are not only finite beings, ridden by time, but we also have, to some degree, the capacity to ride time, to give shape and unity to our lives. To fail even to see such possibilities for faithful commitment would itself be profoundly *un*natural.

Such failure will inevitably mean that we can imagine fidelity only as, in Farley's words, "a way of resisting time," of trying to live "as if there were no time." That is to say, having first accepted temporality as the sole law of our being, we will then be unable to imagine fidelity as anything other than an utter negation of what we are. Either we must be in time and our commitments must suffer alteration, or we must be more than human and untouched by change. Whatever the defects of his historical analysis, de

Rougemont sensed this. He suggested that in the myth of courtly love "Tristan is not in love with Iseult, but with love itself, and beyond love he is really in love with death...."[10] And it is striking to note that Richard Maple is as well. He has a recurring fantasy of his own funeral, of how the women he has loved will attend and weep "at his eternal denial of himself to them." This will, he fantasizes, offer "a satisfaction for which the transient satisfactions of the living flesh were a flawed and feeble prelude.... In death, he felt,...he would grow to his true size." Only in death will he be himself, for only then is he no longer subject to change and alteration. So he must long for death, since he cannot manage a steadfast fidelity within time. Unable to embrace time and give love a history by giving it a future, he must resist its movement. It turns out, therefore, contrary to what Updike writes in his foreword, that death—not temporal human life—becomes "real." Only in death do we reach our "true size." This is the result when we see only our finitude and make temporality alone the law of our being: Human life itself is negated. Perhaps, if we miss the possibility of fidelity within time, we miss the reality of human nature and life.

FIDELITY AS A HUMAN POSSIBILITY

This much we might suggest, simply on the basis of a consideration of our created nature as both free and finite. But those for whom the Christian dogma gives shape to the drama of life will want to say more. When Christ came into this world, he came to his own, John's Gospel says. The divine love, the steadfast commitment Christ displays, cannot therefore be entirely alien to the needs and possibilities of our human nature. Or, to turn again from the language of incarnation to that of resurrection, the risen Christ is Jesus of Nazareth. His resurrection is the vindication of the earthly life he lived as one of us, even if the resurrected life is not simply the natural completion or fulfillment of that earthly life.

Therefore, however contrary to our nature the marriage vow of lifelong fidelity may sometimes seem, however hard and "inhuman" we may sometimes find it, it is, in fact, the perfection toward which our nature is itself directed. "To be in love is both to intend and to promise lifelong fidelity. Love makes vows unasked; can't be deterred from making them.... Eros is driven to promise what Eros of himself cannot perform."[11] The marriage vow and marriage as an institution of agapeic commitment exist to help love reach the fruition toward which it is internally ordered.

It is true, of course, that a man or woman in love may find this hard to believe. When in love, we may think *eros* alone is sufficient to fulfill us. If so, we will soon enough learn how powerful time is. Having made *eros* our god, we will discover how demonic, taken by itself, *eros* can be. When in love, we may find the marriage vow intolerably stifling, since, by making love a duty, the vow seems to remove all spontaneity. In this sense, as de Rougemont noted, marriage may seem to us the grave of love.[12] Marriage may seem so, but it is not—or not only that. Christians should be able to imagine more, since they have been taught that maturity is measured by "the stature of the fulness of Christ," who is a living Lord. Not that we could, or should wish to, remove the mystery here—as if we could not understand how someone might think of marriage as the grave of love. For the mystery of human love perfected and completed by being taken into the life of God in Christ is the paschal mystery. "Perfection [of our love] always includes transformation," Josef Pieper writes. And "this transformation perhaps resembles passing through something akin to dying.... Thus it is much more than an innocuous piety when Christendom prays, 'Kindle in us the fire of Thy love.'"[13] "Perhaps later on," de Rougemont notes, on the other side of that transformation that may seem akin to dying, "a man or woman may find that the happiness he or she has forgone is being restored, even as Isaac was restored to Abraham. But this can only happen if he or she has not expected it."[14]

We must grant the mystery: fulfillment may come the other side of sacrifice. Nevertheless, the possibility of such steadfast commitment cannot be entirely alien to our nature—not if, as the Athanasian Creed teaches, the incarnation means that "God has taken humanity into himself," though without transforming deity into humanity. Were we to look simply at our own possibilities and inclinations, lifelong fidelity might well seem an alien ideal—not suited for our nature, too far to go. The marriage vow would then quite rightly seem irrational. As a prediction rather than a commitment, it could make little sense, at least in our world. Asked to promise lifelong faithfulness, we could only look at the statistics and the experience of our friends and calculate our chances. Indeed, in such a world it would seem almost wrong to ask anyone to make such a vow, if we think simply in terms of what is reasonable to predict "in this nation of temporary arrangements" (as Updike puts it in one of the Maples stories). This, however, would be to isolate our nature from the relation with God established in our creation and affirmed and redeemed in the incarnate and risen Christ, as if we had not been touched by the Eternal. To suppose that we could thus isolate and abstract our nature from the God-relation is to get human nature wrong—and to live a lie. Again, de

Rougemont is on target: "When a young engaged couple are encouraged to calculate the probabilities in favour of their happiness, they are being distracted from the truly moral problem."[15] Which is: they are being offered the possibility of commitment. If they suppose that they are being asked only to predict the likelihood that their marriage will endure, they miss the call to covenant—"the decision in itself is made to seem secondary or superfluous."[16] They are simply ridden by time.

This claim is not intended as a denial of what is also true of our human nature, that we sometimes fail in our commitments and cannot sustain them. We live in the tension between this present evil age and the age to come already inaugurated in the resurrection of Christ, and we must live in hope. As we are always still "on the way" and in need of transformation and perfection, we may sometimes experience that transformation as something akin to dying. Commitment is, in Margaret Farley's words, "love's way of being whole when it is not yet whole, love's way of offering its incapacities as well as its power."[17] But whatever our weaknesses, they alone do not ultimately define human nature. We are both finite and free. We are constituted by our finite attachments and commitments, but they cannot stand alone. They must be drawn into the transforming power of God's love. And they can be, for our nature has been taken into the divine life through Christ. The "real" is not the temporal taken by itself but the temporal bond transformed by God's love. It is the glory and the terror of marriage that in it we attempt to let our earthly commitments be touched and transformed by the Eternal. And it is very much in accord with our nature that we should learn again to pray: "Kindle in us the fire of Thy love."

3

MARRIAGE IN COUNTERPOINT AND HARMONY

If one were to seek a connecting thread that runs through the biblical witness, a good candidate would be "faithfulness." Robert Jenson has written that faithfulness is "the theological heart of the Bible," and that, in turn, marriage is "the paradigm case of an ethic of faithfulness."[1] But in a creation marred and distorted by sin, this faithfulness is always threatened. The sword is placed not only at the entrance to the garden but also between the sexes—and, even, between husband and wife. What Karl Barth characterizes as our "being-in-fellow-humanity," our creation as male and female signifying that we are made for covenant community with each other (and, ultimately, with God), becomes a source of misunderstanding, tension, rivalry, and anger.[2] As the curse of Genesis 3:16 puts it: "Your desire shall be for your husband, and he shall rule over you."

Marriage is, therefore, a sphere of life in which we must struggle to enact our faithfulness. Here we learn what a price permanent, faithful commitment to just one person who is completely other than ourself may exact. Nevertheless, in this earthly bond we are called to be images of the love God wills for the creation and bestows upon humankind in Jesus. "This mystery is a profound one, and I am saying that it refers to Christ and the church."[3] Of course, not all are called to marriage, and Barth is correct to see in it the typical but not necessary expression of our being-in-fellow-humanity; yet, in this bond, many—perhaps most—of us begin to learn the meaning of mutuality in love.

It has, therefore, become something of an embarrassment that the biblical words that most clearly establish Christ's faithful love for the church as paradigmatic for the marital bond, words that depict the bond of husband and wife as one of mutual love in which equal submits to equal "out of reverence for Christ," should also be words that enjoin the husband to be Christlike by being "the head of the wife as Christ is the head of the church."[4] If, however, we want to explore the meaning of marriage as a sphere of faithfulness, a covenant community in which a man and a woman begin to learn the meaning of faithful obedience, it is imperative that we consider the problems raised by these words in Ephesians 5. Any full treatment of marriage would, of course, be far more extensive, but our concern is a narrow one: to explore the bond between husband and wife in which they attempt to forge a union in which each submits to the other but neither tries to occupy the place of the other. The standard set forth in Ephesians 5 seems to suggest that within a partnership of mutual subjection there will be different parts to play. The union of husband and wife is to be a sharing among those who remain as different as their biological structures are different, though as complementary as those biological structures are complementary.[5]

COUNTERPOINT AND HARMONY

This is certainly not the only kind of union we might imagine. Consider an alternative very nicely displayed by Dorothy L. Sayers in one of her detective stories, *Gaudy Night.*[6] The story is far more than a mystery, and one of its central themes is the relationship between Lord Peter Wimsey and Harriet Vane. He had once saved her life when she was unjustly accused, and she is now unable to avoid the feeling that she owes her life to him. Wimsey is madly in love with Harriet, but she fears commitment, believing that it must inevitably involve dependence and loss of self. Out of a sense of obligation she will give herself to him if he wishes, but then, of course, it will not be the kind of giving he desires. Eventually the two elements in the plot—the mystery and the love story—come together. Wimsey, determined not simply to possess Harriet, permits her to endanger herself and risk her life investigating the mystery. He resists the impulse to solve it for her—as, it turns out, he could have—and in so doing offers back the life she felt she owed him.

This is more than a touch of romance to spice up a story; it is Sayers's depiction of the ideal relationship between a man and a woman. In one musical metaphor, in particular, she brilliantly captures her ideal. Peter is being his most eccentric self—playing the piano and singing to Harriet while waiting for a shopkeeper to box a chess set he has bought. Harriet joins in. They begin singing some of Morley's *Canzonets for Two Voices.* Peter tells Harriet that she can sing, "[w]hichever part you like—they're exactly the same."

> "This kind of thing," said Peter, as tenor and alto twined in
> a last companionable cadence, "is the body and bones of

music. Anybody can have the harmony, if they will leave us
the counterpoint."[7]

Sayers returns to this musical image at the end of the story, shortly
before Harriet accepts Peter's proposal. They attend a concert at
which Bach's Concerto in D Minor for two violins is being played.
Wimsey is absorbed in the music. Harriet

knew enough, herself, to read the sounds a little with her
brains, laboriously unwinding the twined chains of melody
link by link. Peter, she felt sure, could hear the whole intricate
pattern, every part separately and simultaneously, each
independent and equal, separate but inseparable, moving over
and under and through, ravishing heart and mind together.

She waited till the last movement had ended and the
packed hall was relaxing its attention in applause.

"Peter—what did you mean when you said that anybody
could have the harmony if they would leave us the counterpoint?"

"Why," said he, shaking his head, "that I like my music
polyphonic. If you think I meant anything else, you know
what I meant."

"Polyphonic music takes a lot of playing. You've got to
be more than a fiddler. It needs a musician."

"In this case, two fiddlers—both musicians."

"I'm not much of a musician, Peter."

"As they used to say in my youth: 'All girls should learn
a little music—enough to play a simple accompaniment.' I
admit that Bach isn't a matter of an autocratic virtuoso and a
meek accompanist. But do you want to be either? Here's a

gentleman coming to sing a group of ballads. Pray silence for the soloist. But let him be soon over, that we may hear the great striding fugue again."[8]

The point is clear and the image a memorable one. In counterpoint two independent melodies interweave. It does not offer the independence of the soloist; yet the unity it offers is quite different from that of harmony. Neither of the independent melodies in counterpoint depends upon the other; that is, each could stand alone as an independent piece. Yet, together they are in some way enriched. Harmony, by contrast, suggests a kind of interdependence; neither part could very satisfactorily stand alone. And it is counterpoint, not harmony, that Sayers offers as an image for the proper relation of husband and wife.[9]

This provides us with a clear—and alluring—alternative to the one seemingly presupposed in Ephesians 5. It is alluring precisely because it offers an image by which we can envision the bond of husband and wife as a union involving genuine exchange, yet a union of two equal and independent beings. Is this good enough for Christian thought? It may, of course, have to be. Certainly it is better than some of the current alternatives available in our society. There is, for instance, a radical feminism that pictures the male-female relation as one of unrelieved oppression and that tends to be separatist over against men. Thus, for example, Janice Raymond has argued *against* a feminism that seeks equality of women with men. To aim at that is already to cast one's thinking in terms of "hetero-reality": the view that woman exists always in relation to man. Instead, Raymond argues, women must begin the companionship of self and those like the self—with "the autonomy, independence, and love of the female Self in affinity with others like her Self—her sisters."[10] About such an alternative, Christians who see in the community of male and female the paradigmatic expression of our creation for covenant community must say with philosophers Mary Midgley and Judith Hughes: "A project whose only live example is apartheid can scarcely be a hopeful one."[11] Sayers, by contrast, offers a vision far more Christian, and it may be that in the years ahead we shall simply learn from experience whether it is adequate. Human reason may gradually come to understand more fully the meaning of our creation for co-humanity as male and female. In the present moment we can only think tentatively about the sort of union Sayers envisions, probing its fitness.

What, if anything, does it lack that a Christian understanding might need? What it lacks—and lacks intentionally—is an appreciation of marriage as communion between those who are not interchangeable and who, in their otherness, are interdependent. It is marriage so understood that begins to teach us the meaning of faithful commitment to the One who is The Other, for communion with whom we are created. In counterpoint the two melodies are joined, and their union is a lovely one, but either could stand alone as an independent piece. They are essentially interchangeable, as Peter says to Harriet: "Whichever part you like—they're exactly the same." The imagery cannot work perfectly for marriage, of course, since husband and wife are, at least, biologically other. What may give Christians—and some who are not Christians— pause, however, is that the biological differentiation seems to count for so little here.

Christians have struggled often and in many different settings against their own recurring tendency to deprecate our creation as embodied beings. It has been a constant struggle to remember that we are to find personal significance in that embodied condition, to affirm and value it. And it is the body, the bodily differentiation between husband and wife, that signifies the extent and difficulty of the project they are called to undertake: to be faithful to one who is not a mirror of the self; one not fully fathomable; one who is harsh, resistant, other. To care about such a one, to be faithful to such a one, to be at peace in communion with such a one—that is the fundamental meaning of marriage and the task spouses undertake. It should be no surprise that we often flee the task—if not literally, then at least by refusing to let the spouse stand forth in his or her otherness. But in fleeing it we lose the meaning of embodiment, of our creation as male and female.

The image of counterpoint that I have drawn from Sayers can make relatively little of this biological differentiation—and, hence, of the task that flows from it. The distinction will, of course, play a role in reproduction, but the assumption—extraordinary if we think about it—seems to be that everything bodily about us could be different, yet everything remain the same in the cultural sphere. Every cell in our bodies is sexed; yet the human person—the real person—is thought of as untouched by such bodily influence.

Seeing this we begin to comprehend how deeply implicated is Sayers's ideal in the modern Western affection for individualism and autonomy. Thus, for example, Midgley and Hughes write: "We have a choice. We can either extend the individualism which has been a religion in the West since the eighteenth century consistently to *both* sexes, or we can admit its limitations, treat it with more caution, and put it in its place as only one element in a more realistic attitude to life for everybody."[12] Thus also theologian Lisa Sowle Cahill also characterizes the androgynous ideal as a new version of "the liberal ideal of the autonomous agent, unconstrained—indeed undefined—by any significant communal or physical boundaries."[13]

And because it gives relatively little significance to our creation as embodied male and female, Sayers's vision inevitably transforms somewhat the task that marriage involves. The project is not that of shaping a union in which we learn the meaning of faithfulness to one who is other than ourself and in which, by being ourself and permitting the spouse to be himself or herself, we become the image of our fellow humanity; rather, the task is to gain the pleasures of submission without relinquishing independence. A difficult task, to be sure, but perhaps not clearly a school in which the meaning of faithfulness is as readily learned.

MAKING SENSE OF "HEADSHIP"

It is, of course, no great trick to discover something that may be lacking in a position. Far more difficult is finding a better alternative. We can consider both the promise and the problem of alternatives by looking at two such views. In each there is an attempt to make some sense of the "headship" Ephesians 5 ascribes to the husband and to explain its place even within a bond of equal partners. Consider the following two passages:

> **(1)** The need for some head follows from the idea that marriage is permanent. Of course, as long as the husband and wife are agreed, no question of a head need arise; and we may hope that this will be the normal state of affairs in a Christian marriage. But when there is a real disagreement, what is to happen? Talk it over, of course; but I am assuming they have done that and still failed to reach agreement. What do they do

next? They cannot decide by a majority vote, for in a council of two there can be no majority. Surely, only one or other of two things can happen: either they must separate and go their own ways or else one or other of them must have a casting vote....

If there must be a head, why the man?... The relations of the family to the outer world—what might be called its foreign policy—must depend, in the last resort, upon the man, because he always ought to be, and usually is, much more just to the outsiders. A woman is primarily fighting for her own children and husband against the rest of the world. Naturally, almost, in a sense, rightly, their claims override, for her, all other claims. She is the special trustee of their interests. The function of the husband is to see that this natural preference of hers is not given its head. He has the last word in order to protect other people from the intense family patriotism of the wife.[13]

(2) This freedom of decision granted to the wife, which frees her from the one-sided authority of the husband, cannot mean that the wife can make her decision in the name of her own individuality and its untrammeled development. On the contrary, she is bound to bring her work and the choice of her domicile into harmony with the primary obligation which is laid upon her by responsibility as a wife and mother. In this case her equality of rights can mean only that the husband cannot settle the question of the wife's working and domicile on his own authority, but rather that the wife makes this decision on her own responsibility....

The freedom granted to the wife by the principle of equal rights therefore cannot mean an emancipation from the marriage and the obligation to seek the building of a common will on the part of the spouses. Rather this freedom can mean only that this common will cannot be one-sidedly dictated by the husband, but must be achieved in partnership....

These problems naturally come to a critical point in the borderline cases. What happens when a meeting of minds does not take place? What happens, for example, when the spouses make different decisions about two possible places to domicile?...

The...problem [of] the rearing of the children makes far more difficult...demands upon the interpretation and administration of the principle of equal rights. In this case too the problem becomes more acute in the borderline cases, namely, when united educational authority of the parents is jeopardized by differences of opinion between the married partners....

In the "normal" cases it would be a matter of the parents' arriving at a common agreement through discussion. In the "borderline" cases, where there is disagreement, however, it would be inevitable that one of the parents should have the right to make the final decision.... At this point where a choice simply *has* to be made and where the exceptional character of a borderline situation prevails, a theological ethics cannot abstain from declaring, in line with the tradition of Christendom based upon the Holy Scriptures, that the father holds the final decision. Though it is true that the New Testament does not recognize any spiritual subordination of the wife to the husband...it nevertheless upholds this subordination in the earthly affairs of marriage....

And even if it does come to the point where the borderline situation exists, and the father exercises his right to make
the final decision, it is important that the responsible person
is one who is constantly aware of the other person in the marriage itself and must accept the consequences of his decision
while continuing to live with the other partner.[14]

For each of these authors—C. S. Lewis and Helmut Thielicke
respectively—it turns out to be no accident that the New
Testament passage that most clearly articulates the call to
Christlike faithfulness within marriage should, at the same time,
speak of "headship" in the marriage. The fundamental assumption—and by far the most important claim—is that husband and
wife should be committed to a permanent, lifelong union. They are
not to imagine that they could "separate and go their own ways."
They must make decisions "while continuing to live with the other
partner" and taking account of the need to make such a shared life
possible. This is the ground floor on which each of these discus-
sions of headship rests. Both Lewis and Thielicke seem to care
about headship chiefly because they discern a connection between
it and the permanence of the marital bond. Without a commitment
to permanence, they would simply accept the fact that, under certain circumstances, spouses—unable to be reconciled to the "otherness" of the partner—would agree to disagree and go their
separate ways. This suggests, in turn, that a culture not committed
to permanence in marriage—or committed to it as little more than
a fond dream, nice if one can manage it, but not the ground floor
on which all else is built—is unlikely to be able to make much
sense of headship in marriage.

Even if a commitment to lifelong fidelity were to require headship, however, why should the lot always or ever fall to the husband rather than to the wife? She may, after all, be more astute, more judicious, or more responsible. At this point Lewis and Thielicke part company, offering quite different rationales. It may prove instructive to consider each briefly.

Lewis grounds the husband's headship in a certain trait that he considers more characteristically masculine than feminine: namely, the tendency to adopt a relatively more universal, disinterested, and impartial stance toward those with whom one stands in no special bond. That is to say, he thinks that justice will be best served in this way. Lewis's argument is, it seems to me, rather wooden. But when we concentrate on the particular reason he gives, it is thought-provoking to see how analogous it is to certain moves in recent feminist thought. What we should make of this I don't know, but the connections are intriguing to contemplate. Most well known, for example, are the claims of Carol Gilligan about differences in moral development and moral reasoning in males and females. These are, it is important to see, *differences*— not superiorities or inferiorities. Gilligan is interested in exploring two different modes of moral thought that, as it happens, seem empirically to be somewhat correlated with gender.[15]

Gilligan's studies had as their central point the questioning of Lawrence Kohlberg's theory of moral development. For Kohlberg the highest stage of moral development involved reasoning that is in accord with principles of universal applicability, principles that leave no room for special preferences or connections—in short, for a justice that abstracts from the particular web of relationships connecting one life to another in special ways. The paradox that triggered Gilligan's concern and study was this: the nature of women has often been associated with traits emphasizing attachment, intimacy, caring, etc. Yet these are the very traits that signify a deficient—because less than impartial—moral development for one who thinks in Kohlberg's terms.[16]

At her best, Gilligan discerns two ways of thinking morally, each of them important, neither necessarily superior to the other.[17] These are an "ethic of justice" and an "ethic of care." The former emphasizes rights, equally shared by all, whether near or far. The latter emphasizes a contextual mode of judgment, bound to the particulars of time and place. These are, she says, "two different moralities whose complementarity is the discovery of maturity."[18] Or perhaps, we might add with Lewis in mind, the discovery of a good marriage.

In a somewhat similar vein, Carol McMillan suggests that our tendency to think of reason only in terms of universal abstract cognition has ignored or failed to appreciate the more characteristically feminine way of reasoning—one that does not picture affection and emotion as irrational.[19] We have tended to use a term like "intuitive" to describe such reasoning, thereby suggesting a certain immaturity or undeveloped character. By contrast, McMillan argues that to call knowledge intuitive is only to focus attention on the way in which a particular set of facts strikes a particular person. It does not imply that there has been no process of thought involving sustained effort. It simply emphasizes a kind of learning that happens in a distinctly individual—rather than universal—way.[20] And she argues, in turn, that it is very important that women should think and learn to think in this way.

It is crucial that, for the most part, women are taught to think at the level of the particular and the affective because the relationship between mother and child is a relationship between two individual human beings. The mother loves her child (or is expected to) simply because it is her child, and equally the child loves its mother (or is expected to) simply because she is its mother. And however primitive or instinctive the relationship between mother and child may seem to us, it never occurs automatically. If the conceptual background and the affective surroundings that make it both possible and intelligible for a woman to take up an attitude of love towards her infant are not present, there will be no such love.... Deep maternal love is a possibility for many women in our society only because of the way we think and act in all sorts of other situations.[21]

Whatever their differences, Gilligan and McMillan are alike in this way: They do not respond to male domination by asking—or demanding—that women learn to think like men. Neither do they argue that, since male ways of organizing human life have exacted so great a price, it is good to think like a woman, however undeveloped or irrational such thought may seem. Rather, they affirm two ways of thinking in their respective otherness *and* complementarity. Benjamin Barber has described five premises of such thought:

(1) It holds that men and women are biologically differentiated in ways that condition our moral development and social institutions. These cultural distinctions built upon biological

differentiation are not wholly inevitable, but neither can they be eradicated.

(2) These differences are, in fact, "life-enriching" and should be cultivated.

(3) Androgyny is undesirable in its "homogeneous uniformity."

(4) Women's special connection to "generativity, nurturing, and affection" gives them "a unique appreciation of (and responsibility for) the ethics of caring and of affiliation indispensable to the preservation of a civilization."

(5) The quest for justice should not be a search for symmetry. "Instead, ways must be found to preserve (or create) political and economic equality in the face of differing social roles, distinctive gender needs, and contrasting, if (ideally) complementary approaches to moral development and reasoning."[22]

It is, of course, improbable that either Gilligan or McMillan would be greatly attracted to the language of headship within marriage. Nor do I know that either would think of commitment to lifelong fidelity as basic to the marital bond and related to headship in the way it is for Lewis and Thielicke. Nonetheless, it is striking to see the congruence of their arguments with what I have termed Lewis's rather wooden suggestion. They put some flesh on the bones of that suggestion, making it seem less like an example of misogyny and more like an insight.

All this should not blind us to the dangers in Lewis's approach. I recall the frustration I experienced the first time I read Karl Barth's discussion of marriage (and headship) in Volume III/4 of his *Church Dogmatics*. Many have been frustrated by that discussion, of course, but for most the frustration arises simply from Barth's insistence that there must be headship—an "order" of "preceding and following" in the relation of husband and wife.[23] But if we get out of our contemporary skins enough to grant Barth that point, we might still be frustrated that he should insist on the necessity of such order while refusing to say anything specific about what the order should be like. To be sure, the husband precedes; the wife follows. He imitates the attitude of Christ; she the attitude of the community. But Barth will at once add: "In carrying out this imitation, which of the two cannot be described as both preceding and following?"[24] There must, he insists, be this order; yet it seems he can say almost nothing about its form or shape.

It is, of course, hardly likely that Barth was too timid to set himself against the current of opinion already growing in his day. The hesitation is, I think, grounded elsewhere: in Barth's rejection of "every phenomenology or typology of the sexes," even those he personally found rather persuasive.[25] Such rejection is, in his view, required if we are to remain open to the divine command. Any typology of gender roles within marriage would seem to enable us to specify in advance appropriate activity for husband or wife— thereby undercutting the freedom of the Divine Commander.[26]

I am inclined to put the matter somewhat differently. Any such typology will be grounded in our embodied nature, and we have already granted the importance for Christian thought of taking that embodiment seriously. But the human being is not only finite body. We are also free spirit—with a freedom that is constantly transcending old limits and adding new and unforeseen contours to human life. We are nature—but also history. Christian thought must always struggle to hold the two together, lest it should fail to affirm the wholeness of our created being. This means, when thinking about sexuality, that we should trust that the meaning of our life as masculine or feminine cannot be severed from our creation as biological male or female. But it also means that our respect for human freedom should make us hesitant to affirm too quickly—whether with Lewis, Gilligan, or McMillan—many limits on the historical permutations that gender distinctions may take. To that degree one might say with Barth that "we can here only ask questions to which ethics can give no answer in advance."[27]

This suggests that we ought to consider the other attempt—by Thielicke—to make sense of the headship requirement. He affirms the headship of the husband but, unlike Lewis, without making any claims about its appropriateness based on traits ascribed to men and women, claims that our historical freedom might one day make obsolete. Yet he does not entirely sever nature and history, as if freedom without limit were the sole truth about human beings. He is willing to consider that there might be a limit that we can in our freedom surpass but, in order to remain faithful to our created nature, ought not.

For Thielicke even more than for Lewis, the importance of headship clearly lies only in its relation to lifelong fidelity in marriage. Thielicke reserves the exercise of such headship for those borderline cases when it is needed for the marriage to survive. In such moments agreement is needed, and headship provides the means to it. But we may still want to ask again, why should the headship be the husband's? Not for Thielicke, at this point, any claims about masculine and feminine ways of being or reasoning. Maybe they are well grounded; maybe not. They need not, as we have seen, imply any inequality between husband and wife; yet we quite easily turn them into superior and inferior ways of being, into capacities that make the husband somehow more deserving of headship. For Thielicke, by contrast, it is very clearly not a matter of capacity or qualification. It is, rather, "the tradition of Christendom based upon the Holy Scriptures." That is all there is to be said for the husband's headship—though, of course, for Christian conscience it is a great deal indeed.

It is worth our seeing one great strength of this view. The husband's headship is not grounded in any superior or distinguishing traits or capacities; rather, it is simply the exquisitely arbitrary burden of office. Precisely in this arbitrariness it sets us free from false typologies of masculine and feminine. Men are not more qualified to exercise headship. It is just that—needing consensus in faithful marriage, but finding no guarantee of it—God tapped men and said, "You do it." It is rather like a point Chesterton once made, not about marriage, but about kingship.

> Next to a genuine republic, the most democratic thing in the world is a hereditary despotism. I mean a despotism in which there is absolutely no trace whatever of any nonsense about intellect or special fitness for the post. Rational despotism— that is, selective despotism—is always a curse to mankind, because with that you have the ordinary man misunderstood and misgoverned by some prig who has no brotherly respect for him at all. But irrational despotism is always democratic, because it is the ordinary man enthroned....
>
> Hereditary despotism is, then, in essence and sentiment democratic because it chooses from mankind at random. If it does not declare that every man may rule, it declares the next most democratic thing; it declares that any man may rule.[28]

To think of Thielicke's position from this angle is to see that he too—despite the simple appeal to authority—is attempting to make sense of headship. But if Lewis's view has some costs, so does Thielicke's. Precisely by grounding his explanation of headship in an appeal to authority, he loses much of the richness in relationship, the complementarity in interdependence, that one can read into the view of Lewis. Risking less in his discussion of headship, he may also gain less.

In any case, in these two illustrations we can see both the promise and the problem of attempts to take seriously headship within marriage. By now it should at least be clear what is at stake in the concept. It offers a way of trying to live with the differences that mark our fellow-humanity within the communion of marriage—to permit those differences to enrich and help preserve the bond without reducing it to a contrapuntal union of interchangeable persons. Not to see this is to miss the point. Articulating a vision of headship (whether in Lewis's or Thielicke's manner) is a way of saying that the marriage bond is not simply a means to individual self-realization. It is a way of saying that the liberal individualism that has served—and, in my judgment, continues to serve—us well in the political sphere is not as appropriate within the bond of marriage. Even "equality" is a quantitative term, and therefore the love that nourishes marriage may better be characterized in terms of mutuality—the giving and receiving, in countless different ways appropriate to the differentiation that marks our humanity, of mutual submission to each other out of reverence for Christ.

In a sinful world, a world in which women flee for shelter to escape another battering by their husbands, we do well to keep clearly in mind that husband and wife submit to each other, as Ephesians puts it, "out of reverence for Christ." Barth quite rightly emphasizes that, in seeking to find and fill their different roles within marriage, husband and wife submit not so much to each other as to the order itself—that is, to Christ.[29] Submission is out of place where there is no serious attempt on the part of husband and wife to nourish a mutual spirit of giving and receiving within their communion.

This means, perhaps paradoxically, that those most willing to accept the order of Ephesians 5 are least likely to have to appeal to it. For in a good marriage the focus and emphasis will not be on headship but on faithfulness. Those spouses who are antecedently committed to a permanent bond will take as part of their task fostering the differentiation that marks our fellow-humanity. Perhaps for some the understanding of that task, which seems to be presupposed in Ephesians, may lack appeal. For them the contrapuntal vision of Sayers can be recommended as an alternative vision—to see whether a union of interchangeable persons really is the meaning of marriage. Perhaps over time they, and we, will learn from their attempt. But perhaps it will turn out that Sayers's vision does not capture the full richness and meaning of the harmony of marriage, does not sufficiently heal the wound of our individuality within a faithful bond of those who are different—and is not, therefore, adequate to sustain the call to permanence in marriage.

In any case, for Christian spouses who understand marriage as a sphere in which we begin to be trained in the meaning and discipline of fidelity, marriage will be understood as a task. Committing themselves to lifelong union, they must learn in the countless ways appropriate to different marriages the meaning of our fellow-humanity, the hard work of being faithful in the whole of life to one who is not just an-other person but who—within this marriage—remains "other." C. S. Lewis came to marriage late in life, long after writing the passage I have cited above. But he was able to say, after the death of his wife, what commitment to that bond made possible. He wrote:

> [W]e did learn and achieve something. There is, hidden or flaunted, a sword between the sexes till an entire marriage reconciles them. It is arrogance in [men] to call frankness, fairness, and chivalry "masculine" when we see them in a woman; it is arrogance in [women] to describe a man's sensitiveness or tact or tenderness as "feminine." But also what poor, warped fragments of humanity most mere men and mere women must be to make the implications of that arrogance plausible. Marriage heals this. Jointly the two become fully human. "In the image of God created he *them*." Thus, by a paradox, this carnival of sexuality leads us out beyond our sexes.[30]

To begin this work of correction and transformation is a task at the very heart of the marriage bond.

4

HOMOSEXUALITY IN CHRISTIAN PERSPECTIVE

In his *Large Catechism* Luther writes that God established marriage as "the first of all institutions, and he created man and woman differently (as is evident) not for lewdness but to be true to each other, be fruitful, beget children, and support and bring them up to the glory of God."[1] That is the perspective from which I begin. In whatever way those who are not Christians may approach this topic, for Christians there should be no discussion of homosexuality that is not also a discussion of marriage and its purposes. It is equally important to emphasize at the outset that I take up this subject as a problem for theological ethics. I will not address directly hard questions of pastoral practice or psychological counseling. Those are important questions, but our approach to them depends upon an ethic already in place. And the position I will be explicating has been stated, about as directly as one could ask, by the noted German theologian Wolfhart Pannenberg:

> If a church were to let itself be pushed to the point where it
> ceased to treat homosexual activity as a departure from the

biblical norm, and recognized homosexual unions as a personal partnership of love equivalent to marriage, such a church would no longer stand on biblical ground but against the unequivocal witness of Scripture. A church that took this step would cease to be the one, holy, catholic, and apostolic church.[2]

Before tracing the steps by which one might arrive at such a judgment, it is important, especially perhaps in contemporary American culture, to note briefly the place of moral reflection in the life of the church. No one can say "Jesus is Lord" except by the Holy Spirit (I Cor. 12:3). We are "justified by faith apart from works of law" (Rom. 3:28). It is "for freedom [that] Christ has set us free" (Gal. 5:1). Protestants, in particular, love to ring the changes on these crucial Pauline themes—almost suggesting, on occasion, that doing so could substitute for moral guidance and direction. And certainly the church is constituted and continually reconstituted only by the word of the gospel announcing that God has vindicated Jesus as his Son. The faith that acknowledges Jesus likewise vindicates us before God. To such faith, no conditions may be added, as if something more were needed to enter the kingdom that Jesus establishes. Nevertheless, it would be a mistake to suppose that the Scriptures exist only to bear witness to Christ, as if they were the norm for the church's faith but not also for her life.

The temptation to make such a mistake regularly expresses itself in a certain type of question. How can we articulate norms for Christian life without thereby establishing conditions for entry into the kingdom? Without supposing that something more is required than the confession "Jesus is Lord"? Such questions seem to press inexorably down a road at the end of which no ethic remains, at the end of which we are unable to distinguish between actions that follow Christ and actions that turn against him. But to distinguish between those deeds that can be done in Christ and those that turn against him—a distinction the church has always struggled to make—is not to add any conditions to the faith that acknowledges Jesus. The church's moral discipline does not set up conditions for entering the kingdom; rather, it offers a description of what the life of discipleship should be like—a description of what it means to follow Christ. In setting forth such a description of her way of life, in understanding that description as a discipline to be undertaken, the church does not raise any other standard than the Christ who is confessed. On the contrary, the church seeks "solely to explore and expound what the standard" is.[3] We seek, that is, to give content and structure to the meaning of love.

LOVE IS NOT ENOUGH

A marriage that neither begins in love nor gives rise to love falls short of what Christians hope for in a bond that analogically participates in the union of Christ and his church. Nevertheless, in a world in which the languages of love and consent have gradually come to trump all other moral language, we do well to remind ourselves at the outset that marriage, the first of all institutions, is not simply about love in general. It is about the creation of man and woman as different yet made to be true to each other; it is about being fruitful, begetting and rearing children. This pours content and structure into our understanding of sexual love, and it takes seriously the body's character within nature and history.

We should not deny, of course, the significance for human life of the person-uniting, love-expressing dimension of sexual love. In such love we are drawn out of our isolated subjectivity, into a relationship that may seem to offer fulfillment and satisfaction. Wherever such love and affection are present, something of great human significance occurs. "A being which can still love is not yet a devil."[4] And even a distorted and perverted *eros*, in its longing to give love to and receive love from another, still bears "the traces of…divinity," as Plato well knew.[5] True as this is, however, it alone does not and cannot constitute a satisfactory Christian ethic. To locate moral meaning only in the love-giving dimension of our sexuality will, for example, leave us unable to explain why the sexual relation must be given a history, why fidelity to one's spouse is required, even when love draws us toward another possible partner. It will not, that is, explain why adultery is an action that turns against Christ. To locate meaning only in the love-giving dimension of our sexuality, rather than in the union of its love-giving and life-giving dimensions, will leave us unable to explain why the giving and receiving of sexual love should in its very nature be ordered toward procreation. It will not, that is, explain why the conception, gestation, and rearing of children should not be separated from the bond of marital love. To locate meaning only in the love-giving dimension of our sexuality will leave us unable to explain why the trust expressed by partners in sado-masochistic acts, as they make themselves vulnerable to harm while trusting that their lover will not go too far, is a degrading rather than a dignifying of our humanity. In short, emphasis upon the quality of the relationship alone, upon the giving and receiving of love within a consensual relationship, does not and cannot by itself provide the necessary content and structure for love as Christians have understood it.

The body is the place of our personal presence. And moral significance must therefore be found not only in the spirit that characterizes our relationships with others—not only in mutuality and communion—but also in the bodily relationship itself. To suppose that mutual love is all that is needed to make a relationship right is to ignore the moral significance of the body. It is, in fact, a kind of dualism that separates our true self from the body. Therefore, if we want to know how rightly to use the body. if we want to distinguish between fulfilling and corrupting sexual relationships, we cannot talk only of love, consent, and mutuality. However much my neighbor's wife and I are drawn to each other, our bodies are already promised to others. However deep and intense may be a father's affection for his adult daughter, to give himself sexually to her is a perversion of love, not its fulfillment.

In countless ways, therefore, a spirit of love is not enough. Spirit must be present in and through the body, and the body is rightly given only in certain ways, to certain people, under certain circumstances. In a world uncorrupted by human sin, spirit and body would, no doubt, be harmoniously integrated, but that, of course, is not the world in which we live. Therefore, human nature as we experience it—a nature in which body and spirit have quarreled—cannot itself provide the norms for human sexual behavior. What seems "natural" to us may, in fact, be contrary to our nature as God's creatures. Behavior that is natural in the sense that we are readily drawn to it, may in fact be unnatural—inappropriate to who we truly are. Experience alone—the prompting of love alone—cannot here be our sole tutor and guide; for our experience is broken and distorted. It must be reshaped and redirected with the guidance of Scripture.

THE MEANING OF MARRIAGE

Published in 1995 by a theological working group responding to a request of the Church of England Evangelical Council, the St.

Andrew's Day Statement articulated the proper starting point for Christian reflection on homosexuality when it stated:

> The primary pastoral task of the church in relation to all its members, whatever their self-understanding and mode of life, is to re-affirm the good news of salvation in Christ, forgiveness of sins, transformation of life and incorporation into the holy fellowship of the church. In addressing those who understand themselves as homosexual, the church does not cease to speak as the bearer of this good news. It assists all its members to a life of faithful witness in chastity and holiness, recognizing two forms or vocations in which that life can be lived: marriage and singleness (Gen. 2:24; Matt. 19:4-6; 1 Cor. 7 passim). There is no place for the church to confer legitimacy upon alternatives to these.[6]

This constitutes our proper starting point, because it makes clear that whatever we say about homosexuality must be grounded in what we say about marriage and the creation of humankind as male and female.

In his book, *The Moral Teaching of Paul*, Victor Furnish begins his discussion of homosexuality with a succinct statement of a view that is commonly expressed: "As we begin an investigation of the biblical teaching about homosexuality, then, we must keep our sense of proportion. We are not dealing with a fundamental biblical theme. We are not dealing with a major biblical concern. We have to hunt for relevant passages."[7] This is a form of biblicism that one does not expect to find in a distinguished critical scholar. But a topic as volatile as the one we are discussing can give rise to such biblicism. We can readily grant that there are only a few biblical texts that speak directly to the issue of homosexuality, and I will make my way toward them before I am done.

But surely *sexuality* is a very fundamental biblical theme. Indeed, as Jesus says, "from the beginning of creation, God made them male and female" (Mark 10:6). God creates woman, not as the mirror image of man, but as his counterpart—like him and yet unlike him. Because she is flesh of his flesh, man and woman correspond to each other and are made for relation with each other; and so, because she is not simply his mirror image, they can become "one flesh." This is not just a spiritual truth about human beings or about "gender." It is written into our sexuality, our embodied selves. Two people—sharing a common nature, yet as different as their genitalia are different—are drawn out of themselves in order that they may learn something of what it means to be true to each other. And by God's grace, this fleshly bond is oriented toward the creation of succeeding generations—toward begetting children, supporting and bringing them up. The sexual union of man and woman is at the center of our nature and sustains our history.

Moreover, our creation for covenant community as male and femalemirrors the still more fundamental relation of Israel and her Lord, who is not only her maker, but also her husband (Isaiah 54:5–6). Even when Israel is unfaithful to this covenant, God sends his prophet Hosea to reclaim her as his wife, to woo her and speak tenderly to her as he once did in the wilderness, so that she will again say to him "my husband" and they will be betrothed in faithfulness (Hosea 2:14–3:1). So also the church is the bride of Christ—here and now in the profound mystery of their union (Eph. 5:31–32), at the end of the age when the new Jerusalem is revealed as the bride adorned for her husband (Rev. 21:2). To be faithful to our creation as male and female is, therefore, to reflect in our lives still deeper truths about God's election of and steadfast faithfulness to his people. To acknowledge *this* God as Lord is to recognize and affirm, as Richard Hays has put it, "that God constituted a normative reality by making them male and female and joining them together as one flesh."[8] We are, then, dealing with a fundamental biblical theme—one, in fact, that comes very near the heart of the gospel, which announces God's faithfulness in Christ.

How do we live in accord with this normative reality—the creation of humankind as male and female? A good starting place would be Luther's explanation of the sixth commandment in his *Small Catechism.* We should seek to "lead a chaste and pure life in word and deed, each one loving and honoring his wife or her husband." Although the sixteenth-century Reformers often exalted the importance of marriage, especially as part of their attack on monastic vows, marriage itself is not the fundamental requirement. Chastity is. And chastity means far more than disciplined control of one's appetites. Were that all it meant, there would be no need or place for chastity in heaven, when we no longer will experience the pull of sinful appetite. Chastity means that we offer our sexual life back to God, presenting our bodies "as a living sacrifice, holy and acceptable to God" (Rom. 12:1). It means not being conformed to the world but being "transformed by the renewal of your mind, that you may prove what is the will of God, what is good and acceptable and perfect" (Rom. 12:2). And, of course, this does then, in our present sinful condition, imply the necessity also of discipline and self-control. According to St. Paul, marriage serves now to restrain our sinful impulses—impulses that, if given free rein, would often satisfy themselves outside the bond of marital commitment (I Cor. 7 passim). We need not enter into a sexual relationship; we can, either by choice or by necessity, bypass that and seek to devote our bodies directly to God as members of Christ's bride, the church. But if we do give ourselves sexually, then it is to be done in accord with the order God establishes in creation. "For this is the will of God, your sanctification, that you abstain from unchastity..." (I. Thess. 4:3).

The central and typical expression of our creation as male and female is, therefore, marriage, together with the procreation of children who, by God's grace, bring to fruition the union of husband and wife. Some marriages may be involuntarily childless, or perhaps, on occasion, deliberately childless in order for husband and wife better to devote themselves to God's service (I Cor. 7:25–35; Matt. 19:10–12). Some men and women may be unmarried—perhaps because they have not yet found a suitable spouse, perhaps because they are widowed. Nevertheless, those who are married but childless and those who are single, when in chastity they offer their bodies to God in holiness and honor, live in accord with the order God has established in creation, an order Jesus himself reaffirms. These men and women do not deliberately set themselves against the grain of the creation. Rather, what they say in essence is: "Marriage and procreation are good. They were once good for me; or they may some day be good for me; or they would be good for me were it not for the special tasks of service laid upon me."[9] With good consciences and glad hearts they take their place in the community of the faithful, who form the bride of Christ.

Having emphasized the significance of our creation as male and female, the biblical story also qualifies it. We tend to suppose that sexual fulfillment is of ultimate importance and that no life can be well lived without it, but we must come to see sexual fulfillment as an image of what is truly ultimate. Our creation for covenant community as male and female points toward the eternal communion of Christ and the church. A day will come when image becomes reality and the marriage supper of the lamb is consummated. Then our creation for one-flesh union will be seen to have offered us something far more important than sexual fulfillment— namely, an inkling of the divine glory in which we have a share. In heaven, Jesus says, they neither marry nor are given in marriage (Mark. 12:25). Not that our created nature as male and female will disappear; for, as C. S. Lewis once put it, "[w]hat is no longer needed for biological purposes may be expected to survive for splendor. Sexuality is the instrument both of virginity and of conjugal virtue; neither men nor women will be asked to throw away weapons they have used victoriously."[10] Knowing this, we are given a vantage point from which to evaluate claims about the importance of sexual expression or satisfaction in human life. On the one hand, our creation as male and female, as sexual beings, is part of the meaning of our humanity. On the other hand, it cannot divulge the final meaning of that humanity, for it is only a pointer toward the true fulfillment God will one day give.

HOMOSEXUALITY AND THE BIBLE

Against this background we may now turn our attention more directly to the Bible's evaluation of homosexual behavior. And the most important passage that demands our attention is, of course, in the first chapter of Romans, where Paul writes:

> Therefore, God gave them up in the lusts of their hearts to impurity, to the dishonoring of their bodies among themselves, because they exchanged the truth about God for a lie and worshipped and served the creature rather than the

Creator, who is blessed for ever! Amen. For this reason God gave them up to dishonorable passions. Their women exchanged natural relations for unnatural, and the men likewise gave up natural relations with women and were consumed with passion for one another, men committing shameless acts with men and receiving in their own persons the due penalty for their error. (Rom. 1:24–27)

In the larger context of this chapter, Paul is laying bare the human condition before God.[11] All stand under God's wrath, condemned in their sins, but this divine judgment "takes the ironic form of allowing them the freedom to have their own way."[12] We try to live free of any limits. With this freedom we wrap ourselves ever more firmly in the chains of vice—and it is not insignificant for Paul that we do so, in part, by using our freedom to distort and corrupt the very sexuality intended to sustain human life, and which, by giving rise to those who will take our place, points to the limits of our mortal nature. But we try to live without limit. By turning against the created meaning of our humanity as male and female, homosexual behavior claims the freedom to give our own meaning to life and thereby symbolically enacts a rejection of God's will for the creation. Paul assumes that his readers will, together with him, view homosexual behavior as wrong; indeed, the structure of his argument rests precisely upon such an assumption.

What makes it wrong? In part, of course, it is wrong for Paul because it is condemned in Torah, as for example in Leviticus 18:22: "You shall not lie with a male as with a woman; it is an abomination." In that passage, we should note, an act is categorically prohibited. Its moral quality does not depend upon the spirit or the circumstances in which it is done, and Jews have historically understood it that way. But the prohibition in Torah cannot be all that stands behind Paul's words in Romans 1. For one thing, the Leviticus passage condemns only male homosexual behavior, whereas Paul also depicts female homosexual behavior as a rejection of the Creator's intent. And for another, Christians—following precisely Paul's lead—have regarded some commands in Torah as no longer binding. One might argue that the levitical prohibition of homosexual behavior as an abomination represents only ancient Israel's understanding of ritual purity and is not a moral judgment that should govern our actions today. Were we orthodox Jews we might still regard this prohibition as binding in our lives. Since we are not, we have to distinguish, one might say, between what the Bible narrates—the purity laws by which Israel ritually separated itself from the surrounding peoples—and what the Bible teaches and requires of us.

This move is not likely to get us very far, however. In the same eighteenth chapter of Leviticus, God's people are forbidden to engage in incestuous behavior, forbidden to "lie carnally" with a neighbor's wife, forbidden to devote their children by fire to Molech. Shall we regard these prohibitions merely as ritual purity requirements? I think not. Torah itself does not distinguish for us between moral law and ritual requirement. But that does not mean we cannot or should not or need not make such distinctions; it only means that we must do what the Old Testament does not do for us. "In each case, the church is faced with the task of discerning whether Israel's national norms remain in force for the new community of Jesus' followers."[13] And quite clearly, one of the norms that Paul here regards as still in force for those who seek to live in Christ is that prohibiting homosexual behavior. Far from being an action that could now be done in Christ, it is one manifestation of the "ungodliness and wickedness" in which our lives are deeply involved and against which the wrath of God is directed (Rom. 1:18). The question our churches have to face, therefore, is not really what Paul thinks and teaches but how we are prepared to respond to what is taught.

This is a hard saying, however, and a variety of strategies have been used to avoid it. For example, even granting that Paul regards homosexual behavior not simply as ritually impure but as morally wrong, perhaps his judgment is limited in some way by the circumstances of his day. Thus, some have argued that Paul is condemning only a form of pederasty known to him at the time and that the expression of sexual love between men in his world was never fully voluntary, nor between equals, nor part of a long-term romantic relationship. Paul, according to this view, knew only of pederastic relationships between a man and a younger boy—relationships lacking in mutuality and almost inevitably exploitative. When he condemns them, we can join him in his condemnation without likewise condemning all homosexual relationships as we know them today.

Unfortunately for the argument, however, the facts are otherwise, as Mark D. Smith has recently demonstrated.[14] First, not all pederastic relationships in the ancient world were exploitative; some were characterized by mutuality and shared pleasure. Second, and more important, the homosexual behavior Paul would have known in the Roman world was no longer chiefly pederastic, if indeed it ever had been. The most common form of homosexual behavior among females had, in fact, "involved mutually consenting women of roughly equal age."[15] And more generally, even in the three centuries before Paul, the practice of pederasty among males was not the most common form of homo-

sexual behavior in the Greco-Roman world. Hence, Smith concludes his exhaustive examination of the evidence this way: "I
believe that the only interpretation that does justice to the literary
and historical context is that Paul probably did know of at least
several different types of homosexual practices among both men
and women. He used general language in Romans 1, because he
intended his proscription to apply in a general way to all homosexual behavior, as he understood it."[16] He was familiar with a
range of homosexual behavior not unlike the range in our world,
and that range of behavior he condemned.

Another way in which we might attempt to confine Paul's
words in Romans to his time alone would be to note that he could
not possibly have had our contemporary understanding of sexual
orientation according to which some people—even if perhaps only
a very small percentage—have, for as long as they have known
themselves as sexual beings, experienced a consistent pattern of
attraction directed exclusively toward members of their own sex.
Because this concept of a fixed sexual orientation emerged only in
the nineteenth century, it could not have affected Paul's thinking.[17]
In condemning those who "exchanged natural relations for unnatural," he could only have had in mind those who, despite being
primary het*ero*sexuals, perversely acted contrary to their own natural inclinations.

Here again, however, it is difficult to make the facts fit the
argument—and that for several reasons. To be sure, the nineteenth
century concept of "orientation" does not seem adequate to Paul's
world, but it is also inadequate to our own. Human sexual experience is varied indeed. If we speak of homosexuals and heterosexuals, we must also speak of bisexuals. Human sexual desire ranges
across a continuum, and the moral question is not why our desires

draw us in one direction or another but what behavior is right or wrong. The diversity of sexual desire in our world is, it turns out, very much like the world Paul knew, with a kaleidoscopic variety of sexual desires and behaviors.[18] The truth may be, as Mary Stewart Van Leeuwen has put it, that "our Old Testament and New Testament ancestors were correct in treating homosexual acts...as behaviors to which any person could potentially be tempted, and that is why they remind their readers to be on guard against them."[19] The important question, in other words, is not about sexual "orientation" but about behavior—both in Paul's world and in ours. Indeed, the language of "orientation" has proven to be a dead end for serious moral reflection.

But suppose we were to grant that such an orientation exists and that some people experience themselves as primary homosexuals—constituted by a consistent attraction toward those of the same sex. Does this mean that Paul's condemnation of "unnatural" sexual activity does not apply to their behavior? That will be a hard case to make. *Philosophically*, "natural" is a word to conjure with. If the "natural" denotes simply the desires some people consistently have, the whole bewildering variety of such desires that exists in our world, we will lose our grip on norms entirely. Indeed, that notion of the natural is incompatible with any understanding of ethics or moral law, for it has no standard by which to judge or evaluate the desires that come "naturally" to us. Then we very quickly find ourselves without the conceptual resources needed to speak ethically about incest, bestiality, and adultery. *Theologically*, the case is equally hard to make. The "exchange" Paul has in mind—when he writes of those who "exchanged natural relations for unnatural"—does not refer to "individual life decisions; rather, it is Paul's characterization of the fallen condition of the pagan world."[20] The Creator's will for human life has been exchanged for sinful human will. Homosexual behavior—whatever orientation it enacts—is contrary to our created nature and is one more evidence of our alienation from the Creator. That is Paul's point. He is offering a moral and theological assessment of behavior that was common in his time and place but is not unlike behavior common in our time and place.

As far as we are aware, of course, Paul did not know churches in which there were people who understood themselves as both committed homosexuals and committed Christians, who wanted to set their experience of homosexual behavior as positive and good over against and in judgment upon the witness of Scripture. In the face of such experiential claims from believing Christians, might Paul have found reason to modify his moral and theological assessment? We have, as I noted, no instance to which we can turn in which Paul responded to such claims. He might have responded "as he did to the Corinthian Christians, for all we know committed church members," who were going to prostitutes.[21] "Do you not know that your bodies are members of Christ? Shall I therefore take the members of Christ and make them members of a prostitute? Never." (I Cor. 6:15).

It is also theoretically possible, of course, that he might have responded more as he did when the earliest Jewish Christians were reluctant to accept into the church Gentiles who, because they were uncircumcised and did not observe dietary laws, were ritually unclean. Theoretically possible, but unlikely. It is hard to find in Paul any warrant for such a response. Richard Hays has articulated the crucial point with clarity and precision:

[E]xperience must be treated as a hermeneutical lens for reading the New Testament rather than as an independent, coun-
terbalancing authority. This is the point at which the analogy
to the early church's acceptance of Gentiles fails decisively.
The church did not simply observe the experience of
Cornelius and his household and decide that Scripture must
be wrong after all. On the contrary, the experience of uncircumcised Gentiles responding in faith to the gospel message
led the church back to a new reading of Scripture. This new
reading discovered in the texts a clear message of God's
intent, from the covenant with Abraham forward, to bless all
nations and to bring Gentiles (*qua* Gentiles) to worship
Israel's God.... Only because the new experience of Gentile
converts proved hermeneutically illuminating of Scripture
was the church, over time, able to accept the decision to
embrace Gentiles within the fellowship of God's people.[22]

An analogous argument, taking seriously the biblical understanding of our creation for community as male and female and showing that homosexual behavior can be a fulfillment rather than a
repudiation of this creation, has not been made—and, I think,
cannot be made. Hence, we can only say what, at the outset, I cited
Wolfhart Pannenberg as having said: the unequivocal witness of
Scripture is that homosexual activity departs from the norm God
has established for human life, and homosexual partnerships
cannot be understood morally as the equivalent of marriage. There
is no persuasive evidence that this scriptural view applies only to a
world now lost. In allowing her public teaching to be governed by

this scriptural witness, the church faithfully distinguishes actions that follow Christ from actions that turn against him.

For me this has been a long, arduous argument. And it is important to recall now what I said at the very outset: I have taken up this subject, not as a question of counseling, but as a matter for theological ethics. We are asking what the church's public teaching ought to be, if it wishes to be faithful to Scripture, and I think we have found the answer to that question. We have not, of course, answered every difficult question that might arise in pastoral or clinical care.

But we dare not permit the church's public teaching, on the matter of homosexuality or any other matter, to be taken over and determined by a desire—however sincere and well intentioned—to "affirm" every person in whatever state he or she may be. That is not the gospel. To articulate the Christian norm for life is not the church's only task, but it is a necessary task. If we fail here, affirmation of, and compassion for, those who fall short mean little. Indeed, once we can no longer say what it means to "fall short," we have little need for compassion and few problems for pastoral practice. But then we also are poorly positioned to take seriously the law written in our hearts, the desire of human beings for what is noble and God-pleasing, the good news that we have been set free from captivity to our own distorted images of what it means to be satisfied and fulfilled. For the sake not only of those who have been baptized into Christ's body, but also for the sake of a world which, even if only inchoately, wants to follow the way of life, we have a responsibility to conform our public teaching to what we have ourselves been taught by Scripture about our creation as male and female and about marriage as the first of institutions. We have no authorization to do otherwise.

PART 2

Parents and Children

5

I WANT TO BURDEN MY LOVED ONES

Recently I was a speaker and panel member at a small educational workshop on "advance directives" sponsored by the ethics committee of our local hospital. The workshop was an opportunity to provide information about, and discuss the relative merits of, living wills and health care powers of attorney as different ways of trying to deal in advance with medical decisions that might have to be made for us after we have become incompetent. This was not the first such workshop for me, and I suppose it will not be the last. And I was struck, as I have been before, with the recurrence of a certain theme.

Many people come to such a workshop already quite knowledgeable about the topic to be discussed. They come less for information than for the opportunity to talk. Some earnestly desire the chance to converse about a troubling issue; a few just want to express themselves. In either case, however, it is remarkable how often they may say something like the following: "I'm afraid that if my children have to make decisions about my care, they won't be able to handle the pressure. They'll just argue with each other, and they'll feel guilty, wondering whether they're really doing what I would want. I don't want to be a burden to them, and I will do whatever I can in advance to see that I'm not." And after someone has spoken words to this effect, there will be a chorus of assent from others who, evidently, share the speaker's view.

Now, of course, we can in many ways understand and appreciate such a perspective. None of us wishes to imagine his children arguing together about who really knows best how he should be treated (or not treated). We hate to think that our children's last thoughts of us would be interwoven with anger at each other, guilt for their uncertainty about how best to care for us, or even (perhaps) a secret wish that we'd get on with the dying and relieve them of this burden.

Nonetheless, as the workshop wore on, I found myself giving it only a part of my attention, because I couldn't help musing on this recurring theme. Understandable as this theme is in many respects, there is, I am convinced, something wrong with it. I don't know how to make the point other than a little too crassly—by saying that I want to be a burden to my loved ones. But, rightly understood, I think I do.

The first thought that occurred to me in my musings was not, I admit, the noblest: I have sweat in the hot sun teaching four children to catch and hit a ball, to swing a tennis racket and shoot a free throw. I have built blocks and played games I detest with and for my children. I have watched countless basketball games made up largely of bad passes, traveling violations, and shots that missed both rim and backboard. I have sat through years of piano recitals, band concerts, school programs—often on very busy nights or very hot, humid evenings in the late spring. I have stood in a steamy bathroom in the middle of the night with the hot shower running, trying to help a child with croup breathe more easily. I have run beside a bicycle, ready to catch a child who might fall while learning to ride. (This is, by the way, very hard!) I have spent hours finding perfectly decent (cheap) clothing in stores, only to have these choices rejected as somehow not exactly what they had in mind. I have used evenings to type in final form long stories—far longer than necessary—that my children have written in response to school assignments. I have had to fight for the right to eat at Burger King rather than McDonald's. Why should I not be a bit of a burden to these children in my dying?

This was not, I have already granted, the noblest thought, but it was the first. And, of course, it overlooks a great deal—above all, that I have taken great joy in these children and have not really resented much in the litany of burdens recited above. But still, there is here a serious point to be considered. Is this not in large measure what it means to belong to a family: to burden each other—and to find, almost miraculously, that others are willing, even happy, to carry such burdens? Families would not have the significance they do for us if they did not, in fact, give us a claim upon each other. At least in this sphere of life we do not come together as autonomous individuals freely contracting with each other. We simply find ourselves thrown together and asked to share the burdens of life while learning to care for each other. We may often resent such claims on our time and energies. We did not, after all, consent to them. (Or, at least, if we want to speak of consent, it will have to be something like that old staple of social contract theorists, tacit consent.)

It is, therefore, understandable that we sometimes chafe under these burdens. If, however, we also go on to reject them, we cease to live in the kind of moral community that deserves to be called a family. Here, more than in any other sphere of life, we are presented with unwanted and unexpected interruptions to our plans and projects. I do not like such interruptions any more than the next person; indeed, a little less, I rather suspect. But it is still true that morality consists, in large part, in learning to deal with the unwanted and unexpected interruptions to our plans. I have tried, subject to my limits and weaknesses, to teach that lesson to my children. Perhaps I will teach it best when I am a burden to them in my dying.

This was my first thought. It led to a second. Perhaps it is a good thing, lest we be tempted to injustice, that the dying burden the living. Some years ago Robert Burt wrote a book about medical decision-making for incompetent patients. The book's title was *Taking Care of Strangers*. Burt's point, which carried a *double entendre*, was essentially this: patients who are unable to make decisions for themselves are often in a state (e.g., severely demented, comatose) in which they become strangers to us. They make us uneasy, and we react with ambivalence. And to say of such a patient, "I'll take care of him," may be a statement freighted with ambivalence. Burt worries that, no matter how devoted our care, our uneasiness with a loved one who has become a stranger to us may prompt us to do less than we ought to sustain his life. (Nor, we should note, are physicians immune to such uneasiness.) It is, therefore, essential that we structure the medical decision-making situation in such a way that conversation is forced among the doctor, the medical caregivers, the patient's family, and perhaps still others, such as pastor, priest, or rabbi. Advance directives— designed to eliminate the need for such extended conversation, lest it should burden loved ones—are, from this perspective, somewhat problematic. They may not force us to deal with our own ambivalence in "taking care of" a loved one who is now a burdensome stranger.

This does not mean that advance directives are entirely a bad idea. It does suggest, however, that a health care power of attorney—in which we simply name a proxy to make decisions in the event of our incompetence—is better than a living will in which we attempt to state the kinds of treatment we would or would not desire under a variety of medical circumstances. At this point in my life, for example, I would surely turn over to my wife my power of attorney. In doing so I simply announce to medical caregivers: "Here is the person with whom you must converse when the day comes that you cannot talk with me about my medical care." I myself do not particularly like even the recently fashionable attempts to combine the two forms of advance directives by naming a proxy *and* giving that proxy as much detail as possible about what we would want done. That move—though, again, it will be seen as an attempt to avoid burdening the loved one who must make such decisions—may not, in any case, accomplish our aim. It commits us to an endless, futile search to determine what a now-incompetent person would wish. Still more important, it is one last-ditch attempt to bypass the interdependence of human life, by which we simply do and should constitute a burden to those who love us.

I hope, therefore, that I will have the good sense to empower my wife, while she is able, to make such decisions for me—though I know full well that we do not always agree about what is the best care in end-of-life circumstances. That disagreement doesn't bother me at all. As long as she avoids the futile question, "What would he have wanted?" and contents herself with the (difficult enough) question, "What is best for him now?" I will have no quarrel with her. Moreover, this approach is, I think, less likely to encourage her to make the moral mistake of asking, "Is his life a benefit to him (i.e., a life worth living)?" and more likely to encourage her to ask, "What can we do to benefit the life he still has?" No doubt this will be a burden to her. No doubt she will bear the burden better than I would. No doubt it will be only the last in a long history of burdens she has borne for me. But then, mystery and continuous miracle that it is, she loves me. And because she does, I must of course be a burden to her.

6

THE MEANING OF THE PRESENCE OF CHILDREN

W hy have children? The question carries its own pathos, and we might be tempted to reply that those for whom the question is a live one probably should not. But our society is greatly confused about this question. Many couples have difficulty summoning the courage to proceed. They doubt their readiness—and that not only for economic reasons. Ellen Goodman wrote a column a few years back, reflecting on a survey that had been taken to determine whether people felt "ready" to have children. She doubted the wisdom of such an undertaking.

> I know a dozen couples who can't decide to have children. They can't even decide how to decide. They want a rational actuarial kind of life-plan, and this test feeds right into their anxiety. The search is on to unearth the "right reason" to have children and to find out who are the "right people" to have them…. Parenting demands a risk and not a scoreboard.

It is my aim here to explore the venture of parenthood, the inner meaning of the family bond. And because such an exploration must always have a location, I will examine the meaning of fecundity from within the perspective of Christian faith—which has, after all, been one of the principal sources of our culture's formation on this question, and which, on this question, may help to point us in the direction of a true humanism.

Such a humanistic perspective, and something of the meaning of the presence of children, has been provocatively exemplified in P. D. James's novel *The Children of Men*.[1] The story is set in Great Britain in the year 2021. No children have been born anywhere in the world since 1995, a year in which all males—for reasons unknown—became infertile. We see what such a world means through the eyes of Theodore (Theo) Faron, an Oxford historian.

Because of his fascination with a woman named Julian, Theo makes contact with a revolutionary group to which she belongs. But their plans for revolution against the dictatorship ruling Britain suddenly take a back seat to an unexpected turn in the plot: Julian discovers that she is pregnant (by Luke, a priest, who is also a member of the small band of rebels). Needing help to escape detection until Julian gives birth, the group turns to Theo. He comes by night to their hiding place, unable to believe that Julian could truly be carrying a child. She places his hand on her abdomen, and he feels the child kick. Then she tells him to listen to its heartbeat. In order to do so, he kneels beside her.

> It was easier for him to kneel, so he knelt, unselfconsciously, not thinking of it as a gesture of homage but knowing that it was right that he should be on his knees. He placed his right arm around her waist and pressed his ear against her stomach. He couldn't hear the beating heart, but he could hear and feel the movements of the child, feel its life. He was swept by

a tide of emotion which rose, buffeted and engulfed him in a turbulent surge of awe, excitement and terror, then receded, leaving him spent and weak.[2]

There is mystery in the presence of the newly created child—and Theo rightly kneels. But we can and should also explore a little the human meaning of this mystery.

THE VENTURE OF PARENTHOOD

There is, I claimed at the outset, a certain pathos in the question, Why have children? It suggests a loss of spontaneous confidence in life and an impoverishment of spirit. This does not mean that such a question is unreasonable, particularly for those whose circumstances make hope difficult. I do not seek to judge the difficulties facing any particular married couple or their special circumstances; rather, I seek to reflect upon the social significance of our attitude toward the presence of children.

The formation of a family is most truly human, a sign of health, when it springs from what Gabriel Marcel called "an experience of plenitude."[3] To conceive, bear, and rear a child ought to be an affirmation and a recognition: affirmation of the good of life that we ourselves were given; recognition that this life bears its own creative power to which we should be faithful. In this sense Marcel could claim that "the truest fidelity is creative."[4] The desire to have children is an expression of a deeply humanistic impulse to be faithful to the creative power of the life that is mysteriously ours. This impulse "is not essentially different from that of the artist who is the bearer of some message which he must communicate, of some flame which he must kindle and pass on...."[5] The power of art will have dried up in an artist who no longer feels impelled to create and who must ask, Why write? or, Why sing? or, Why paint? She will no longer be in touch with the powerfully creative Muses that were hers—and yet, of course, not simply hers; they were forces beyond her control in which she was a confident and hopeful participant.

This does not mean that we are most truly human when we simply reproduce often and almost by chance. We can distinguish, Marcel notes, between forming a family and producing a brood.[6] Nor does it mean that the marriage bond should be thought of simply as a means to the end of production of offspring, as if the relation of husband and wife were not itself centrally related to the meaning of our humanity. Nor yet does it mean that "planning" is inappropriate in the formation of a family, as if to be human were only to be subject to a life-force and not to exercise our freedom and reason. But granting all such provisos, there is still a sense in which planning alone cannot capture the "experience of plenitude" from which procreation, at its best, springs. There is, after all, no necessity that human beings exist—or that we ourselves *be*. That something rather than nothing exists is a mystery that lies buried in the heart of God, whose creative power and plenitude of being are the ground of our life. That life should have come into existence is in no way our doing. Within this life we can exercise a modest degree of control, but we deceive ourselves if we forget the mystery of creation that grounds our being.

To form a family cannot, therefore, be only an act of planning and control—unless we are metaphysically deceived. It must also be an act of faith and hope, what Marcel termed "the exercise of a fundamental generosity."[7] There is, as he quite rightly noted, a fundamental difference between deciding to produce an heir and deciding to reproduce ourselves (by having a son and a daughter)—between such instrumentalist attitudes and a fidelity to life that is creative, in the sense that a man and woman, "in a sort of prodigality of their whole being, sow the seed of life without ulterior motive by radiating the life flame which has permeated them and set them aglow."[8] Years ago I read a set of newspaper articles comparing the attitude toward children of two married couples.[9] One couple had decided to have no children; the other had, at least by our contemporary standards, a large family. Certainly there was nothing illogical in the first couple's decision.

> They are distrustful as well of what children can do to a marriage. "When you have children," says Michael, "the focus changes from the couple to the kids. Suddenly everything is done for them. Well, I'm 27, I've used up a good portion of my life already. Why should I want to sacrifice for someone who's still got his whole life ahead of him?"

How instructive is the image this man used. Life is held in a container. We must hold on to as much of it as we can, be careful not to give too much of it away, avoid pouring out the container's contents precipitously. One could not ask for a better contrast with Marcel's claim that the creation and sustaining of a family is an act of self-spending. And if there is nothing illogical about this man's attitude, there is, nonetheless, a failure to probe deeply the mystery of human life. As if our very existence were not itself an act of entirely gratuitous self-giving on the part of the Creator—an act for which no logical ground or explanation can be given! And in response to that primal act of self-giving we can respond with that fidelity to life which is itself creative—or we can turn the mystery of life into simply a problem to be controlled by our own attempts at planning and mastery.

To the extent that we moderns have understood the family as a problem to be mastered, and not a mystery to be explored faithfully, we have quite naturally come to adopt a certain attitude toward our children. They have been produced, not out of any spontaneous confidence in life, but as the result of our own planning. We are, therefore, tempted to suppose that we must—and can—become their protectors, the guarantors of their future. Paradoxically, having lost the metaphysical underpinnings of procreation as a participation in the Creator's own gracious self-spending, having lost much of the real significance of the family, we make of it more than it is. We invest it with more emotional freight than it can bear, as we cling ever more tightly to the children we have. The paradox is, in fact, understandable: to ask of an earthly good more than it can offer is an inescapable result of idolatry. In order to make of the family neither more nor less than it ought to be, we may be helped if we think of its inner meaning in two ways—as a biological community and a historical community.

THE FAMILY AS BIOLOGICAL COMMUNITY

Lines of kinship and descent embed us in the world of nature so that from birth we are individuals within a community. Like the other animals, human beings "bring forth...according to their kinds" and, in more peculiarly human fashion, pass on to their children their image and likeness.[10] Our personhood is marked by that inheritance, for we incarnate the union of the man and the woman who are our parents. They are not simply reproducing themselves, nor are they simply a cause of which we are the effect. In reaching out to each other, they forge a community between two beings who are different and separate. When, from their oneness, they create a new human being, that act testifies to the truth that love for someone other than the self is a love that does not seek simply to see its own face in the loved one. This love creates community.

And the bond between parents and children does in fact bind; with it come obligations. Parents have, whether they want it or not, the honor and responsibility to stand before their children as God's representatives, for it is his creative power in which they are sharers. Children have that most puzzling of duties: to show gratitude for a bond in which they find themselves without in any way having chosen it. For the "problem" of their existence is simply, in miniature, the "problem" of all existence—the mystery that anything should exist at all. Hence, in what seems to be a biological fact, moral significance is embedded. The psalmist writes that children are "a heritage from the LORD."[11] The child, therefore, as a gift of God and the fruit of our fidelity to and participation in God's continuing creative work, is a sign of hope and of God's continued affirmation of his creation. Still more, the presence of the child indicates that the parents, as co-creators with God, have shared something of the mystery of divine love: their love-giving has proved to be life-giving. That such gratuitous self-spending should, in fact, give new life is the deepest mystery of God's being and we see faintly the image of that mystery in the birth of a child.

We are, of course, free in many ways to transcend our embeddedness in nature, but we ought also to respect the embodied character of human life. As parents of children and children of parents, we are marked by the biological communities in which we find ourselves. We are not just free spirits, free to make of ourselves what we will. There is, in part at least, a "givenness" to our existence that limits us. Part of the task of a faithful life is to learn to receive that givenness with thanksgiving and to be trustworthy in the duties it lays upon us.

If this is in part the inner meaning of the bond of parents and children, we should be clear about one important truth. This bond may very often make us deeply happy; indeed, it may have the capacity to bring some of the greatest joys into human life. But we ought not have children chiefly for that reason. Though it often fulfills us, the bond does not exist for the sake of our fulfillment. Parents are not reproducing themselves; they are giving birth to another human being, equal to them in dignity and bound to them in ties of kinship but not created for their satisfaction. To desire a child of "one's own" is understandable, but such language should be used only with great caution. Biological parenthood does not confer possession of children. Rather, it calls us to the traditional tasks of rearing, nurturing, and civilizing our children so that the next generation may achieve its relative independence. And it calls us to seek to impart that spontaneous confidence in life that is the fundamental ground of the family.

Self-giving, therefore, not self-fulfillment, lies at the heart of the parents' vocation. If such self-giving should prove to be deeply satisfying, we have reason to be thankful. But such a symmetrically satisfying result is not guaranteed, and seeking it is not the best way to prepare for the vicissitudes of parenthood. To give birth is a venture that must be carried out in hope and in faith that the Creator will continue to speak his "yes" upon the creation.

THE FAMILY AS HISTORICAL COMMUNITY

In love, a man and a woman turn from themselves toward each other. They might, however, miss the call of creative fidelity to life and be forever content to turn toward each other alone, to turn out from themselves no more than that. But in the child, their union, as a union, quite naturally turns outward. They are not permitted to think of themselves as individuals who come together only for their own fulfillment. In the child they are given a task. Their union plays its role in a larger history, and it becomes part of their vocation to contribute to the ongoing life of a people. Certainly both Jews and Christians have commonly understood the bond of parents and children in this way:

> I will utter dark sayings from of old,
> things that we have heard and known,
> that our fathers have told us.
> We will not hide them from their children,
> but tell to the coming generation
> the glorious deeds of the LORD, and his might,
> and the wonders which he has wrought.
> He established a testimony in Jacob,
> and appointed a law in Israel,
> which he commanded our fathers
> to teach to their children;
> that the next generation might know them,
> the children yet unborn,
> and arise to tell them to their children,
> so that they should set their hope in God.[12]

In many respects this is the most fundamental task of parents: transmission of a way of life. When the son of the ancient Israelite asked, "What does this mean?" his father told again the story of the mighty acts of God, the story of their common life as a people. When a woman of Israel appeals to the biological bond and cries out to Jesus, "Blessed is the womb that bore you, and the breasts that you sucked," he responds: "Blessed rather are those who hear the word of God and keep it."[13] He points, that is, to a further bond that must be built upon the basis of biological community and is finally more crucial: initiation into a way of life. The apostle writes that fathers should not provoke their children to anger but should "bring them up in the *paideia* and instruction of the Lord."[14] That task of *paideia*, of nurture and inculcation of a way of life, is the calling of parents.

Of course, these biblical passages refer to the transmission of a religious tradition: the story of God's care for his people. But they also point more generally to something fundamental. Parenthood is not just biological begetting. It is also history—a vocation to nurture the next generation, to initiate it into the human inheritance of knowledge and obligation. If today many feel that the family is "in crisis" or wonder why they should have children, that may be in large part because parents have little commitment to or sense of a story to pass on.

To think of the family as a biological community points us, we noted earlier, toward the importance of self-giving love. The same is true when we envision the family as a historical community. Here, even more clearly and starkly, the risk and venture of parenthood come into view. Parents commit themselves to initiating their children into the human inheritance and, more particularly, into the stories that depict their way of life. In so doing they shape, mold, and civilize their children.

But there are no guarantees that the final "product" of this process will be what the parents anticipated. Parents know this, of course, and are therefore understandably anxious about their children's future. However understandable such anxiety may be, it also constitutes a great temptation—the temptation to try to be the guarantor of our children's future, to protect them from all disappointment and suffering. To give in to such temptation would be, in effect, to deny their freedom to be an-other like us, equal to us in dignity. This means that parents must seek more than their own satisfaction in rearing their children. They must give themselves in faith and hope, recognizing that they are not more than co-creators and that they cannot shape the future.

WHY CHILDREN?

Viewing the family from these two perspectives, we can understand why Marcel would suggest that parenthood, at its best, implies a certain fundamental generosity. And if this is true, if the family is a community that demands a great deal of us, we may often wonder why we should undertake the effort it involves. The ultimate answer, I think, is the one with which I began—that there is no answer if we lack all spontaneous confidence in life. But perhaps we can now press a little further and find a purpose or *telos* in the family bond. Both a social and a theological case can be made for commitment to the family, and we can begin with the lesser and move toward the greater.

Renewal of the species and rearing of the next generation might take place apart from anything remotely resembling the family. That is a very old idea. Plato had Socrates propose it when constructing the ideal city in *The Republic*. Socrates suggests that by making kinship universal we could eliminate the divisive passions that ordinary family preference involves. In today's setting, we could establish a universal system of day-care centers to which children were given at birth and in which everyone had a hand in the care of all children—and in this way begin to approximate

Socrates' proposal. If, however, the family is the sort of community I have described, doing this would make war on elements written very deeply into our nature. And no doubt Aristotle had something like that in mind when he suggested that Socrates' proposal would do more than combat divisive passion: it might also dilute a sense of concern and responsibility for those who come after us.[15]

We can expand a little upon his claim. A parent, after all, is not simply a public functionary charged with looking after a certain number of children. The special attachment that characterizes the parent-child bond serves, at its best, as a kind of guarantee of love— almost an analogue to divine grace. (That it does not always work this way indicates only that it is no more than an analogue and that quite often we are not at our best.) The child is loved unconditionally, for no particular reason. I love my children not because they are especially talented or qualified in one way or another, but simply because they have been given to me and placed in my care. And only such love, founded on no particular quality or attribute, can offer something approaching unconditional acceptance.

If I love my daughter because she plays the piano well, or my son because he executes the pick-and-roll with precision, if that is the ground of my special attachment, then it is subject to change. There can be little certainty that my commitment will endure, for it is likely that others will play both piano and basketball better. But when, by contrast, parental love is grounded in the facts of biological and historical bonding, the child lives in a setting that offers the kind of acceptance human beings need to become capable of adult commitment—a setting in which individuals who are separate but connected can grow and flourish. Thus, Michael Walzer perceptively commented that

[o]ne might...liberate women from childbirth as well as parents from child care, by cloning the next generation...or by purchasing babies from underdeveloped countries. This is not the redistribution but the abolition of parental love, and I suspect that it would quickly produce a race of men and women incapable even of the commitment required for an affair.[16]

At least this much can be said about the social purpose of the family. But from a Christian perspective our commitment to the family cannot and ought not to be grounded simply in its importance for our common life, for training the generation that will succeed us. However important, this remains only penultimate. The family is also something more than a basic social unit, and this something-more limits it, helping us to make of it neither more nor less than it should be. It is a sphere in which God is at work on us, shaping and molding us, that we may become people who genuinely wish to share his life of love. The overarching interpretive rubric within which to understand the spheres of life—here, in particular, the family—is Augustine's statement that the servants of God "have no reason to regret even this life of time, for in it they are schooled for eternity."[17] The family is a school of virtue in which God sets before us, day after day, a few people whom we are to learn to love. This is the *paideia* of the heavenly Father at work upon both children and parents, building upon the love that comes naturally to us in our families, but transforming it also into the image of divine love.

Such straightforward religious talk may, of course, seem alien to the common life of our society, and no doubt it is, to some degree. Yet it may be precisely the language for which we are searching, language that points the way toward a true humanism.

We tend to make of the family both too much and too little. Too much is made of it, as parents seek to reproduce themselves in their children, feverishly seek children "of their own," and try as much as possible to protect those children from all experience of suffering and sacrifice. In doing this we ask of the family more than it can give, and we place upon it expectations that must inevitably be disappointed. At the same time we make too little of the family—seldom seeing in it anything more than an arena for personal fulfillment and failing to see it as a community that ought to transmit a way of life.

What we really need is language that can take seriously the venture of parenthood without depriving the family bond of a still greater *telos*, a larger aim and meaning. The family understood as a school of virtue—the place where citizens capable of adult commitment are formed, the place where we begin to learn the meaning of love—can provide that larger context.

THE IMPORTANCE OF AN IDEAL

One might argue, of course, that the vision sketched above—whether true or false—is largely irrelevant to our circumstances. The creative fidelity to which the venture of parenthood calls us rests upon the virtue of hope—and, perhaps, many in our world have little reason to hope. Until we change the conditions and circumstances of their lives, this vision of the family is worthless. We might well be tempted to think in that way, but we would then fail to appreciate the importance of an ideal.

In his engagingly titled book *What's Wrong with the World*, G. K. Chesterton argued that his fellow citizens could not repair the defects of the family because they had no ideal at which to aim. Neither the Tory (Gudge) nor the Socialist (Hudge) viewed the family as sacred or had an image of what the family at its best might be:

> The Tory says he wants to preserve family life in Cindertown; the Socialist very reasonably points out to him that in Cindertown at present there isn't any family life to preserve. But Hudge, the Socialist, in his turn, is highly vague and mysterious about whether he will try to restore it where it has disappeared.... The Tory sometimes talks as if he wanted to tighten the domestic bonds that do not exist; the Socialist as if he wanted to loosen the bonds that do not bind anybody. The question we all want to ask of both of them is the original ideal question, "Do you want to keep the family at all?"[18]

The result of such confusion, Chesterton thought, was that in his own day "the cultured class is shrieking to be let out of the decent home, just as the working class is shouting to be let into it."[19]

In such circumstances one needs an ideal—a point from which to begin and on the basis of which to think about the world. Chesterton began "with a little girl's hair":

> That I know is a good thing at any rate. Whatever else is evil, the pride of a good mother in the beauty of her daughter is good. It is one of those adamantine tendernesses which are the touchstones of every age and race. If other things are against it, other things must go down.... With the red hair of one she-urchin in the gutter I will set fire to all modern civilization. Because a girl should have long hair, she should have clean hair; because she should have clean hair, she should not have an unclean home; because she should not have an

unclean home, she should have a free and leisured mother; because she should have a free mother, she should not have an usurious landlord; because there should not be an usurious landlord, there should be a redistribution of property; because there should be a redistribution of property, there shall be a revolution. That little urchin with the gold-red hair, whom I have just watched toddling past my house, she shall not be lopped and lamed and altered; her hair shall not be cut short like a convict's; no, all the kingdoms of the earth shall be hacked about and mutilated to suit her. She is the human and sacred image; all around her the social fabric shall sway and split and fall; the pillars of society shall be shaken, and the roofs of ages come rushing down; and not one hair of her head shall be harmed.[20]

That captures vividly the importance—and the power—of an ideal. And until we rediscover the inner meaning of the venture of parenthood as a mystery to be lived rather than a problem to be controlled, we will be poorly equipped to deal with the ills we confront.

7

CLONING AND BEGETTING

Because I have been invited to reflect on the moral implications of human cloning specifically as a Protestant theologian, I have chosen my concerns accordingly.[1] I do not suppose, therefore, that the issues I address are the only issues that deserve our attention. Thus, for example, I will not address the question of whether we could rightly conduct the first experiments in human cloning, given the likelihood that such experiments would not at first fully succeed. That is an important moral question, but I will not take it up. Nor do I suppose that I can represent "Protestants" generally. There is no such beast. Indeed, Protestants are specialists in the art of fragmentation. In my own tradition, which is Lutheran, we commonly understand ourselves as quite content to be Catholic except when, on certain questions, we are compelled to disagree. Other Protestants might think of themselves differently. It is also important to emphasize that reflecting from this particular perspective should not be understood as an attempt for the "Protestant interest group" to weigh in on public policy deliberations. On the contrary, theological language, at least as I shall use it here, has sought to uncover what is universal and human. It begins epistemologically from a particular place, but it opens up ontologically a vision of the human. The faith which seeks understanding may sometimes find it.

Lacking an accepted teaching office within the church, Protestants had to find some way to provide authoritative moral guidance. They turned from the authority of the church as interpreter of Scripture to the biblical texts themselves. That characteristic Protestant move is not likely, of course, to provide any very immediate guidance on a subject such as human cloning. But it does teach something about the connection of marriage and parenthood. The creation story in Genesis 1 depicts the creation of humankind as male and female, sexually differentiated and enjoined by God's grace to sustain human life through procreation.

Hence, there is given in creation a connection between (1) the differentiation of the sexes and (2) the begetting of a child. We can begin with that connection, making our way indirectly toward the subject of cloning. It is from the vantage point of this connection that our theological tradition has addressed questions that are both profound and mysterious in their simplicity: What is the meaning of a child? And what is good for a child? Such questions are, of course, at the heart of many problems in our society today, and it is against the background of such questions that I want to reflect upon the significance of human cloning. What Protestants found in the Bible was a normative view: namely, that the sexual differentiation is ordered toward the creation of offspring and that children should be conceived within the marital union. By God's grace the child is a gift who springs from the giving and receiving of love. Marriage and parenthood are connected—held together in a basic form of humanity.

To this depiction of the connection between sexual differentiation and child-bearing as normative, it is, of course, possible to respond in different ways.[2] We may welcome the connection and find in it humane wisdom to guide our conduct, or we may resent it as a limit to our freedom and seek to transcend it. Members of our society, whether theoreticians or eminently practical people, are often drawn to a vision of human nature that sees the "essence" of being human—as an older language would have put it—to be simply our freedom to make and remake ourselves. Hence, limits to our freedom are resented. If we are able to separate child-bearing from the sexual relation of a man and woman, and if we have reason to make the separation, we chafe at any suggestion that we ought not do what we can do. But recent "advances" in human reproduction, and certainly the possibility of human cloning, might give us pause. Is the freedom to make and remake ourselves really what is most fundamental about being human? That it is one important aspect of our being is undeniable. But at least as important, I think, is the affective bond that ties the generations together, and that bond is grounded in our biology and in the procreative relationship of a man and woman. Some recent "advances" in reproductive technology have already begun to threaten the bond between the generations, and cloning would constitute a decisive rupture. We would willfully give rise to relationships we hardly know how to name—when, for example, a woman's "daughter" is, in some sense, her twin "sister." We would willfully undertake something like a deliberate rejection of the otherness within relationship—and perhaps of relationship altogether—that sexual reproduction always requires us to acknowledge. We would willfully subvert the web of relationships across the generations, one of the constitutive elements of our humanity. A decision to clone, therefore, would demonstrate paradigmatically the way in which our freedom is not only creative, but also destructive.

We did not need modern scientific breakthroughs to know that it is possible—and sometimes seemingly desirable—to sever the connection between marriage and begetting children. The possibility of human cloning is striking only because it breaks the connection so emphatically. It aims directly at the heart of the mystery that is a child. Part of the mystery here is that we will always be hard pressed to explain *why* the connection of sexual differentiation and procreation should not be broken. Precisely to the degree that it *is* integral to our humanity, as integral as freedom, it will be hard to give more fundamental reasons why the connection (between marriage and begetting children) should be welcomed and honored when, in our freedom, we need not do so. But moral argument must begin somewhere. To see through everything is, as C. S. Lewis once put it, the same as not to see at all.

If we cannot argue *to* this norm, however, we can argue *from* it. If we cannot entirely explain the mystery, we can explicate it. And the explication comes from two angles. Maintaining the connection between procreation and the sexual relationship of a man and a woman is good both for that relationship and for children.

It is good, first, for the relation of the man and the woman. No doubt the motives of those who beget children coitally are often mixed, and they may be uncertain about the full significance of what they do. But if they are willing to shape their intentions in accord with the norm I have outlined, they may be freed from self-absorption. The act of love is not simply a personal project undertaken to satisfy one's own needs, and procreation, as the fruit of coitus, reminds us of that. Even when the relation of a man and

woman does not or cannot give rise to offspring, they can understand their embrace as more than their personal project in the
world, as their participation in a form of life that carries its own
inner meaning and has its *telos* established in the creation. The
meaning of what we do then is not determined simply by our
desire or will. As Oliver O'Donovan, a well-known contemporary
Anglican theologian has noted, some understanding like this is
needed if the sexual relation of a man and a woman is to be more
than "simply a profound form of play...."[3]

Maintaining the connection between procreation and the
sexual relationship of a man and a woman is good, second, for the
child. For when the sexual act becomes only a personal project, so
does the child. No longer, then, is the bearing and rearing of children thought of as a task we should take up or as a return made
in recompense for the gift of life we have received; instead, it is a
project we undertake if it promises to meet our needs and desires.
Those people—both learned commentators and ordinary folk—
who have described cloning as narcissistic or as replication of one's
self point to something important. Even if we grant that a clone,
reared in different circumstances than those of its immediate
ancestor, might turn out to be quite a different person in some
respects, the point of that person's existence would be grounded in
our will and desire.

Hence, retaining the tie that unites procreation with the sexual
relation of a man and a woman is also good for children. Even
when a man and a woman deeply desire a child, the act of love
itself cannot take the child as its primary object. They must give
themselves to each other, setting aside their projects, and the child
becomes the natural fruition of their shared love—something quite
different from a chosen project. The child is therefore always a

gift—one like them who springs from their embrace, not a being whom they have made and whose destiny they should determine. This is light years away from the notion that we all have a right to have children—in whatever way we see fit, whenever it serves our purposes. Our children begin with a kind of genetic independence of us, their parents. They replicate neither their father nor their mother. That is a reminder of the independence that we must eventually grant to them and for which it is our duty to prepare them.[4] To lose, even in principle, this sense of the child as a gift entrusted to us will not be good for children.

In C. S. Lewis's *That Hideous Strength*, subtitled "a modern fairy tale for grown-ups," the National Institute of Coordinated Experiments (acronym: NICE) is undertaking an ambitious attempt to control and shape nature. A member of NICE named Filostrato explains how this applies to human beings. "What," he asks, "are the things that most offend the dignity of man?" And he answers, "Birth and breeding and death."[5] Organic life, having done its work in producing mind, can now be transcended by the free human spirit. Death can be conquered, and reproduction need no longer involve copulation. We are able now to see just how prescient Lewis was—how offensive birth and breeding are to a society in which control of our nature and destiny has become for some the central cultural project. But such control is, I have suggested, bad for both the sexual relation of a man and a woman and for children. In particular and especially, the child becomes a chosen and willed product, one whom we have shaped and whom we thus may control.

I will press this point still further by making one more theological move. When early Christians tried to tell the story of Jesus as they found it in their Scriptures, they were driven to some rather complex formulations. They wanted to say that Jesus was truly one with that God whom he called Father, lest it should seem that what he had accomplished did not really overcome the gulf that separates us from God. Thus, while distinguishing the persons of Father and Son, they wanted to say that Jesus is truly God—of one being with the Father. And the language in which they did this, language from the fourth century Nicene Creed, one of the two most important creeds that antedate the division of the church in the West at the Reformation, is language that describes the Son of the Father as "begotten, not made." Oliver O'Donovan has noted that this distinction between making and begetting, crucial for Christians' understanding of God, carries considerable moral significance.[6]

What the language of the Nicene Creed wanted to say was that the Son is God just as the Father is God. It was intended to assert an equality of being. And for that what was needed was a language other than the language of *making*. What we beget is like ourselves. What we make is not; it is the product of our free decision, and its destiny is ours to determine. Of course, on this Christian understanding human beings are not begotten in the absolute sense that the Son is said to be begotten of the Father. They are *made*—but made by God through human begetting. Hence, although we are not God's equal, we are of equal dignity with each other. And we are not at each other's disposal. If it is, in fact, human begetting that expresses our equal dignity, we should not lightly set it aside in a manner as decisive as cloning.

I am well aware, of course, that other advances in what we are pleased to call reproductive technology have already strained the connection between the sexual relationship of a man and a woman and the birth of a child. Clearly, procreation has to some extent become reproduction—making rather than doing. I am far from thinking that all this has been done well or wisely, and sometimes we may only come to understand the nature of the road we are on when we have already traveled fairly far along it. But whatever we say of that, surely human cloning would be a new and decisive turn on this road—far more emphatically a kind of production, far less a surrender to the mystery of the genetic lottery that *is* the mystery of the child.

I am also aware that we can all imagine circumstances in which we ourselves might—were the technology available—be tempted to turn to cloning: Parents who lose a young child in an accident and want to "replace" her. A seriously ill person in need of embryonic stem cells to repair damaged tissue. A person in need of organs for transplant. A person who is infertile and wants, in some sense, to reproduce. Once the child becomes a project or product, such temptations become almost irresistible. There is no end of good causes in the world, and they would sorely tempt us, even if we did not live in a society for which the pursuit of health has become a god, justifying almost anything. As William F. May has often noted, we are preoccupied with death and the destructive powers of our world. But without in any way glorifying suffering or pretending that it is not evil, Christians worship a God who wills to be with us in our dependence, teaching us "attentiveness before a good and nurturant God."[7] We learn, therefore, that what matters is how we live, not only how long—that we are responsible to do as much good as we can, but this means, as much as we can within the limits morality sets for us.

I am also aware, finally, that we might for now approve human cloning but only in restricted circumstances—for example, the cloning of preimplantation embryos (up to fourteen days) for experimental use. That would, of course, mean creation solely for purposes of research on human embryos—human subjects who are not really best described as *pre*implantation embryos. They are *un*implanted embryos—a locution that makes clear the extent to which their being and destiny are the product of human will alone.

Proponents of human cloning sometimes suggest that the kinds of concerns I have noted here cannot be determinative of public policy in a pluralistic society such as ours. Even if I have successfully pointed to certain dangers or suggested certain wrongs that we might do, all such claims will be branded as "speculative." Perhaps human cloning will help to create a world in which we think of children principally as the product of will and choice, a world in which the affective bond that ties the generations together will be radically altered, a world in which human equality will be threatened. But if such wrongs do not indubitably lead to physical harm, they are only "speculative." That is, they put forward a kind of metaphysical vision of what is good in human life—profound perhaps and, even, on some occasions compelling, but never worthy of any special place in the formulation of public policy. What must then be said in response is that the alternative view, which seeks to make place in our common life for human cloning, is every bit as "speculative." It too, then, must be said to be grounded in a disputed vision of what is fundamentally human. For against the vision of the human good that sees children as the fruit of an ecstatic union of a man and a woman, the defender of cloning puts forward a speculative metaphysic according to which rational will and choice are what characterize our humanity. There is no reason to give such a vision of humanity pride of place in our public deliberations.

Protestants have often been pictured—actually erroneously in many respects—as stout defenders of human freedom. But whatever the accuracy of that depiction, they have not had in mind a freedom without limit, without even the limit that is God. They have not located the dignity of human beings in a self-modifying freedom that knows no limit and that need never respect a limit that it can, in principle, transgress. The meaning of the child—offspring of a man and a woman, but a replication of neither; their offspring, but not their product whose meaning and destiny they might determine—that, I think, constitutes such a limit to our freedom to make and remake ourselves. In the face of that mystery we do well to remember that "progress" is always an optional goal in which nothing of the sacred inheres.[8]

8

ABORTION AND THE MEANING OF PARENTHOOD

Consider the following three "cases" and what we might want to say about them:

(1) A pregnant women undergoes amniocentesis to test for genetic abnormalities in the fetus she is carrying and is told that she will give birth to a normal male child. It turns out, however, that she has a baby girl who is afflicted with Down's Syndrome. The woman, contending that she would have aborted the fetus if she had been given accurate prenatal diagnosis, sues the hospital that administered the test. She sues on behalf of her child, arguing that the child is entitled to damages for "wrongful life."

(2) A thirty-six-year-old woman gives birth to a child with Down's Syndrome and related physical abnormalities. While pregnant, this woman had been offered amniocentesis by her physician, but she had declined it. The child's father, acting on behalf of the child, sues the mother, seeking damages for wrongful life.

(3) A pregnant woman has placenta previa—a serious condition in which part of the cervix is blocked by the placenta, leading

to a risk of hemorrhage for the mother and oxygen deprivation for the fetus. The woman has been advised by her physician that while pregnant she should not use amphetamines, should not have sexual intercourse, and should go to the hospital at once if she begins to bleed. Her child is born with severe brain damage and dies within weeks. It turns out, however, that the woman had delayed going to the hospital for a number of hours after beginning to bleed, had been using amphetamines (indeed, had taken them as recently as the day she went into labor), and on that same day had sexual relations with her husband. The woman is charged with a misdemeanor under child abuse laws.

The first and third of these are versions of cases that have actually occurred and made their way into our courts. The second is a not unlikely scenario for the future. Taken together, they raise a number of important and provocative questions, some of them having to do with the very meaning of the vocation of parents.

ABORTION AND PARENTHOOD

We can begin by thinking about the last of these cases. It could, of course, have many different variants. The pregnant woman could be a heavy smoker or drinker, or a narcotic drug user. She could need to follow a very restrictive diet throughout pregnancy in order to avoid damage to the fetus (e.g., from PKU). The fetus could need surgery while still *in utero*—a kind of science fiction possibility gradually becoming reality, a possibility that must also, of course, mean surgery on the pregnant woman. What should the responsibilities of such a woman be? Should she be not merely encouraged but also required to alter her behavior and way of life for the sake of the fetus? To submit to restrictions or hazards for its sake? If, because of her unwillingness to alter her behavior, her child is born with harms that could have been avoided, should she be penalized?

Although courts have, in fact, sometimes enforced such restrictions, we might well worry about attempts at legal restriction. It is one thing to argue that a pregnant woman (or any parent of any child) should not be permitted to take action that aims at her child's death (as abortion in most circumstances does). It is harder to argue that she must avoid behavior that may harm her child or that the law should make significant restrictions on her way of life with that end in view. Yet, it might be persuasively argued in some instances. After all, the law does punish both child abuse and neglect that occur after birth. And even if a woman is free to abort a fetus and thereby end a pregnancy, we might hold that she is not free to carry it to term while engaging in behavior that carries serious risk of harm for that child.

Suppose we were considering a law that would require a pregnant woman who intended to carry the pregnancy to term to alter her behavior in significant ways (or even undergo surgical procedures) for the well-being of the child. We can begin to appreciate the meaning of abortion for the parental vocation if we consider one argument that might be offered against such a law. One might say: "That sort of law treats the fetus as if it were an independent entity, physically separate from the woman. It ignores the fact that the woman cannot simply walk away from the fetus."

Except that, abortion being legal, she can walk away from it. Abortion makes that possible. Notice what this means. The possibility of abortion has a peculiar effect on the relation of mother and fetus. The "natural" connection is no longer tight. She can walk away. This might seem to give her greater freedom—the freedom to see herself and her child as separate entities. The freedom to affirm the connection of these two entities if she wishes...or to reject the connection. But if the law we are hypothetically considering were to be passed, this way of thinking would lead to less freedom for the woman who chooses not to abort. Since she hasn't walked away, she has taken on some pretty stringent obligations. This is what happens when we cease to think of the fetus as the "fruit of the womb" and think instead of the mother-fetus connection as a chosen, willed one. If the woman can choose, she must be in control. But then, perhaps, some will begin to think we must hold her responsible (even legally liable) in new ways.

An argument analogous to this one is central to the important and provocative book by Barbara Katz Rothman titled *The Tentative Pregnancy*.[1] Although she favors the legal right to abortion, Rothman worries about how that right—and especially the prenatal diagnosis that so often accompanies it—may alter our understanding of what it means to be a parent and, in particular, a mother. The technology that appears to confer new freedom ultimately controls and reshapes the way we think. It encourages us to think in terms of separation and individuation, of the mother as simply the environment of the fetus. More traditionally, we might have pictured mother and child as beginning with complete, inseparable attachment—and moving from that point through a separation that begins at birth and widens thereafter. But the technology of prenatal diagnosis and abortion that encourages us to picture pregnancy as a willed, chosen relation between two wholly separate individuals reverses this way of thought. We learn to think of birth as the moment of "bonding," of pregnancy as moving from separation to attachment (p. 114f.).

The "tentative pregnancy" is one, therefore, in which a mother cannot really acknowledge the presence of her child until it has been given a clean bill of health. Only then can she choose to bond with it. The irony, of course, as Rothman notes, is that even our technology can never guarantee a perfect baby—or that the perfect baby will remain that way after birth. She writes:

> The possibility of spending the rest of one's life caring for a sick or disabled child can *never* be eliminated by prenatal testing.... [M]otherhood is, among other things, one more chance for a speeding truck to ruin your life (p. 252f.).

To think of the bond between a parent and child as chiefly a chosen and willed one—quite different, for example, from thinking of the child as God's gift or of the parents' role simply as that of co-creators with God—turns out to undermine the kind of unconditional commitment so central to the vocation of parenthood. It happens simply to be a fact that children need from their parents such unconditional commitment if they are to flourish. They need to know that they can be and are loved with an acceptance that does not depend on any qualifications or merits they may bring. They need, that is, to know that their parents love them in precisely the way we all need to know that God loves us.

FREEDOM AND RESPONSIBILITY

When, however, parents love more tentatively, the result is that—forsaking the call to try to love as God does—they end up having to try to be godlike. What they get in place of unconditional commitment is a new, and more stringent, sort of responsibility. They take on the role of creator with respect to their children. And they must, in turn, bear an equivalent responsibility. No longer need children hold God responsible for the cruel joke life has played on them. The culprit will be nearer to hand. The old problem of theodicy—justifying the ways of God in our world—will have to be applied to parents. The child whose life of pain or disability might have been avoided by abortion might learn to reason thus: "If my parents have the power to keep me from living such a life, and if they really loved me, they would not let me endure this. But I am enduring it, and they had it within their power to abort me. They must not really love me." To exercise godlike control over one's child—to learn to think of the bond as purely chosen and willed—is to risk becoming the object of such reasoning. That is what happens when the child becomes a product for whose quality of life parents are responsible.

This brings us back to the other two cases with which I began, cases of "wrongful life" as they have begun to be called. If parents have a nearly godlike responsibility for the nature and well-being of their children, if children have become a kind of commodity, then it only makes sense that we should ask of parents some "quality control." Indeed, in a nice turn of phrase, Rothman calls wrongful life suits "a form of product liability litigation" (p. 92). And in fact, wrongful life suits are a good prism through which to view the meaning of parenthood. In the past, courts have been reluctant to permit such suits—reluctant, in large part, to grant that existence itself could be an evil on the basis of which one had standing to sue. But a few such suits have been successful in recent years, and it would probably be foolish to wager that the day will not come when a child wins such a suit, not just against a hospital or a physician, but against parent(s).

We may be uneasy about such possibilities, but it is hard to say why. Having taken on greater responsibility for the very nature of children than we ever have before, we may find ourselves wanting to step back and abdicate at least some measure of the newly acquired responsibility. For example, Rothman counsels women who undergo prenatal diagnosis not even to ask whether the fetus is male or female; for, having such knowledge, we may be tempted to take control not only of what clearly seems to be a defect, but also of the child's person more generally. The techniques that offered freedom begin to control us. They, not we, are in the driver's seat, and we end with a responsibility too awesome for human beings to accept. Sensing that, we wisely draw back from some portion of that responsibility, but we may no longer be able to say why.

FREEDOM AND FINITUDE

It would be a mistake to turn my argument into one that denies all human responsibility for shaping the world in which we live and, even, the children whom we beget and rear. We are not simply gods, we are not simply our freedom to shape and reshape the world. We are not to think of the world—and, in particular, other people and our children—as infinitely plastic to our desire for control. Nevertheless, if we are not simply freedom, we are called to exercise our freedom in responsible ways—as co-creators, though not as gods. Human beings are made from the dust of the ground and are, therefore, finite beings who should respect the limits of our human condition; for in respecting such limits we recognize that we are not God, and we acknowledge the Creator. But made from the dust of the ground, we also have within us the God-breathed spirit that rightly seeks to exercise an appropriately benevolent dominion within creation. We seek to cure illness, to overcome disability, to discover new ways to enrich human life. In short, if we are not simply free to be as gods, we are not simply finite animals either. We quite rightly exercise many kinds of control every day of our lives.

If wrongful life suits make us uneasy, it is because they force us to think about the line that is so hard to draw: between our freedom and our finitude, between the exercise of freedom that is rightful dominion and the exercise of freedom that gives in to the temptation to be as gods. This is not a line that can always be clearly drawn in advance, but to see the issue in these terms is to appreciate that our uneasiness has its roots in some of the most basic questions—religious questions—about the world in which we live.

Who finally is the lifegiver? Parents? Physician? Both together? Or are they only cooperators in and with a power greater than their own? Does the natural tie of mother and child (or, more broadly, parents and child) itself have any moral claim upon us apart from our own willing and choosing? And, are there possible exercises of freedom that we *ought* to reject or kinds of responsibility that we *ought* to view as inappropriate for human beings? Such issues, which can only be termed religious issues, lie deep within our public uneasiness about developments like the wrongful life suit.

We can press the issue yet a bit further if we consider a world in which God (and even nature) has faded from consciousness, but a world in which we remain morally serious. If God is no longer around to bear responsibility for bringing good out of evil—out of, for example, the suffering of an infant born with serious disabilities—then we must look elsewhere for someone to shoulder the burden of responsibility. If an avoidable evil has been permitted to occur and God cannot be blamed, then who is the most likely candidate for such responsibility and blame? Surely it is we ourselves. To see our situation in this light is to see what it might mean really to learn to think of ourselves not just as co-creators with a power greater than our own but, instead, simply as creators.

Our public debates about abortion have tended to shy away from such seemingly metaphysical issues. Thus, for example, even when we oppose abortion done on grounds of "fetal defect," we usually oppose it on the ground that we ought not make judgments about the comparative worth of human lives. And that is a perfectly respectable argument to which I, at least, am quite ready to assent. Perhaps, however, we also need to think about some other issues—fuzzier ones and harder to clarify, but very important. How we think about a child, and the relation of mother, father and child, is not simply a given. It can change over time, and it is the very possibility of abortion that brings about some of those changes and teaches us to think in new and different ways about the "nature of human nature" and the meaning of being a parent or a child.

If (to use some old-fashioned language) the essence of our humanity consists in our freedom, in taking control, we will have to think of parenthood in a corresponding way. But that may mean the loss of much humane wisdom—the wisdom that sees a parent as one who stands before the child as God's representative but certainly not as God, the wisdom which knows that to accept full responsibility for what our children are and become is to cut the root that will nourish them as children, the root that is the unconditional love of a parent. Concerns such as these are at stake in our public debate about abortion, and we do well to pay them some heed.

PART 3

Place and Possessions

9

C. S. LEWIS AND A THEOLOGY OF THE EVERYDAY

"One is sometimes (not often) glad not to be a great theologian. One might so easily confuse it with being a good Christian."[1] Thus, C. S. Lewis wrote in *Reflections on the Psalms*. Similarly, Lewis's religious writings are full of asides to the effect that he is not a theologian and that what he says is subject to correction by real theologians. In part, of course, let us recognize this for what it is: a smart rhetorical strategy that gets the reader on his side over against the presumably elitist theologians. But there is a worrisome sense in which Lewis's readers might be all too ready to hear such a message, all too ready to suppose that faith is simple and clear, that theologians are largely in the business of making complicated what ought to be simple.

That is a temptation whose seductions we should resist. Indeed, to the degree that Lewis is often characterized as a "popular" religious thinker, I am inclined to think the characterization misleading and, in part, I fear, a result of a peculiar academic prejudice against anyone who writes clearly and is widely read. Lewis's readers actually get a rather heavy dose of serious religious reflection, though generally in quite alluring literary style.

Nevertheless, theology is and must remain an elite activity. It is not, in fact, aimed at the masses. And there is a sense in which we might better say that Lewis's writing is "religious" rather than "theological." This sense is one that he would himself, I believe, affirm. He makes such a distinction, for example, in the incomplete, posthumously published essay "The Language of Religion."[2] There he develops a distinction between ordinary language ("It was very cold") and two other kinds of language, each of which transforms ordinary language in the interest of certain purposes. Scientific language ("The temperature was minus 5 degrees Fahrenheit") seeks language that has a certain kind of precision lacked by our ordinary speech—a precision that we can quantify and test, that can be used to settle disputes about how cold it actually is. But this scientific language does not itself give us any sense of how a very cold day "feels," a sense of its "quality." If I have spent my entire life in a tropical climate, and you tell me that it is minus 5 degrees Fahrenheit where you live, such language will not help me feel what it's like to be there.

Ordinary language might do a little better in communicating this "feel." "Your ears will tingle." "It will hurt just to breathe." But poetic language exists in large part to try to improve ordinary language on just this point: to convey the quality, the feel, of experience. Lewis uses Keats's poem "The Eve of St. Agnes" as illustration: "Ah, bitter chill it was! The owl, for all his feathers was a-cold; The hare limped trembling through the frozen grass, And silent was the flock in wooly fold: Numb'd were the Beadsman's fingers." This language cannot be quantified or tested, but it may,

Lewis suggests, convey information that we can get in no other way. Perhaps it may even convey the quality of experiences we ourselves have never had.

Religious talk, like all talk, begins with ordinary language, but, depending on our purposes, it may quickly turn in directions more like the scientific or the poetic. Theological language, as Lewis describes it, is, strictly speaking, an alteration rather like the scientific. It seeks a precision that is needed and useful for clarifying uncertain or disputed points and for settling disagreements. As such, it is absolutely necessary. Elitist in a certain sense, it is, nonetheless, not to be belittled. Indeed, its precision can be a thing of beauty. But one thing it cannot do: it cannot, by itself, convey understanding of what in its very nature transcends our ordinary experience. For that we need language that is religious but not, in this sense, theological—language more like the poetic. To say "God is the Father of lights" is such language—religious, though not exactly theological.

A good bit of Lewis's success can, I think, be attributed to the fact that he actually writes relatively little "theology" in this technical sense. Clearly, he's read a good bit of it and been instructed by it; he does not in any sense belittle it; but he tends to seek language that captures and communicates the quality, the feel, of living and thinking as a Christian. As Austin Farrer put it: "[Lewis's] real power was not proof; it was depiction. There lived in his writings a Christian universe that could be both thought and felt, in which he was at home and in which he made his reader feel at home."[3] That is the universe I want to explore. It illumines the everyday, so that we may find in it shafts of the divine glory that point to God, so that we may sense the eternal significance of ordinary life.[4]

THE ETERNAL IN THE EVERYDAY

In his famous and powerful work *Fear and Trembling,* Søren Kierkegaard describes the "knight of faith" who has made the double movement of infinite resignation and of faith.[5] Having given up the sense that anything is his possession to claim, having surrendered all for the sake of an immediate relation to God, the knight of faith nevertheless trusts that God will give it back—not in some future life, but in the here and now, in the finite realm. And, as a result, although he has made the first movement of infinite resignation, he is also able to savor the everyday. Kierkegaard describes the knight this way:

> Here he is. The acquaintance is struck, I am introduced. The moment I first set eyes on him I thrust him away, jump back, clasp my hands together and say half aloud: 'Good God! Is this the person, is it really him? He looks just like a tax-gatherer.'... I examine him from top to toe, in case there should be some crack through which the infinite peeped out. No! He is solid through and through.... One detects nothing of the strangeness and superiority that mark the knight of the infinite. This man takes pleasure, takes part, in everything, and whenever one catches him occupied with something his engagement has the persistence of the worldly person whose soul is wrapped up in such things.... He delights in everything he sees....[6]

The knight of faith is therefore, as Kierkegaard puts it, able "to express the sublime in the pedestrian absolutely."[7]

That characterization—to express the sublime in the pedestrian—is an apt description of something that makes Lewis's religious writing so effective. "[O]nly supernaturalists really see Nature," Lewis says.

> You must go a little away from her, and then turn round, and look back. Then at last the true landscape will become visible.... Come out, look back, and then you will see...this astonishing cataract of bears, babies, and bananas: this immoderate deluge of atoms, orchids, oranges, cancers, canaries, fleas, gases, tornadoes and toads. How could you have ever thought this was the ultimate reality?... She is herself. Offer her neither worship nor contempt.[8]

The ordinary pleasures of life—both those simply given to us in nature and those derived from culture—play a large role in Lewis's thinking and account for much of the power of his writing.

He can make domesticity seem enticing—as when Peter, Susan, and Lucy share a meal with the Beavers. And, indeed, the best times in Narnia are not the times when momentous events are occurring. The good times are those when nothing "important" happens, when life goes on in its ordinary, everyday way. Similarly, Lewis finds—surely not by accident—that "cheerful moderation" is an important characteristic in the novels of Jane Austen. "She has, or at least all her favourite characters have, a hearty relish for what would now be regarded as very modest pleasures. A ball, a dinner party, books, conversation, a drive to see a great house ten miles away...."[9] He celebrates the appreciation of "middle things" that he finds in the writings of Joseph Addison. Granting that Addison does not stir one's soul as some writers do, Lewis nonetheless finds a kind of strength and goodness in Addison's affirmation of "the common ground of daily life." "If I were to live in a man's house for a whole twelve-month, I think I should be more curious about the quality of his small beer than about that of his wine; more curious about his bread and butter and beef than about either."[10]

And few readers of *Surprised by Joy* are likely to forget Lewis's description of what was for him a "normal day" during the time he was living with and being tutored by Kirkpatrick.

> [I]f I could please myself I would always live as I lived there. I would choose always to breakfast at exactly eight and to be at my desk by nine, there to read or write till one. If a good cup of tea or coffee could be brought me about eleven, so much the better. A step or so out of doors for a pint of beer would not do quite so well; for a man does not want to drink alone and if you meet a friend in the taproom the break is likely to be extended beyond its ten minutes. At one precisely lunch should be on the table; and by two at the latest I would be on the road. Not, except at rare intervals, with a friend. Walking and talking are two very great pleasures, but it is a mistake to combine them. Our own noise blots out the sounds and silences of the outdoor world; and talking leads almost inevitably to smoking, and then farewell to nature as far as one of our senses is concerned.... The return from the walk, and the arrival of tea, should be exactly coincident, and not later than a quarter past four. Tea should be taken in solitude,...[f]or eating and reading are two pleasures that combine admirably. Of course not all books are suitable for mealtime reading. It would be a kind of blasphemy to read poetry at table. What one wants is a gossipy, formless book

which can be opened anywhere.... At five a man should be at work again, and at it till seven. Then, at the evening meal and after, comes the time for talk, or, failing that, for lighter reading; and unless you are making a night of it with your cronies...there is no reason why you should ever be in bed later than eleven.[11]

Such a life Lewis himself describes as "almost entirely selfish" but certainly not "self-centered." "[F]or in such a life my mind would be directed toward a thousand things, not one of which is myself."[12] Lewis, of course, understands that an "almost entirely selfish" approach to life cannot really be recommended. He simply understands its attraction, and he sees that it may, in fact, be better in some respects than a life that seems less selfish.

One of the happiest men and most pleasing companions I have ever known was intensely selfish. On the other hand I have known people capable of real sacrifice whose lives were nevertheless a misery to themselves and to others, because self-concern and self-pity filled all their thoughts. Either condition will destroy the soul in the end. But till the end give me the man who takes the best of everything (even at my expense) and then talks of other things, rather than the man who serves me and talks of himself, and whose very kindnesses are a continual reproach, a continual demand for pity, gratitude, and admiration.[13]

In an epitaph he once composed, Lewis made the same point a little more playfully:

> Erected by her sorrowing brothers
> In memory of Martha Clay.
> Here lies one who lived for others;
> Now she has peace. And so have they.[14]

Thus, Lewis has a keen delight in the ordinary and the everyday. But I think this appreciation for the everyday goes yet a little further than simple delight—which, taken by itself after all, might be chiefly a matter of temperament. The deeper point is that the ordinary is the stuff of most of our lives most of the time. It is, therefore, where we most often find our callings, our opportunities for faithfulness, and our temptations. Something like that is the point of Lewis's sermon "Learning in War-Time," a sermon preached in the Church of St. Mary the Virgin in Oxford on the evening of Sunday, October 22, 1939—when people in England had a genuine crisis, very much out of the ordinary, on their hands. Even such a moment of crisis does not, Lewis suggests, alter the fundamental situation in which we always find ourselves. For every moment of life is lived in the presence of the Eternal, in every moment of life we are "advancing either to heaven or to hell," and those high stakes are played out in the most mundane of decisions.[15] Lewis's ability to see that, and help us to see it, is part of the enduring power of *The Screwtape Letters*. Screwtape knows how much the ordinary and the everyday count in our spiritual life. He knows, for example, of a human being who was once "defended from strong temptations to social ambition by a still stronger taste for tripe and onions."[16] He knows that Wormwood has blundered badly when he permits his "patient" to read a book simply because he enjoys it or to take a walk through country he enjoys.[17] He knows that, when it comes to separating a human being from God, the ordinary can also be Wormwood's greatest ally. The important choices in life seldom present themselves in extraordinary appearance. "It does not matter how small the sins are, provided that their cumulative effect is to edge the man away from the Light and out into the Nothing. Murder is no better than cards if cards can do the trick. Indeed, the safest road to Hell is the gradual one—the gentle slope, soft underfoot, without sudden turnings, without milestones, without signposts."[18]

This sense that eternal issues are at stake in the mundane choices of our everyday life helps, I think, to account for the fact that, in this country, Lewis has been so popular among evangelical Protestants. An analysis of the theological structure of his religious writings would, I am convinced, show clearly that this structure is more adequately described (to paint in broad strokes) as "Catholic" than as "Protestant." Faith as trust does not play a large role in his depiction of the Christian life. That life is not conceived primarily as a turn from consciousness of sin to the proclamation of grace. Instead, it is conceived of as a journey, a process of perfection, and Jesus is the way toward that goal. From start to finish this journey is, to be sure, the work of grace, but that grace is primarily the power to finish the journey, not simply a pardoning word of forgiveness. The end of this journey is the beatific vision—to see God and to rest in God—and that vision is granted only to those who are perfected, to the pure in heart.

In good Aristotelian fashion, therefore, Lewis thinks of all the ordinary decisions of life as forming our character, as turning us into people who either do or do not wish to gaze forever upon the face of God. When "night falls on Narnia" and we get the great scene of final judgment, all the inhabitants of that world have no choice about one thing. All must march past Aslan and look upon him. Some see there the face they have always longed to see, which they have learned to love, and they enter Aslan's world. Others see a face they can only hate, for that is the sort of person they have become. They go off into nothingness. Every choice counts. Every choice contributes to determining what we ultimately love.

Protestant readers may, I believe, be especially drawn to this picture because, though they might not articulate the matter this way, it supplies something that is often missing from standard Protestant talk of forgiveness and faith, pardon and trust. Lewis's picture suggests that our actions are important not only because they hurt or harm the neighbor, but also because—under grace—they form and shape the persons we are. There are, to be sure, some theological dangers embedded in such a vision of the Christian life, but in Lewis's hands we can also see its power and its allure.

If we ask ourselves, therefore, what accounts for the success Lewis's writings have clearly had in reaching a wide range of readers and in shaping a religiously informed vision of life, we cannot overlook his appreciation of the everyday. His notion of the everyday comes, of course, with a distinctively British flavor, but that does not seem to have created insurmountable obstacles for his readers. It is not just that he appreciates the everyday, however; it is also that he understands and evokes its significance for our moral and spiritual life. In ordinary pleasures, shafts of the divine glory, God touches our lives to draw us to himself. In *Surprised by Joy*, Lewis tells his own life story as one whose underlying theme is *Sehnsucht*—the longing for joy. Just as Augustine said that our restless hearts could find the rest they desire only in God, so Lewis suggests that the ordinary goods and pleasures of life draw us beyond themselves and beyond ourselves to the only One who is Goodness itself.

But, as Augustine also said in a passage that Lewis places as an epigraph at the start of the last chapter of *Surprised by Joy*, "It is one thing to see the land of peace from a wooded ridge...and another to tread road that leads to it." The ordinary and the everyday count immensely in our moral and spiritual life. In them, God touches us to call us to himself. That means also, however, that the stakes there are very high, that seemingly minor decisions may help to shape a person who one day will say—with a tone of utter finality—either "*my* will be done," or "*thy* will be done." God calls to us in the pleasures of everyday life, but we can miss the message. We can refuse to let ourselves be called out beyond the ordinary, we can try to hang on to the everyday—ignoring what is terrible and mysterious about it. Then the manna that we have tried to save rots, the pleasures fade, and we are left with something less than the everyday: with only ourselves. Something like that, surely, is the picture Lewis paints in *The Great Divorce*. The choice is, finally and simply, between heaven and hell. But the choice is made, and eternal issues determined, in our everyday decisions and actions. Every moment of life is momentous—touched by and equidistant from the Eternal.

THE GOD WHO HURTS

This is, I have suggested, part of the religious power of Lewis's vision of human life. But there is still more. If we take it only this far, in fact, we probably miss the most penetrating and compelling aspects of his thought. For the God who meets us in the ordinary and the everyday in order to call us to himself is not simply a God who makes us happy. To be sure, he will do that—will make us happier than we can even imagine. But Lewis offers no "feel-good" religion, no books about how to live the abundant life. If there is a biblical theme that pervades all his writing it surely is: only the one who loses his life for Jesus' sake will find it. The ordinary pleasures of life give us just an inkling of what true pleasure must be, and Lewis is a master at using them to depict the happiness God will one day bestow on those who love him. But "it is one thing to see the land of peace from a wooded ridge...and another to tread the road that leads to it." And the road that leads to it may be painful indeed.

The Christian life hurts. God hurts. That's what Lewis really has to say, and it is, I think, the deepest reason for the power of his writing. "[T]he Divine Nature wounds and perhaps destroys us merely by being what it is," Orual reflects in *Till We Have Faces*.[19] This theme—that God hurts—is perhaps most pronounced in some of Lewis's last works—especially in *Till We Have Faces*, *A Grief Observed*, and *The Four Loves*. And it is perhaps not insignificant that each of these three works, in different ways, was influenced by Lewis's acquaintance with and, finally, marriage to Joy Davidman Gresham. But, in fact, this theme was present in Lewis's writing almost from the very beginning. Near the end of *The Pilgrim's Regress*, John, the pilgrim who has finally made his way back to Mother Church, sings a song about "the tether and pang of the particular." It may not be great poetry. Despite Lewis's aspirations to be known as an epic poet, it turned out that his talent was for prose. Nevertheless, this very early poem makes clear how the turn or (re-turn) to God wounds our nature.

Passing to-day by a cottage, I shed tears
When I remembered how once I had dwelled there
With my mortal friends who are dead. Years
Little had healed the wound that was laid bare.

Out, little spear that stabs, I, fool, believed
I had outgrown the local, unique sting,
I had transmuted away (I was deceived)
Into love universal the lov'd thing.

But Thou, Lord, surely knewest Thine own plan
When the angelic indifferences with no bar
Universally loved but Thou gav'st man
The tether and pang of the particular.

Which, like a chemic drop, infinitesimal,
Plashed into pure water, changing the whole,
Embodies and embitters and turns all
Spirit's sweet water to astringent soul.

That we, though small, may quiver with fire's same
Substantial form as Thou—not reflect merely,
As lunar angel, back to thee, cold flame.
Gods we are, Thou hast said: and we pay dearly.[20]

Rather abstractly put, perhaps, but to the point. Lewis put flesh
and bones on this abstraction in *The Magician's Nephew*, where
Digory is forced to choose between obedience to Aslan's command

and an action that may save the life of his dying mother. And, although the poem from *The Pilgrim's Regress* surely betrays the influence of philosophical idealism on Lewis's thought, it also shows certain Christian assumptions about what it means to be human. We are created as both finite and free—made from the dust of the ground, tied to particular times and places, but also made for something more, a something more that is finally God.

Thus, the poem recognizes our finitude: we are not angels who love only universally, simply reflecting back the divine love. We also love particularly, with "the tether and pang of the particular." We never outgrow "the local, unique sting," nor transmute it into universal love alone. Yet, we are also free, made for God. We must therefore learn how to love more universally—and, ultimately, how to love God, who is by no means ours alone. We live with this duality of our being, with our hearts both tied to what is local and unique and drawn toward the universal. Living within that tension, as the poem puts it, "we pay dearly."

The movie *Shadowlands* got it right, therefore, in a conversation it imagines between C. S. Lewis and Joy. During the period when her illness is in remission, Joy and Jack are on a trip and, taking shelter from the rain, suddenly find themselves talking about what lies ahead. Jack expresses his fear, fear of the pain he will feel when he loses her. To which Joy responds: "The pain then is a part of the pleasure now. That's the deal." The pleasure now is grounded in a particular commitment of the heart, and such a commitment makes us vulnerable. It sets us up to be hurt. But we can avoid that pain only by refusing right now to give our heart to anyone whom we might one day lose. We can, that is, avoid future pain, only by retreating entirely into the self, by caring about nothing outside the self. But that, of course, would be hell—a retreat into the "ruthless, sleepless, unsmiling concentration upon self" that Lewis calls "the mark of Hell."[21]

Even in his stories for children, Lewis does not hesitate to emphasize the appropriateness and necessity of suffering. When, in *The Last Battle*, "night falls on Narnia" and Aslan pulls down the curtain on Narnian history, the children who are friends of Narnia find themselves in Aslan's world—an even more wonderful place to be. But Lucy begins to cry at the thought of what they have left behind. "What Lucy!" Peter says. "You're not *crying*? With Aslan ahead, and all of us here?" To which Tirian, last of the kings of Narnia, who has come into Aslan's world with the children, replies, "Sirs, the ladies do well to weep. See I do so myself. I have seen my mother's death. What world but Narnia have I ever known? It were no virtue, but great discourtesy, if we did not mourn."[22] Likewise, expressing and reflecting upon his own very deep personal anguish in *A Grief Observed*, Lewis writes that what he wants in his bereavement is to continue to live his marriage "well and faithfully" in and through his loss. "We were one flesh. Now that it has been cut in two, we don't want to pretend that it is whole and complete."[23]

We could try to avoid this pain by holding on to the beloved—if only in memory—as if she were ours, our possession. That would, of course, be futile, but, still more important, it would be to miss the call of God that comes to us in and through the loved one. It would be to mistake the gift for the Giver. Or we could try to avoid this pain by telling ourselves that there has been no real loss. God's will has been done, and the loved one is now better off. But true though this is from one angle, it does less than justice to that "local, unique sting" that should and does characterize our loves. Lewis puts the point very directly and insightfully, again in *A Grief Observed*:

> If a mother is mourning not for what she has lost but for what her dead child has lost, it is a comfort to believe that the child has not lost the end for which it was created.... A comfort to the God-aimed, eternal spirit within her. But not to her motherhood. The specifically maternal happiness must be written off. Never, in any place or time, will she have her son on her knees, or bath[e] him, or tell him a story, or plan for his future, or see her grandchild.[24]

This theme—of the tension or rivalry between our natural loves and love for God—is given its most systematic treatment by Lewis in *The Four Loves*, a book that deserves, I believe, to be considered a minor classic in Christian ethics. What makes the book so powerful is that Lewis by no means contents himself only with noting the possible rivalry between particular loves and love for God. With each of the natural loves that he takes up—affection, friendship, and erotic love—he begins where I began above: by depicting for us the sublime within the everyday. Thus, he finds in each of the natural loves an image of what divine love itself is in part. We see one facet of God's love, for example, in the undiscriminating character of affection. Given familiarity over time, almost anyone can become an object of affection. Hence, this love manifests an implicit openness to the worth of every human being. Friendship, by contrast, is clearly a discriminating love, for we are friends only with certain people whom we have chosen for particular reasons. But, at the same time, friendship is, unlike affection, the least jealous of loves. Our circle of friends will be open to anyone who shares the interest that binds us together, and in that sense friendship is implicitly universal. If affection is jealous but undiscriminating, and friendship is discriminating but not jealous, *eros* is both discriminating and jealous. How, then, might it provide us with the image of divine love? In selfless devotion *eros* plants "the interests of another in the centre of our being. Spontaneously and without effort we have fulfilled the law (towards one person) by loving our neighbour as ourselves. It is an image, a foretaste, of what we must become to all if Love Himself rules in us without a rival."[25]

Thus, Lewis's first move is to evoke the beauty and the splendor of the natural loves, the way in which they give pleasure. And surely, part of the hold of this book upon several generations of readers has been its ability to evoke delight—to help us appreciate the beauty of the natural loves and find in them shafts of the divine glory. But Lewis's discussion never stops there. He never forgets that "the Divine Nature wounds and perhaps destroys us merely by being what it is." And so, with each of the loves he notes also its insufficiency—the way in which, even and especially at its very best, it may go wrong. Affection is prone to jealousy and wants to possess the loved one. Still more, it needs to be needed. In affection we desire only the good *we* can give, which is not always the good the loved one needs. The love of friendship is always tempted to exclusivity. Rightly excluding those who do not share our special interests, we may easily take pride in our circle of friends and come to value exclusivity for its own sake. And so powerful, almost godlike, is the claim of *eros* upon us, that we may do great injustice in its name. Left to itself *eros* is likely to be fickle and unfaithful, to work harm and havoc in human life.

Therefore, each of the natural loves, beautiful and splendid as they are in themselves, must be transformed by charity, by love of God. They must be taken up into a life directed toward God and be reborn—transformed and perfected as "modes of charity." Lewis's concluding chapter on charity in *The Four Loves*, among the most powerful pieces of his generally powerful prose, is a haunting depiction of the way in which this needed transformation is likely to be painful. We say that the natural loves are transformed and perfected, but that language does not quite capture the truth of our experience. It may sometimes feel more like death—that the natural loves must be put to death so that a new life marked by charity can arise. With just such an idea in mind—namely, that the needed transformation of our natural loves may seem akin to dying—Josef Pieper once recalled that charity has been pictured by Christians as a consuming fire, and that it is therefore "much more than an innocuous piety when Christendom prays, 'Kindle in us the fire of Thy love.'"[26]

At their very best, therefore, the natural loves fall short. In themselves they are good, but they were never meant to be simply "in themselves"—to be isolated from the God-relation, to be anything other than modes of charity. But in our sin we do isolate and idolize them, refusing to recognize that they are and must remain *creaturely* loves. Because we do so, we can only experience the transformation of our loves as painful. When God redirects them to himself, it hurts. We can, of course, say, with perfect justification, that this redirection is a restoration of them to what they are meant to be. It is a liberation of their true beauty and is in the service of their genuine flourishing. In the Augustinian language that underlies Lewis's treatment in *The Four Loves*, it is the restoring of inordinate love to right order. It is the restoration of harmony between nature and grace.

All true—and truly said. But we cannot always—perhaps not even often—experience this restoration as liberation and fulfillment for all that is "far away in 'the land of the Trinity'," and we remain pilgrims on the way.[27] Along the way, nature may often seem wounded by grace. When, in the theological struggles to which the Reformation gave rise, Protestants depicted a nature so thoroughly corrupted by sin that death and rebirth were necessary, Catholics sometimes thought that this demonstrated an insufficient appreciation of the continuing goodness of creation, of its ability to point us to God. And so, Catholics responded by saying that "grace does not destroy nature, but perfects it." That is, over against an image of death and resurrection they set an incarnational image—not a destruction of the natural life and a new birth, but the natural life taken up into and perfected within a graced life.

Lewis, mere Christian that he seeks to be, sees the worth of both pictures of the Christian life—and sees it quite profoundly. As always in his view, the real truth of things is captured in the Catholic formulation: the natural life is God's good gift; he will not destroy but perfect it. The natural loves are transformed when they become incarnate as modes of charity. But the Protestant formulation captures something very important about the truth of our experience, about what this transformation may feel like. It hurts.

Lewis's most haunting depiction of nature wounded by grace must certainly be one of his least read books, *Till We Have Faces*. Before the story is over, Orual comes to see the harsh truth about her love for Psyche and others. It had been a "gnawing greed." She comes to see that the kingdom of "Glome was a web—I the swollen spider, squat at its center, gorged with men's stolen lives."[28] Yet, her natural loves of affection, friendship, and *eros* were not mere selfishness. They were, in some ways, the natural loves at their best. As Lewis once put it in a letter to Clyde Kilby, Orual is an example of "human affection in its natural condition, true, tender, suffering, but in the long run tyrannically possessive and ready to turn to hatred when the beloved ceases to be its possession."[29]

Sin builds its throne at the heart of what is best in our nature, and, then, when God draws us toward himself, it may feel the way it felt to Orual when the divine surgeons went to work on her. What she experienced was loss and suffering—so great, indeed, that she finally cries out: "That there should be gods at all, there's our misery and bitter wrong. There's no room for you and us in the same world."[30] Striving for independence, striving to isolate her natural loves from the only context in which they could ultimately flourish, Orual had been making war on the reality principle of the universe. How can the gods meet us face to face, she finally asks, till we have faces? She had to be broken to be transformed.

I do not believe there is any theme more central to Lewis's vision of human life in relation to God, and I think there are very few indeed who have managed as well as he to evoke simultaneously in readers both an appreciation for and delight in our created life, and a sense of the pain and anguish that come when that life is fully redirected to the One from which it comes. "To love at all," Lewis wrote in *The Four Loves*, "is to be vulnerable.... The alternative to tragedy, or at least to the risk of tragedy, is damnation. The only place outside Heaven where you can be perfectly safe from all the dangers and perturbations of love is Hell."[31] The whole of life, therefore, every ordinary and everyday moment of it, every choice that we make, is charged with the significance of an eternal either/or. Which means, I guess, that no moment is simply ordinary.

Here, I think, we find the truth behind the remarkable staying power of Lewis's writings. He is not exactly writing theology for the masses. In fact, in the strict sense, he can hardly be said to be writing theology. He gives us something better—the feel, the quality, of a life truly lived before God. He gives us the everyday—in all its splendor, terror, pain, and possibility. And through what is ordinary and everyday he invites us to enter into that "mystical death which is the secret of life."[32]

10

ON BRINGING ONE'S LIFE TO A POINT

I n February of 1994, in what was its March issue, *First Things* published a statement on the homosexual movement, signed by twenty-one people, of whom I was one. An excerpt from that statement was published in the *Wall Street Journal* on February 24. I do not intend here to rehearse the argument of that statement or to defend it. In my own view, it was certainly not perfect, and I see ways we could have made it better. Moreover, I think the *Wall Street Journal* excerpt was inadequate, losing part of the point of the statement. But I have not changed my mind on the question involved; and a reader, in order to understand what follows, will have to keep that in mind and, if he or she disagrees with the statement, bracket such disagreement for the moment.

The day the *Wall Street Journal* excerpt appeared, things began to explode on the campus of Oberlin College, where I teach. Since Oberlin has been described by *Newsweek*, for example, as a "gay mecca," perhaps this was not surprising, though I could never have predicted the intensity of the reaction. In order to provide a context for what follows, I must describe briefly the reaction at Oberlin. But just as I do not seek to rehearse again the argument on the issue, so also I do not intend here to take up the topic of "political correctness." My experiences provide in many ways a textbook example of that phenomenon, but I am more interested in something I regard as ultimately more important.

What happened? Posters went up around the campus photocopies of the *Wall Street Journal* piece, with arrows pointing to my name and various statements written on the posters ("rampant homophobia," "read this and fear"). Over the next few days several more rounds of posters appeared, attacking me, for example, as "super bigot." It is not too much to say that an uproar had been created. Students expressed outrage that such views were held by someone at Oberlin. They called for a boycott of my classes in the coming fall (since I was on leave during the spring semester of 1994). One student was quoted in the student paper as calling for a march past my home, though I did not expect that to take place, and it did not. The student senate voted to reprimand me, and the student paper editorialized against me, charging that I had compromised my "academic objectivity." Students talked publicly about bringing charges against me through the college's judicial system, and a student who is co-chair of the Lesbian Gay Bisexual Union was quoted as saying, "Some people would like him out of here." Fifty-one members of the faculty (about a quarter of the total) signed a letter criticizing the statement on homosexuality—charging that it engaged in "repugnant stereotyping," was "intellectually naive," and provided "sanction for a homophobic agenda."

For at least the first week, while the uproar was at its height, I felt largely isolated—an experience that is almost paralyzing, since one hardly knows how to respond in such circumstances.

Over time, at least the appearance (though not, in truth, the reality) of some balance was restored when letters providing support of various kinds for me appeared in the next week's edition of the student paper. (I myself did respond in writing to the letter signed by members of the faculty.) Some defended the right of free speech, some testified to my good character (which I appreciated greatly, though there is something unsettling about having to be defended on such grounds), and a very few expressed substantive agreement with my views. A couple of brave students wrote letters expressing such support. One member of the faculty did so also. At this point he remains the only member of the faculty to have publicly expressed agreement with the position adopted by me and other signers of the *First Things* statement.

Events such as these remind us that, despite torrents of talk about diversity at our elite colleges, they lack anything resembling genuine intellectual diversity. But, although this much summary has been necessary to give the reader some context for the reflections that follow, I repeat that I do not intend here to add another chapter to debates about political correctness. What follows is, as best I can manage, "emotion recollected in tranquillity." Although I have over the years defended in print a number of positions that are relatively unpopular in our society, this experience is unlike any other I have had. And I have found myself reflecting on what it means to bring one's life to a point—which is, on the one hand, a place of solitude and, on the other, a moment of significance. (The irony has not escaped my attention that this is not unlike the way gays sometimes speak about the experience of "coming out of the closet." But to take up the similarities and differences would draw me back into substantive discussion of the argument, which is not my aim. The reader who disagrees with my normative views is simply going to have to stop reading or prescind from such judgment for a while.)

PUTTING THE MOMENT IN CONTEXT

The experience involved for me an act of *recovery*—and this in several ways. In the midst of unrelenting public attack, one regains some sense of what counts in one's life—not what I would like to count, but what does in fact count for me, what matters to the person I have become. In that sense I recovered myself within my deepest commitments.

Thus, for example, I reclaimed the significance of the local community of believers. The Lutheran congregation that I attend (which I attend for the simple reason that it is here in Oberlin) is neither particularly large nor noteworthy. It has the virtues and the vices of many small congregations, and I have to admit that worshipping there seldom stirs my soul deeply. But, as the apostle writes, we are many members with many gifts, but one body in which burdens are mutually borne. The reaction of many people in the congregation (when a local newspaper carried an article about the controversy at the college) was immediate and powerful. They spoke words of support in conversations with me. Several said something like, "I would like to write a letter on your behalf, but I know I probably wouldn't get it right, so I am praying for you." Which was, of course, precisely right. Many members with many gifts—I am probably better at offering arguments, but they did what they did better than I might have, had the tables been turned. One body—reminding me how foolish I would be if I thought, finally, that I could offer arguments simply on my own apart from the way of faith and life that the entire body sustains.

There are, however, other ties that are also very important in a person's life—chief among them, at least for me, is the bond of the family. A few years ago I wrote a little piece titled "I Want To Burden My Loved Ones." It was written in fun, but also in all seriousness, arguing—in relation to questions about care for dying patients and advance directives about one's own care at the point of death—that the impulse to handle these problems autonomously was mistaken, that the family was a context in which we are quite properly burdened by others. And my experience at, remember, a small college in a small town, where anyone's business is everyone's business, reminded me of how deeply implicated we are in the lives of our family. One might think that my signature on a document does not involve my wife or children, but life teaches otherwise. The experience intrudes into their own lives in conversations with friends or teachers, and they are, in a sense, forced to make it their own. They didn't ask for it, but it found them. And if I have burdened them as I have, perhaps I have also—to the best of my ability—helped them to understand how important it may be to bring one's life to a point.

I recovered also some of the psalms that I have never quite known what to do with, psalms that have been a puzzle for me. Christians use them regularly in worship, but what are we thinking when we do? A few examples, which could readily be multiplied, may suffice:

> Be gracious to me, O LORD!
> Behold what I suffer from those who hate me,
> O thou who liftest me up from the gates of death,
> that I may recount all thy praises,

that in the gates of the daughter of Zion
I may rejoice in thy deliverance. (9:13–14)

Keep me as the apple of the eye;
hide me in the shadow of thy wings,
from the wicked who despoil me,
my deadly enemies who surround me.
They close their hearts to pity;
with their mouths they speak arrogantly.
They track me down; now they surround me;
they set their eyes to cast me to the ground. (17:8–11)

Consider how many are my foes,
and with what violent hatred they hate me.
Oh guard my life, and deliver me;
let me not be put to shame, for I take refuge in thee.
(25:19–20)

Save me, O God, by thy name,
and vindicate me by thy might.
Hear my prayer, O God;
give ear to the words of my mouth.
For insolent men have risen against me,
ruthless men seek my life;
they do not set God before them. (54:1–3)

Enough. We get the picture—of one who has attempted in integrity
to be faithful to God, who because of that is surrounded by enemies, and who brings that situation before God. I suspect that
most Christians are uneasy with making the prayers of such right-

eous Israelites their own. We are uneasy because such claims to our own integrity are difficult for those who, with St. Paul, have taken seriously the deep division even within the self that seeks to serve God and have learned to claim Christ as their righteousness.

This note of the righteous sufferer is, of course, not the only note sounded in the Psalter. A Lutheran pastor, having heard of the controversy at Oberlin, wrote to thank me for the position I had taken and to offer encouragement and support. But she also, very nicely, reminded me not to suppose that this cause was simply my own to assert, and she in turn cited the psalmist.

> Keep back thy servant also from presumptuous sins;
> let them not have dominion over me!
> Then I shall be blameless,
> and innocent of great transgression. (19:13)

That is, of course, one very important way to deal with psalms that are puzzling and troubling in their protestations of righteousness. We set them in the context of other psalms that remind us that we cannot plumb the depths of our own self and must finally hand that self over to God for judgment and safekeeping.

But what do we do with the psalms themselves—those which assert one's integrity and ask for deliverance from enemies who surround one? I myself have generally made two moves in dealing with them. The first I learned from C. S. Lewis, who suggests that we place ourselves not with the righteous sufferer but with the evil-doers—that, in making such psalms our own prayers, we remember soberly that we might have brought others to a point where they felt as isolated as the psalmist sometimes feels. The second—and for Christians ultimately more telling—I learned from Dietrich

Bonhoeffer, who reminds us that we make these prayers our own only when we see Jesus as this righteous sufferer. We pray them as our own only "in him," *the* righteous sufferer who calls on God for vindication.

Bonhoeffer's reading is, I think, the first and last reading that a Christian ought to give such psalms—but, I now believe, not the only one. For between those first and last readings may come another that is closer to the psalmist's own experience, one that enters into the text's own trajectory (as we like to say these days). For this is, in fact, what it may feel like to try—as best one can—to be faithful. No one should seek such experience, and perhaps we should even be hesitant about assuming that it is our own, but if others persuade us that they do indeed surround us, then we can pray these psalms as our own, as—perhaps—that righteous Israelite did. Cautious as Christians must inevitably be to make such a move, I am not prepared to say we cannot or ought not.

But, of course, the final reading remains that one in which they are the prayer of Jesus, and it did not escape my attention that my experience took place during Lent. How casually I tend to read the New Testament texts that speak of sharing in Christ's suffering and even most puzzlingly (in Colossians) of completing "what is lacking in Christ's afflictions for the sake of his body, that is, the church." One could, melodramatically, make too much of such passages—as Ignatius, bishop of Antioch early in the second century, so famously did in a letter written on the way to his martyrdom: "Let me be fodder for wild beasts—that is how I can get to God. I am God's wheat and I am being ground by the teeth of wild beasts to make a pure loaf for Christ." The spirit that could seek such experience is, I confess, alien to my own. But to accept what comes when one has attempted to be faithful, and to make it one's own by drawing it into an *imitatio Christi*, seems right to me, and surely Lent exists in part to ask us to take such possibilities seriously in life. We read these psalms as the prayer of Jesus, accepting—even if not seeking—a share in the sufferings of his body. Some people said to me at the height of the uproar: "It will pass; a new cause will come along." Which is true. (Indeed, a little more than a month later the college's administration was kind enough to provide, through one of its personnel decisions, a new cause, a new object for hostility, thereby giving me some breathing space.) But the passing of a moment is not the same as taking it up and bringing one's life to a point around it. When the moment passes, life continues, more or less as it had before. But if we take up the moment, accepting a certain kind of death that it brings, we may be renewed—which is quite different from the simple continuation of life.

LESSONS FOR THE MORAL LIFE

Beyond the recovery of such obvious truths, an experience like mine may also uncover some of the deeper meaning of the moral life, meaning that cannot be taught in the classroom. At one point, a couple weeks into the uproar, I had a short conversation with a faculty colleague, a little older than I, whose judgment I respect and whose counsel I have often sought. Although sympathetic to the concerns of the statement I had signed, he could not himself affirm its view, though he could and did offer support from his own perspective. But when we spoke, he commented that the standard upheld in the statement was a very "difficult" and "demanding" one. (He had in mind the larger concerns of the statement, its concern not simply with the homosexual movement but with the results of the sexual revolution more generally in our society. And, in fact, some of the strongest language in the statement—language entirely omitted in the *Wall Street Journal* excerpt—dealt with standards that applied to heterosexuals.) Our standard, he said to me, was such a demanding one that he was reluctant to affirm it. He could not say that he himself had always lived up to it.

That set me to thinking about how we render moral judgment today. Beginning perhaps with the generous thought that we should not "impose" on others standards that we ourselves do not meet, we end with a morality that demands less even of ourselves than we ought. The norms to which I adhere are not those I can keep or do keep; they are those to which I hold myself accountable. I do not see how I could manage to be accountable if there were not ways to recognize my accountability—if, that is, I were not part of a community that regularly confesses its sin and seeks to begin anew. Only from such a perspective, I suspect, could I have the courage to set forth an ideal of which I myself often fall short. The moral life is much more than we can or should teach in a classroom; it involves disciplines such as confession and absolution.

Still more, the moral life involves—how not to put the point too melodramatically?—preparing to die. Thus Epictetus: "Let others study cases at law, let others practice recitations and syllogisms. You learn to die." Thus also Socrates, who speaks of pursuing philosophy in the right way as practicing "how to face death easily." And in death we are, finally, isolated and alone. Others may and should do what Paul Ramsey called "companying" with the dying. They may through the virtue of love actually help to carry our sufferings, but they cannot enter the void with us. Christians believe, of course, that One has kept us company even there, but that belief is experienced as hope, not possession. To learn to die, therefore, we have to learn to be alone.

This we are very reluctant to do—at least I certainly am. We value the ways in which our lives are joined with others in bonds of life, family, property, and reputation (the very bonds to which the second table of the Decalogue points). Therefore, it is rather hard to sing sincerely the words of Luther's great hymn (at least as that hymn was translated before we settled for less poetic translations designed to avoid allegedly sexist language): "And take they our life / Goods, fame, child, and wife, / Let these all be gone, / They yet have nothing won; / The kingdom ours remaineth." Most of the time, if the truth were known, I probably prefer my good name with my colleagues to such a sentiment. And it is therefore useful—indeed, it is central to the moral life—to bring one's life to a point, even if that is experienced as a point of solitude and isolation. This truth also cannot be taught in the ethics classroom, but this is what it means to begin to learn to die.

Once we come to see that our self is at stake in such moments, we will get quite a different slant on the truth we think we understand. It cannot be simply my personal view, my personal cause. For that alone I would scarcely risk or endure isolation. Few "opinions" of mine are likely to mean as much to me as my good name among colleagues. So if it is *my* cause that is at stake, that good name is likely to trump other considerations. No, the truth we think we understand must have about it an impersonality; it cannot simply be one's own private view or opinion. The truth I think I understand and for which I must stand up is, in reality, a truth that I stand under and to which I look up. To put the point again in the language of hymnody, in such moments I prefer

"Beneath the Cross of Jesus / I long to take my stand" to "Stand Up, Stand Up for Jesus."

That the truth we understand must be a truth we stand under is brought out nicely in C. S. Lewis's *That Hideous Strength* when Mark Studdock gradually learns what an "Idea" is. While Frost attempts to give Mark a "training in objectivity" that will destroy in him any natural moral sense, and while Mark tries desperately to find a way out of the moral void into which he is being drawn, he discovers what it means to "under-stand." "He had never before known what an Idea meant: he had always thought till now that they were things inside one's own head. But now, when his head was continually attacked and often completely filled with the clinging corruption of the training, this Idea towered up above him—something which obviously existed quite independently of himself and had hard rock surfaces which would not give, surfaces he could cling to."

This too, I fear, is seldom communicated in the classroom, where opinion reigns supreme. But it has important implications for the way we understand argument. During the course of the uproar at Oberlin I discovered to my own surprise that the cause I defended had become genuinely an impersonal one—not my own. It was not the sort of thing over which one could become personally irritated or annoyed. Indeed, I have on occasion over the years been far more annoyed by minor criticisms of my writing than by the direct and personal attack I now experienced. For it was impossible to regard the position I defended as my own; indeed, I cannot imagine subjecting myself to such criticism for the sake of anything so minor as an "opinion" of mine. In such moments one needs a truth with hard surfaces to cling to and stand under, and this experience has renewed my fear that the mere teaching of ethics seldom offers such truth.

THE POINT OF LIFE

If trying to stand under the truth means the practice of an *ars moriendi,* we begin to see what the moral life really requires. I have been reminded of two favorite passages of mine, the first from Peter Geach, the second from C. S. Lewis.

> Every man is given sufficient grace to make the right choice, but many reject that grace and are lost. How this choice does come a man's way, what chances men have and how they take or reject them, we shall not know till the Day of Judgment. In the stories of the Vikings there is recorded that one Viking was named Bairnsfriend because he would not share in the popular sport of tossing infants from spearpoint to spearpoint; let us hope that he took his chance; in such ways the Grace of God may show itself despite the most corrupting environment.

> In *King Lear* (III:vii) there is a man who is such a minor character that Shakespeare has not given him even a name; he is merely "First Servant." All the characters around him— Regan, Cornwall, and Edmund—have fine long-term plans. They think they know how the story is going to end, and they are quite wrong. The servant has no such delusions. He has no notion how the play is going to go. But he understands the present scene. He sees an abomination (the blinding of old

Gloucester) taking place. He will not stand it. His sword is
out and pointed at his master's breast in a moment: then
Regan stabs him dead from behind. That is his whole part:
eight lines all told. But if it were real life and not a play, that
is the part it would be best to have acted.

Two examples, each quite literally of bringing one's life to a point.
And although our opportunities generally come in far less dramatic ways, we can learn from such examples what is and what is
not within our power.

It has occurred to me any number of times that, were I deliberately to aim to bring my life to a point, the issue of homosexuality would not have been the issue I would have chosen for the
occasion. And, again, had I intended to bring my life to a point—
a point of solitude but also of significance and discovery—I would
have done things a little differently. Certainly I would have
changed a word here and there!

But, in fact, we do not decide to bring our lives to a point. We
are brought. The most important things have always been decided
in advance and are not ours to determine. We can seize the occasion and seek to live faithfully, but we are ultimately not makers
but responders. Hence, any account of the moral life is inadequate
if it does not help us to learn how to deal with what may come
upon us without our choice—illness, suffering, a child, death. Few
of the current approaches to morality do this or even seek to do it.
If, therefore, we are not, like Prufrock, to measure out our lives
with coffee spoons, we need to reclaim an older wisdom that may
help us learn what it means to bring one's life to a point.

11

CREATURES OF TIME AND PLACE

My family and I moved this past summer to Valparaiso from Oberlin, where we had lived for eighteen years. Now, eighteen years is a reasonably long time in anyone's life. It constitutes the bulk of the life of my children and almost the entire life of several of them. It is by far the longest that my wife and I have lived anywhere in our years of marriage. We are told, of course, that ours is a highly mobile society, but those statistical averages reflect quite different experiences. Some people—perhaps because of the demands of work—may move every five years. (In academia we call them "assistant professors"!) That is, I suspect, a different experience from moving after eighteen years in a place. I am sure it has quite a different "feel," and knowing that one will probably move again in five years must have an incalculable effect on the experience. And, of course, some people never move. So what I have to say may reflect not only the peculiarities of my temperament, but also a particular kind of experience. Moreover, because our experiences are different, one has to be cautious when reflecting theologically, as I do here, upon an experience. One's tone must be less prescriptive than exploratory and interrogative.

One other *caveat* is worth mentioning here at the outset. There is an important sense in which it makes no difference at all whether one moves every few years or never moves at all. What does matter—and it is, I suppose, the modest "lesson" toward which I am heading—is that we all learn to understand ourselves as being "on the way." That understanding we may achieve without ever moving from one town to another, although my experience suggests to me that the actual moving is a powerful reminder of more ultimate truths. Still, I am prepared to grant that the experience upon which I reflect is a penultimate one, that it makes no ultimate difference whether one shares it or not. But this does not mean, to paraphrase Helmut Thielicke, that in the dark night of sin all cats are gray. Our task is to hold together—in life more than in theory—the sense that everything penultimate, the whole of our life "on the way," matters morally, *and* the recognition that what finally matters is the judgment of God upon our person. At any rate, such a simultaneous affirmation remains my aim here.

AN EMBEDDED LIFE

I continue to be surprised by the fact that I actually moved. So routinized a creature am I that it seems an almost unbelievably daring thing for me to have done. There are still moments when I catch myself almost supposing that I am on leave and will soon be returning to Oberlin, and there are days when I cannot account at all for the decision. This is one point on which I am pretty certain that not everyone's experience would be the same. It is probably a good thing that not all of us are quite so routinized, so ready to say, as C. S. Lewis once did, "I like monotony." But all of us do and must lead lives that are embedded in particular places, and that fact is worth our reflection.

When contemplating the possibility of this move, I thought about many concerns that are rather obvious. What effect would it have on my children? Was it really all right with my wife, or was she only saying what she thought I might want to hear? Could I afford it financially? Could I, after so many years at Oberlin, really function successfully at a quite different sort of institution? Did I have the energy and the desire to accustom myself to new colleagues, a different set of problems, and new ways of doing things? Could I bring myself to move away from the Cleveland airport, so wonderfully accessible to me, and from the Cleveland Indians, at last a good ball club? Did I want to leave the several Lutheran congregations in the area to which I had become quite close over the years? Did I know people who had moved after so long in one place and for whom the move seemed to be a happy one? Might it be better just to buy my burial plot in Oberlin and leave well enough alone?

What I did not think about, however, and what I now think myself naive to have passed over so quickly, was simply whether I was up to it physically and emotionally—whether, that is, I could uproot and re-embed myself. I recall that when my father-in-law asked me whether I didn't think I was going to miss living in Oberlin, I quickly said that I didn't think that would be a problem.

I now realize that I had forgotten one little matter—what we call the doctrine of creation. Wholly apart even from any work-related questions, over eighteen years one carves out a life in a place. Except in the most extreme of circumstances, I suspect that it doesn't even particularly matter whether that place is generally perceived as desirable. It becomes home, the place where one is located. One walks certain routes, enjoys certain trees, recognizes certain people. We have doctors and dentists, grocery stores and shopping malls, baseball fields and banks, churches and schools. All become deeply embedded in a pattern of life. If ever we find ourselves supposing that we are simply Descartes's *cogito*, located in no particular place, we might try moving. As Dr. Johnson is supposed to have claimed to refute Berkeley's idealism by kicking a stone which turned out to have its matter quite securely in place, so, I am tempted to say, moving after eighteen years is a refutation of any supposition that our self is not in good part a body located in space and time.

Who, for example, would be constantly struck by how big a town Valparaiso is except someone who had spent the last eighteen years in a little town of eight thousand, walking from his office to bank or post office whenever he felt like it? Why are there so few mailboxes to drop mail into on corners in this town? Why so few street lights in our neighborhood? What shall we make of all those train whistles at night? What kind of university—however proud it may be of its recent appearance in the NCAA basketball tournament—would have no squash courts? I guess after all these years I could try to learn racquetball, but how shall I sing the Lord's song in a strange land?

This relates to what some theologians have been getting at in recent years when they have emphasized the categories of story and narrative. The self is always on the way and is not available to us abstracted from the story of one's life—which story is not yet complete. Only God, as St. Augustine said, can catch the heart and hold it still. Only God can see us whole and entire, as we truly are. Hence, we cannot in any complete sense account for ourselves or our decisions, even as I noted that I am often baffled when I try to account for my decision to move. To take the embedded nature of our life seriously is to realize that the story of that life must be precisely what St. Augustine wrote—a *confession* that God knows us better than we know ourselves. We are characters in a story of which we are not the author, caught up in a present moment that is always, in Stephen Crites's felicitous phrase, a "tensed present."[1] Caught between memory of the past and expectation of the future, embedded in a present moment, unable to say in any complete sense who we are, we exist within the tensions of this pilgrim existence.

By disturbing the ground of our life, moving seems to rake up all those tensions. It discloses human life as it has been created by God. It is a finite and bodily life, tied to particular times and places. To give ourselves to no one and no place in particular is not to be more like God; it is just to fail as a human being. We are in large measure the conversations we have had, the games we have played, the books we have read, the work we have done. But we are not only that, for we are also on the way. As spirits made to rest in God, made to live in expectation, we transcend every particular location, and we must learn to live within that tension.

Theologically, I know what I think about all this. I think that even had I stayed in Oberlin until they lowered me into that burial plot, I would have needed to learn to think of myself as "on the way." God ties our hearts to particular times, places, and people— and then the same God tears us away from them so that we may learn to love *him* with all our heart, soul, strength, and mind. And God does it so that we may learn to see this world—with all its beauty—in the way C. S. Lewis once described: It is an inn, a resting place, but we should not mistake it for home.[2] God does it to help us learn that an "otherworldly" Christianity is the only kind that gives deep meaning to this life, that we dare not rest the whole weight of the heart's longing in any finite good.

That is, I say, my theological position on the matter. But one's gut doesn't always follow one's theology immediately or straightforwardly. Thus, before we moved, I went to a piano recital for the seventeenth consecutive year in Oberlin, listened to some pieces I have heard many times over the years, and found it terribly sad that the routine should be coming to an end. I went to my daughter's graduation from Oberlin High School—a ceremony not unlike the graduations of her older brother and sister. I have never liked those ceremonies. They are rather raucous affairs with little of the dignity that a ritualized occasion needs. And yet, I was saddened to be leaving at the end, saddened in part to think that the graduation of our one remaining child would be in a different place. There is, I know, something here of the "my country right or wrong" attitude, and I am prepared to defend it. An embedded life is simply that—not the most desirable life, but one's own. One's own, however, we must hasten to add, because we have been given it and placed there by the Creator toward whom we must make our way. If something within us rebels against being on the way, that is not all bad. For we are both on the way *and* located. Placed here by God and made one day to rest in God. Neither truth about our nature should be denied.

A POSSESSIVE LIFE

To move—especially from a house with a big attic—is to find oneself buried under the accumulation of the years. Four children whom we have taught to love books and who now own far too many books—as does their father. Countless things we have saved over the years for ourselves or our children. Many other things we have kept because we thought "we might need them some time" and wouldn't be able to afford to get them again. Here again, people's experiences may be irreducibly different. Perhaps the truly affluent simply know that if they need something again in the future they can just buy it. Perhaps, paradoxically enough, their affluence permits them to sit a little looser with their possessions. They are perhaps less likely to be buried under the weight of the years. But even they must surely have things they save, not because they must, but because they want to. And those possessions pile up over the years.

Perhaps for all of us there are some possessions—different ones quite probably—that we can hardly do without. Moving made clear to me that our family simply has too many books. We weeded out hundreds. A few we sold. Some I gave to colleagues. Hundreds we donated to the Oberlin Public Library. They can practically hold a book sale with just what we gave them. No doubt, of course, there are many more we could have disposed of, but how wrenching must the experience of moving be?

The most striking thing to me, however, is not the number of books. I recall the last couple of weeks before we moved. By then the books were packed, and we wandered around the house like lost sheep with no books to read. We were busy, of course, but, even so, one looks for time to read. I went to the public library several times those last weeks and checked out books—Robert Parker's "Spenser" mysteries, Larry MacMurtry, some old essays by Joseph Epstein, Elzbieta Ettinger's little book on the Heidegger-Arendt correspondence. I just can't seem to get along without a few books around. Neither, I noted, could my daughters. They wanted to go one last time to the "Bookseller" and look at used paperbacks. It struck me as a crazy idea, given the moaning I'd been doing about all the boxes of books. But we went—and, of course, each of them bought a couple cheap paperbacks to read during the move.

I have found myself wondering, in fact, what I will do if the day comes when I can't read. How will I fill the hours? Perhaps I'll just listen to sports talk on the radio, but I don't know whether that will get the job done. Surely, among those many mansions in our Father's house there must be some lined with book shelves and appointed with old, comfortable chairs where I can read my favorite authors for whom life now so seldom leaves time—John Tunis, Felix Salten, C. S. Lewis, L. M. Montgomery. It's hard to imagine a heaven without their books.

Presumably an embedded life need not be a possessive life. The two, although closely related, are slightly different. I have defended embeddedness. Shall I also defend a certain possessiveness? Is there something wrong or, at least, questionable about all these possessions? I do not, of course, feel about all my possessions as I do about my books. In the course of moving—of buying a new home and trying to sell an old one—I found myself wondering why owning a home has never meant much to me. Perhaps it has something to do with having grown up in a parsonage. Perhaps it is because I am not (to put it mildly) very handy and cannot take joy in fixing things around the house. But more generally, I simply find property to be a burden—a black hole into which one pours time, energy, and money. I feel the same way about automobiles. Necessary, to be sure, but always causing trouble. Not so, however, with things like books and baseball cards. There the possessive tie goes a little deeper.

When we think about possessions, we can hardly help recalling that the Bible, depicting God's people as on the way, often raises questions about our desire to locate ourselves, our desire to possess. Augustine says, in a famous passage, that Cain built a city, but Abel, being a sojourner, built none.[3] Abraham leaves home because God calls him and, as the Letter to the Hebrews puts it, sojourns as a foreigner in the land of promise. The Israelites march for forty years in the desert and never (except for Joshua and Caleb) reach the promised land. There is a strand of opinion in the Bible that prefers the tabernacle to the temple. It could, after all, be picked up and moved from place to place. And Jesus himself is worse off than the foxes and the birds, having nowhere to lay his head.

But we are not Jesus. We are not even called to be like Jesus, but only to follow him at a distance, and human beings need to "nest," to personalize space and make it home. In *Shantung Compound*, his memoir of life in a Japanese internment camp in Northern China in 1943, Langdon Gilkey reflects upon precisely this need. Within the compound the refugees found themselves in something like a state of nature, needing to organize their common life. In such conditions one notices what we usually take for granted. "The importance of space to the well-being, nay the existence, of a person came as a surprise to me," Gilkey writes. "Somehow each self needs a 'place' in order to be a self, in order to feel on a deep level that it really exists. We are, apparently, rootless beings at bottom. Unless we can establish roots somewhere in a place where we are at home, which we possess to ourselves and where our things are, we feel that we float, that we are barely there at all."[4] Possessions are not simply contrary to our created nature.

At the same time, of course, we should not deny the rootless-
ness "at bottom" that Gilkey detects in our nature. As free spirits
made for God, we are always strangers and pilgrims. If Jesus has
nowhere to lay his head, and if he is, as Ephesians puts it, the
image of mature humanity, can a truly human life need such per-
sonalized space?[5] I think so—as long as we understand this need
rightly. If we are on the way, we are on the way to somewhere—to
a place we can call home. For now we may—either from necessity
or duty—have to make do without the "home" our heart desires.
But even the sparrow finds a home and the swallow a nest for herself; hence, the psalmist concludes, our soul should long to be
home in the courts of the Lord.[6] Every home we take possession of
along the way is at least an intimation of that greater home we
cannot make—cannot make because the new Jerusalem comes
down from above and is not of our making. We may sometimes
love these intimations too much, but we cannot be entirely wrong
in wanting them. As Dr. Johnson said in what I cannot help reading as a *double entendre* capturing the duality of our nature, "To
be happy at home is the end of all human endeavor."

It is quite true that there is always danger in possessions—that
where our treasure is our heart will be also. Of course, many of
our possessions are things that no one else would want, so it's
hardly a matter of piling up things that would be treasures for
anyone else. They are just *our* treasures. But no doubt we often
love them too much, and no doubt they sometimes enslave us. In
becoming part of the story of our life, part of us, our possessions
may take possession of us. And so, it cannot be altogether bad to
divest ourselves of some, even if it hurts. That hurt is a reminder
that we are still on the way.

I spent a good bit of the Fourth of July up in the attic packing
boxes and reflecting upon our relation to possessions. One can, of

course, have the moving company pack everything, but how would they do it? Some of these things need to be sifted and sorted. Much of what we keep is, as I noted, only *our* treasure. Boxes of old school papers, programs, and awards for each of the children. Cards the children have made for us at Christmas or Easter. Autographed baseball scorecards. Old newspapers. Favorite toys of each child. Stuffed animals they took to bed when they were little.

When in doubt I usually said "pitch it," and Judy, my wife—wiser as usual—said "keep it." In the long run, she is right. All these papers, ribbons, and records are the things that tie us to our past. They remind us that we are not the independent, autonomous beings our world celebrates. Quite the contrary. We have been formed and shaped by others, to whom we owe a great deal, and gratitude is the appropriate response.

In many of the subjects central to my own professional work the concept of autonomy has been very important. Patients want control over their dying. Women want control of their bodies, even when those bodies carry a newly conceived child. Indeed, men and women generally want control of their reproductive powers. We want to control our environment, to have a sense of mastery. Who can entirely argue with such desires? Human beings are not just puppets, and they should have at least some control over the course of their lives. But a few hours spent packing in my attic suggests the need for caution here. Where we will put all this stuff in our new home that lacks an attic is anyone's guess, but Judy is right: We need to carry a good bit of it with us.

Still, up there in the attic I would often try one more tactic. We are taking this box of stuff, I would say, only so that ten—or twenty—years from now the children will have to go through it and pitch it themselves after we're dead. And no doubt they will pitch a good bit of it, either because they want to or because they must. But they will have to go through it first. They will have to be reminded that they are not like Hobbes's picture of men as mushrooms, springing out of the earth without any engagements or attachments.[7] And in being thus reminded, they will perhaps see that their independence is, at best, relative. A good lesson for parents to teach their children.

A VULNERABLE LIFE

To move, at least to move after having been a long time in one place, means inevitable loneliness. Others may welcome you and seek to ease the transition, but they have their own lives to live—moving along contentedly in familiar paths, as you were only weeks before—and nothing but time can heal the wound. Moving reminds one of the fragility of life. If we fall ill, we no longer have the doctors upon whom we had learned to rely. If our automobile falls ill, we no longer have the trusted mechanic whose counsel we had sought for years. Before moving we had life well under control—or, perhaps better in light of the point toward which I am heading, we *seemed* to have it under control. Now we are uprooted.

The ultimate truth of life might, of course, be that we are nothing but "rootless beings at bottom." One can build a philosophy upon such a vision. Thus, for example, Thomas Hobbes, living in chaotic and dangerous times, pictured human beings as "on the way," but hardly in the (Augustinian) sense that I have used above. For Augustine the goal of this sojourn is to rest in God, and that is true felicity. For Hobbes the goal is simply to outdistance others. In the race course of life

To consider them behind, is glory

To consider them before, is humility

To be in breath, hope

To be weary, despair

To endeavor to overtake the next, emulation

To lose ground by little hindrances, pusillanimity

To fall on the sudden, is disposition to weep

To see another fall, is disposition to laugh

Continually to be outgone, is misery

Continually to outgo the next before, is felicity

And to forsake the course, is to die.[8]

Here is a sobering vision of life, although, of course, a possibly true one. Moving makes one take Hobbes seriously and invites us to consider what life must be like if there is—as Hobbes thought—no "*summum bonum*, greatest good, as is spoken of in the books of the old moral philosophers." Then, indeed, happiness must be what Hobbes says it is: "Felicity is a continual progress of the desire, from one object to another; the attaining of the former, being still but the way to the latter." This "restless desire," Hobbes says, "ceaseth only in death."[9]

If this is a true vision of life, the only reason to move is to get ahead, to pass a competitor on the race course of life. And I would not deny that there is something to this. If we run well, we may manage for long stretches of time to forget the vulnerability that "grounds"—if that can possibly be the right word here—our mad dash to the end of the course. But I think that, for those of us who believe Augustine closer than Hobbes to the truth, the point is not to forget our vulnerability but to be reminded of it. Moving has a way of accomplishing that.

I have always been a good sleeper, but I have found something that can keep me awake at night: two mortgage payments. At least up to the time I write these lines—though, I devoutly hope, not for much longer—we have not sold our home in Oberlin. Two mortgages plus a bridge loan can evoke a sense of vulnerability in one and make Hobbes's picture of the race course, in which to be weary is to despair, seem all too accurate. It is hard for the ordinary person not to lose a little sleep or to avoid feeling vulnerable when he—in company with the banks, of course—owns two homes. I dislike this in myself. Indeed, I have read and pondered several times Jesus' words about trust and anxiety in Luke 12. If by being anxious I cannot add a cubit to my stature, why should I worry more than the lilies of the field? But the theologian's occupational hazard is that he must think about such advice. No doubt, to the degree that I am simply worrying about the uncertainties of my own future, I am failing to trust God as I should. No doubt I need to learn day after day to say with the psalmist, "In peace I will both lie down and sleep; for thou alone, O LORD, makest me dwell in safety."[10]

All this I grant and, at least in my better moments, am prepared to admit my failings here. But, of course, a decision to move affects others as well. It is one thing for me—if I could—to take no thought for *my own* morrow. It is quite another for me to take no thought for the morrow of my children. I am not persuaded that anything in Luke 12 suggests that a little anxiety about their future is not proper for me, even granting that one must always give one's children over, finally, into God's keeping. God, after all, wills to care for them in considerable part through me, and to make myself vulnerable is to make them vulnerable as well.

Here again, however, it seems impossible to know oneself fully. I find that I cannot sort out the good from the bad here. Perhaps I fail my children to some extent by making a financial sacrifice to move. Perhaps, on the other hand, if my vocational reasons are sound, I help them to learn that there are also other things that count in life. What cannot be denied, however—or, at any rate, what I cannot deny—is that moving brings one up short and evokes a sense of the vulnerability of human life. It reminds us that although the "abundant life"—modern evangelical jargon for that *summum bonum* in which Hobbes did not believe—may lie at the end of our way, God makes no promise that it always feels good to be on the way. If moving is this hard, I find myself thinking, what would it be like if Judy were to die? I have been with a decent number of people in such circumstances. They generally seem able to carry on, even with difficulty, but one never quite knows how they manage. Clearly, staying put without her would be infinitely harder than moving with her—and that has seemed hard enough. Yet, of course, if we are both truly on the way, such a day must come. Not to live toward such pain would mean that our lives now were impoverished. Human beings cannot have the richness of love without setting themselves up for the most enormous rupture we can imagine some time in the future. As Joy Davidman says in the movie *Shadowlands*: "The pain then is part of the pleasure now. That's the deal." C. S. Lewis, in one of his early attempts at poetry, expressed precisely this "tether and pang of the particular," which is the source of our vulnerability:

> Passing to-day by a cottage, I shed tears
> When I remembered how once I had dwelled there
> With my mortal friends who are dead. Years
> Little had healed the wound that was laid bare.

Out, little spear that stabs, I, fool, believed
I had outgrown the local, unique sting,
I had transmuted away (I was deceived)
Into loving universal the lov'd thing.

But Thou, Lord, surely knewest Thine own plan
When the angelic indifferences with no bar
Universally loved but Thou gav'st man
The tether and pang of the particular;

Which, like a chemic drop, infinitesimal,
Plashed into pure water, changing the whole,
Embodies and embitters and turns all
Spirit's sweet water to astringent soul.

That we, though small, may quiver with fire's same
Substantial form as Thou—nor reflect merely,
As lunar angel, back to thee, cold flame.
Gods we are, Thou has said: and we pay dearly.[11]

It turns out, then, that the deepest vulnerability does not lie in holding two mortgages but simply in our shared human condition. We are not angels who, because their life is not an embedded one, do not experience "the local, unique sting" and can easily love universally. The God who, while loving universally, loves each person individually has something more than that in mind for us—that, having experienced vulnerability, we may one day "quiver with fire's same / Substantial form" as God himself. That, Josef Pieper once noted, is what we really ask when we pray, "kindle in us the fire of Thy love."[12] Moving reminds us just what it is that we ask in such a prayer, and we ought not do it casually.

A LIFE IN ONE'S CALLING

Where in these reflections is the sense of renewal—the challenge and stimulation of undertaking something new? A reasonable question, to which I now turn under the heading of vocation. In the second stanza of his well-known hymn, "Forth in thy name, O Lord, I go," Charles Wesley expressed succinctly that concept of vocation:

> The task thy wisdom has assigned
> Oh, let me cheerfully fulfill,
> In all my works thy presence find,
> And prove thy acceptable will.

We in the West owe this sense of a "calling" in large part to the Protestant Reformers, even though we have distorted their ideas a good bit by now. The powerful sense that there is work that we are called to do in the world, work that is ours and no one else's, work that will serve the needs of others whether it pleases and fulfills us or not—all that is built into the idea of vocation. This brings joy in the midst of our labor, but we should not suppose that such joy is simply a smile face that suppresses the uncertainty and vulnerability of being "on the way." Calvin, I think, had it about right in the *Institutes* when he wrote: "each man will bear and swallow the discomforts, vexations, weariness, and anxieties in his way of life, when he has been persuaded that the burden was laid upon him by God."[13]

The large and largely unanswerable question, of course, especially when one is contemplating moving, is how we may discern
what task God's wisdom has assigned us. At least for those whose
lives are as routinized as I have confessed my own to be, the force
of inertia must be very strong indeed. Why move? Why assume
God wants me somewhere other than where I happen to be?
Indeed, the one passage in the New Testament from which Luther
drew his understanding of the calling, a few verses in I Corinthians
7, is notably ambiguous on just this question. Translators must
decide whether verse twenty-one is to be rendered: "Were you a
slave when called? Never mind. But if you can gain your freedom,
avail yourself of the opportunity." Or whether it is better rendered:
"Were you a slave when called? Never mind. But if you can gain
your freedom, make use of your present condition instead." Two
translations that lead in quite different directions when one asks
what God desires of us in the calling.

The idea that we will feel the leading of God if only we seek it
seriously is one I admit to doubting. I am more drawn, in fact, to
the language Paul Ramsey once used in telling me that only twice
in his life had he faced vocational decisions that he had "to put his
will to." We must consider our talents and aptitudes, our likes and
dislikes, the needs we are suited to serve—and then "put our will
to" vocational decision.

When one moves there are, of course, always reasons for leaving as well as reasons for coming. For the most part I am largely
uninterested here in the reasons for leaving. Indeed, I have to say
that Oberlin College generously supported my work over the
years, and I suspect that I might not have been as productive elsewhere. Moreover, it gave me for many years the privilege of membership in a department of religion that was always intellectually

aggressive and never facile. Yet, I have found it increasingly difficult simply to believe in liberal education, despite the little talks
about it that I have given to my advisees over the past couple
decades. So often it does not seem to open the mind and heart to
what counts most in life. This lack has, in my view, almost nothing to do with the idea of core curricula and almost everything to
do with the fragmentation of our culture and the identity politics
that dominates so much of academic life. Moreover, the one identity that seems to lack a place in the academy is religious identity.
It becomes hard to recommend such a setting to young people and
disconcerting to think of having given one's most productive years
to an undertaking one is reluctant to recommend.

St. Augustine makes the point perhaps a little too strongly but
still powerfully in his *Confessions*:

> And what good did it do me that I, at a time when I was the
> vile slave of evil desires, read and understood for myself every
> book that I could lay my hands on which dealt with what are
> called the liberal arts? I enjoyed these books and did not
> know the source of whatever in them was true and certain.
> For I had my back to the light and my face to the things on
> which the light shone; so the eyes in my face saw things in the
> light, but on my face itself no light fell.[14]

That light, in truth, is what gives center and cohesion to our study,
what makes the liberal arts what they once meant: study that sets
one free from what is merely necessary or obligatory, free, ultimately, to rest in God—to worship.

Although he might not wish to take credit for its results in my
life, Richard Neuhaus indirectly persuaded me of this in a conver-

sation we had about his decision to become a Roman Catholic. He saw little future for Lutheranism in this country, and I feared—and often fear—he may be right. I noted to him, however, that this makes relatively little difference in my life. I am, for better or worse, pretty much formed by now. If the church dissatisfies me, as it often does, I can muddle along, serving it where I can, ignoring it when I must. His response was to the point: That may be fine for me, but will it work for my children? And, of course, he was on target. He meant that without institutions committed to a way of life—and without people interested in sustaining those institutions—we cannot transmit a valued way of life. We could, of course, follow Fr. Neuhaus to Rome, where they are still willing to run the risks involved in institutional commitment, and that would not be the worst of the choices open to us. A few decades from now it may be the best. But, although it may again be nothing more than that force of inertia in my life, I am not quite ready to give up on Lutheranism. Hence, Valparaiso. I am, of course, acutely aware that it may disappoint me; indeed, I live in fear that such may be the case! That too is part of the vulnerability we incur in making important decisions, and it is part of life in one's calling, which is always personal, always one's own and no one else's.

"We can," Einar Billing wrote in his classic work *Our Calling*, "never foresee the results of our acts, least of all when the goal is the kingdom of God. To maintain that our feeble deeds do serve this infinite goal is and remains a matter of faith."[15] If we understand Billing rightly, we must, of course, appreciate the irony here, and it returns me to where I began. For had I remained at Oberlin I could have said exactly the same: that we can never foresee the results of our acts, and that we can only trust that our feeble deeds serve the goal of God's kingdom. Move or stay—there is a crucial sense in which it makes no difference, for in either case one is "on the way." The great temptation, of course, is then to suppose that what is not of ultimate significance makes no penultimate difference. I have tried to avoid that temptation, tried to reflect upon what it means to be on the move, tried to let the experience remind me of truths too easily forgotten in the rush of life. I have, borrowing and modifying a Wordsworthian description of poetry, tried to recollect emotion in (theological) tranquillity. It should be evident, however, that neither the calling nor theological reflection upon it provides much tranquillity, for they situate us "on the way." There is, however, another, more important kind of tranquillity to be found even along the way, and for that I must give the last word to Billing when he writes: "According to the Lutheran teaching [of the calling], the joy over the forgiveness of sins is the only joy we should seek."[16]

12

TO THROW ONESELF INTO THE WAVE: THE PROBLEM OF POSSESSIONS

The Christian Scriptures provide no single rule governing attitudes and actions in the realm of possessions. Perhaps for this reason, "the church has always been more hesitant to lay down a rule of practice about money than it has...about sexual relations," even though the destructive power of possessions is every bit as great as that of sexuality.[1] There may also be reasons more general in character why we should be reluctant to universalize any single view of possessions as *the* Christian view, a point to which I will return later. But we can begin to think about the problem of possessions by juxtaposing a few biblical texts.

A PARTISAN GOD

Blessed are the poor in spirit, for theirs is the kingdom of heaven. (Matt. 5:3)

Blessed are you poor, for yours is the kingdom of God. (Luke 6:20)

These passages—and the contrast between them in their Matthean and Lukan forms—are well known. Taken together they raise a question. Who are the poor upon whom God's blessing—life in the kingdom—is bestowed? Is God's favor shown to all the poor in spirit, all who know themselves to be beggars before him—who, even when they have done all that is asked of them, say, "We are unworthy servants; we have only done what was our duty" (Luke 17:10)? Or is God's favor shown particularly and preferentially to those who are poor in the goods of this world, those who, like the beggar Lazarus, long for the crumbs that fall from the tables of the wealthy—but who, when they die, are carried by the angels to Abraham's bosom (Luke 16:19 ff.)?

If God's favor is to be understood as preference for those who are poor in the things of this world, the case will have to be made elsewhere than from the Old Testament. For the Hebrew Scriptures also recognize the ambivalence to which the Matthean and Lukan forms of Jesus' beatitude point. Israel's God is one who

> raises the poor from the dust,
> and lifts the needy from the ash heap. (Ps. 113:7)

But the Israelite sage knows that there is another kind of poverty cutting more deeply into the human soul.

> It is better to be of a lowly spirit with the poor
> that to divide the spoil with the proud. (Prov. 16:19)

And at the most fundamental level of human "being," our material condition cannot affect our relation to Israel's God.

The rich and the poor meet together;
the LORD is the maker of them all. (Prov. 22:2)

In the Old Testament there is condemnation of those who oppress and show no concern for the poor, but there is little condemnation of wealth itself.[2] After we have finished calling attention to prophetic woes uttered upon the rich who trample the poor, and after we have taken note of the legal provisions connected with the year of jubilee, we will still have to grant that the legitimacy of possessions is both presupposed and protected by the Decalogue's commandments forbidding theft and covetousness. Radical poverty is not an ideal. The prophetic picture of the day when all peoples come to Zion can be described in terms of a settled life of moderation and contentment once experienced under Solomon: "They shall sit every man under his vine and under his fig tree" (Mic. 4:4; cf. 1 Kings 4:25).

It is therefore something genuinely new when Jesus says, "Blessed are you poor, for yours is the kingdom of God." New and powerful—but not to be taken alone. It does not mean that the Gospel's invitation is addressed primarily or exclusively to those who are poor in this world's goods—"the poor, the maimed, the lame, the blind" (Luke 14:13). We must read this blessing together with the expression of God's favor toward all who, like the tax collector, say, "God, be merciful to me a sinner" (Luke 18:13). Such poverty of spirit frees one from the bondage of both poverty *and* wealth.

Even in Luke's Gospel, with its special attention to the poor and lowly, the relation to God is fundamental. If Luke does not cite Jesus' saying about the first and greatest commandment—love of

God—he nonetheless teaches the lesson in a striking and profound fashion. In chapter ten he recounts Jesus' story of the Good Samaritan—the story that, perhaps more than any other, has powerfully depicted the requirement of love especially for the neighbor in need. Yet, that is followed immediately by the brief account of Jesus' visit to the home of Mary and Martha. This is the Jesus who has just pointed to the Samaritan and said, "Go and do likewise." And when Martha attempts in her own way to do likewise, to serve the needs of Jesus while Mary sits contemplatively at his feet and listens, he says to Martha: "One thing is needful. Mary has chosen the good portion..." (Luke 10:42). That poverty of spirit is asked of every person—rich or poor—and is the one thing needful.

If the church is to be an agent of reconciliation among all who are poor in spirit (even if, perhaps, rich in this world's goods), its calling must be chiefly, though not exclusively, to speak the good news of Christ and to let its faith be active in works of mercy. That offer of God's favor to all who are poor in spirit, even though it may not directly address the most immediate needs of the poor, can never be irrelevant to the human condition. The church's vision must always, in Reinhold Niebuhr's terms, discern the equality of sin underlying the inequality of guilt in human life.[3] What is at stake here is chiefly a question of emphasis, of centrality in the church's mission. For surely it is true that, in addition to speaking the word of the gospel and letting its faith be active in works of love, the church is to let its love seek justice through words of witness. But when the *central* element in the church's mission becomes partisan advocacy in the political arena, "the evangelistic voice of the church is muted.... Even though political activity is mandated by love, it masks love's face in a way that evangelism and direct care of the poor do not."[4]

The church risks irrelevance, in fact, when it makes central in its vocation God's preference for the poor and not his universal favor toward the poor in spirit. For a partisan God, whom we can enlist in political struggle, is a God we can capture and possess. And we may wonder whether, when the day comes that such a God is no longer useful as a means toward our partisan ends, we will not find the message of his favor to have become irrelevant.

SPIRIT AND STRUCTURE

> Do not lay up for yourselves treasures on earth, where moth and rust consume and where thieves break in and steal, but lay up for yourselves treasures in heaven, where neither rust consumes and where thieves do not break in and steal. For where your treasure is, there will your heart be also. (Matthew 6:19–21)

> Either make the tree good, and its fruit good; or make the tree bad, and its fruit bad; for the tree is known by its fruit.... The good man out of his good treasure brings forth good, and the evil man out of his evil treasure brings forth evil. (Matt. 12:33, 35)

Luke Timothy Johnson suggests that when we seek a theological understanding of the proper place of possessions in our life, we should focus primarily on motivation, the chief determinant of Christian character: "We are convinced that our identity is found in our inner heart, where we desire and will, and that God, the discerner of hearts, looks not so much to our actions as to our intentions."[5] From this perspective the problem of possessions is chiefly a problem of getting from "in here" to "out there"—achieving the right attitude, a righteous inner self, so that this self may handle external goods properly.[6] And yet, despite this emphasis, Johnson must grant, a few pages later, that the direction of movement also goes the other way—from "out there" to "in here," from external things to inner self. The way we dispose of external things not only expresses the self we are, but also forms and shapes that inner self.[7] Inner spirit is expressed through external structures—and, indeed, a right inner spirit can probably be expressed through a variety of structural arrangements. But structure also shapes spirit, and anyone concerned for inner virtue cannot ignore the formative influence of the things we use and possess.

We have not exhausted all there is to be said about the Christian life when we have discussed motives and noted that a good tree will bring forth good fruit, for it is also true that our hearts will be shaped by the location of our treasure. Christians have not usually wanted to say, for example, that an inner motive of love would suffice to sanctify any and every sexual act. Because we are embodied spirits, the disposition of the body (and not simply motive) counts morally. Some bodies are already committed in sexual relationships. Some bodies cannot enact the union of those who are other, as male and female are other. There is no reason why structure should not also count when we turn from the issue of sexuality to that of possessions.

The problem of relating spirit and structure does not arise solely when we reflect upon wealth and poverty; it is a perennial difficulty for Christian living. Because structure shapes spirit, moral virtue is simply habit long continued. The inner self—what we are likely to call "character"—is developed and molded by the structures within which we live daily. Only gradually do we become people whose character is established—who, for better or worse, can be depended upon to act in certain ways. All of us believe that structure shapes spirit to this extent. If we did not, we would pay far less attention to the social environment in which we—and others, such as our children—live. Although possessions are not bad, they are dangerous. They can corrupt the spirit: "where your treasure is, there will your heart be also." But spirit cannot be reduced to structure. We cannot guarantee a virtuous inner self by rightly ordering structures. We may give away all that we have, even sacrifice our life, and yet—so the apostle tells us— "have not love" (1 Cor. 13:3). Just as God cannot be captured or possessed by our side in any partisan struggle, so true virtue cannot simply become our possession—as if the mysterious working of God's grace on our inner self had no part to play, as if the tree did not have to be made good before its fruit could be good.

THE AMBIVALENCE OF POSSESSIONS

"One thing you still lack. Sell all that you have and distribute to the poor, and you will have treasure in heaven; and come, follow me." But when he heard this, he became sad, for he was very rich. Jesus looking at him said, "How hard it is for those who have riches to enter the kingdom of God! For it is easier for a camel to go through the eye of a needle than for a rich man to enter the kingdom of God." Those who heard it said, "Then who can be saved?" But he said, "What is impossible with men is possible with God." (Luke 18:22–27)

It would be hard to find a story from the New Testament that has had a greater impact upon Christian history than the story of the rich ruler who came to Jesus with high hopes for discipleship and left sorrowfully, clinging to his possessions. "One thing you lack,"

Jesus says. And generations of Christians, called to what they thought of as special religious vocations, have heard in these words a counsel of perfection—a possibility for Christian living that goes beyond the careful use of possessions required by the commandments. Others have labored with sincere diligence to interpret the passage in ways that made clear that the camel Jesus had in mind could indeed squeeze through the eye of a needle he had in mind. This story, in fact, has all the ambiguity we have noted in the sets of passages discussed above.

We can learn a good bit by considering the story through the eyes of Clement of Alexandria, a Christian philosopher who lived at the beginning of the third century in a city that had become a center of learning, culture, and wealth. Not all Christians who came to him for advice were necessarily prepared to sell all that they had and distribute it to the poor. Nor did Clement think they should. His essay "The Rich Man's Salvation" is a thoughtful and instructive discussion.

Clement notes that what Jesus chiefly asks of his followers (and what he really wants from the rich ruler) is that they rid themselves of the passion for wealth and the anxiety this passion breeds. In speaking to the rich man, Jesus does not, Clement writes, "bid him throw away the substance he possessed, and abandon his property; but bids him banish from his soul his notions about wealth, his excitement and morbid feeling about it, the anxieties, which are the thorns of existence, which choke the seed of life."[8] And if we are likely to think that Clement strains a bit too much in suggesting that Jesus does not bid the young man to abandon his possessions, it is still true that on the essential point he is very near the mark. The danger, Clement believes, lies not simply in external possessions but in the inner spirit of passionate desire for goods. Things themselves he considers neutral; what counts is how we use them, the attitude we adopt toward them. "For it is no great thing or desirable to be destitute of wealth" (p. 94). Clement will not grant that simply being without earthly goods, being destitute and a beggar, makes one "most blessed and most dear to God" (p. 95). On the contrary, he is persuaded that what God is concerned with—and what Jesus was aiming at in his advice to the rich ruler—is a right inner spirit. "It is not the outward act which others have done, but something else indicated by it, greater, more godlike, more perfect, the stripping off of the passions from the soul itself" (p. 95).

This is Clement's basic interpretive move. Possessions themselves are entirely neutral; it is spirit, not structure, that concerns God. What counts is not what we have but how we use it. And yet, he himself realizes that the issue is more complicated that this. What we have *may* affect who we are—possessions may shape character. Clement notes this in a rather backhanded way. Having argued that there is nothing particularly holy about lacking wealth, that we might give away all that we own and still be consumed by the passion for things, he suggests that it might even be dangerous *not* to possess any of this world's goods. "For it is impossible and inconceivable that those in want of the necessaries of life should not be harassed in mind, and hindered from better things in the endeavour to provide them somehow and from some source" (p. 95). Having too little may lead to anxiety and concern—may corrupt the inner spirit. The insight here is not unlike that of the Israelite sage:

> Give me neither poverty nor riches;
> feed me with the food that is needful for me,

lest I be full, and deny thee,

and say, "Who is the Lord?"

or lest I be poor, and steal,

and profane the name of my God. (Prov. 30:8–9)

What this must mean, however, is that things, and the way we structure and possess things, are not entirely neutral. It is, I suppose, not entirely surprising that the point should come through in so "backhanded" a way in Clement. His audience would not be sorry to hear that there might be dangers in *not* possessing. But if there are dangers in poverty, if possessions therefore are not simply neutral, we will have to conclude in turn—what Clement does not note—that there may also be dangers in possession and acquisition.

To see this is not to undermine Clement's central point; indeed, it may be to reinforce it. For, although possessions are not simply neutral, what is clearest is that no particular way of possessing *or* not possessing can guarantee a spirit of trust in God alone for our security. The ideal for life that emerges in Clement's discussion seems at first, therefore, to be one of *moderation*. The acquisitive passions of the soul should be controlled and moderated. To the degree they achieve this, Christians will neither be distressed in times of adversity nor led astray by the seductions of wealth.

There are, however, hints in Clement of an ideal that goes beyond that of balance and moderation. It is possible, after all, that the life of moderation might be largely self-serving. Clement does not entirely forget that Jesus asks something harder of his followers. The ideal is not simply a pure, temperate inner spirit; rather, that spirit is sought, at least in part, because of the action to which it will give rise. Followers of Jesus should have possessions without clinging to them *so that* they are always ready to give to those in need. "For if no one had anything, what room would be left among men for giving?... How could one give food to the hungry, and drink to the thirsty, clothe the naked, and shelter the houseless,...if each man first divested himself of all these things?" (pp. 95–96).

To come this far with Clement is to see again the ambivalence of Christian thought about possessions. How shall we describe the proper attitude as Clement depicts it? We might say: moderate your desires *and* be ready to give to those in need. And yet, at any moment—or every moment?—that readiness to give might reach down and begin to transform the measured tones of one's moderation. It might seem that about at least one thing—giving to the neighbor in need—the Christian should be *im*moderate. There is no place for mediocrity in such service. Clement himself writes that the Christian knows he possesses goods "more for the sake of the brethren than his own" (p. 98). Where will such an *im*moderate spirit of giving lead? Back to Jesus' words, "sell all that you have and distribute to the poor"? Clement does not, of course, mean for that to happen. But to see it reemerge, even as a possibility, from Clement's discussion is to see why Christian thought has been unable to say only one thing about possessions.

We can distinguish at least three attitudes, each of which takes root in the soil of Christian faith:

First, possessions are both a dangerous threat and a good opportunity. To avoid the dangers, we need the virtue of *simplicity*— to choke off the passion for things and moderate our desires. To seize the opportunities for service, we need the virtue of *generosity*.[9]

Second, regularly seizing the opportunity to give to those in need may call for and give rise to something more than a moderation of our desires; it may suggest the need for *renunciation*.

Clement writes to oppose this move, and he is surely correct in seeing that not all Christians are called to such a life—correct also to see that this is no higher way, since it can offer no guarantee of a purer inner spirit. What Jesus says to the rich ruler is the precise truth: *no one* is good but God alone. But Clement's own case suggests—almost against his will—that the way of renunciation may be the way some Christians must go.

Third, an attempt to practice the virtues of simplicity and generosity may give rise to a sense of *tension* within the Christian life—tension that pushes the whole of that life in a relatively *austere* direction. Presupposing the possession of goods, the virtue of generosity seems (like Clement) to call simply for a right inner spirit and by itself sets no limit (other than the neighbor's need) to what we possess. Presupposing the danger of possessions, the virtue of simplicity reminds us that things are not simply neutral. Too much—though also too little—can corrupt the soul. The call for simplicity is essentially a reminder that we are seldom as generous as we think, or as we could be, or as we ought to be. The call for generosity is essentially a reminder that the desire to live a simple life is not the same as the desire to help those in need; it can be largely a self-serving desire. We may, for example, retreat from the life of society; we may choose subsistence for ourselves. But in doing so we are retreating from a life of exchange and interdependence into one of autonomy and independence. The virtues required of us stand in some tension. "Civilization is commanded," C. S. Lewis wrote, "yet civilization can safely be practised only by those to whom it is promised that 'if they drink any deadly thing it shall not hurt them.'"[10] Yet, the virtues of simplicity and generosity need not and will not simply stand in tension within the Christian life. They will often be complementary and, when taken seriously, will together transform the whole of life in a relatively austere direction—a direction perhaps concealed in the "and" by which we held together Clement's two emphases: be moderate in desires *and* desire immoderately to help the needy.

For such a life of moderation and austerity there are, however, no universal rules. The way of renunciation is not a higher form of Christian life than that of simplicity, and simplicity is not always to be preferred to the wealth that makes possible greater generosity. "One of the marks of a certain type of bad man," C. S. Lewis once wrote, "is that he cannot give up a thing himself without wanting everyone else to give it up."[11] At issue here is the nature of Christian vocation. Room must be left for freedom of the Christian life—and, perhaps still more, freedom of the God who calls Christians to different ways of life.[12] Beneficence to others in need is a duty for Christians, but the ways in which that beneficence may be enacted are many, and no single way can be universally required. Thus, Luther offered the following explanation in his *Small Catechism* of the commandment prohibiting stealing: "We should fear and love God that we may not take our neighbor's money or goods, nor get them by false ware or dealing, but help him to improve and protect his property and business." Luther here first articulates a negative prohibition that admits of universalization: no one should take another's goods or get them through deceit. But the positive norm, the beneficence required—to help the neighbor "improve and protect his property and business"— can be enacted in countless ways that love may find but the moral law can neither specify nor require. Since such beneficence must ultimately flow from "fear and love" of God, the problem of possessions is, finally, a problem of trust.

ENJOYMENT AND RENUNCIATION

There is more simplicity in the man who eats caviar on impulse than in the man who eats grape-nuts on principle.

—G. K. Chesterton

Man, please thy Maker, and be merry,
And give not for this world a cherry.

—William Dunbar

Such virtues as contentment, simplicity, temperance, justice, generosity, and hospitality are important. And such vices as greed, avarice, covetousness, envy, and ambition are—because of their destructive power—important. But at the heart of our attachment to things is the need for security. In what or whom do we place our confidence? To say that our life consists not in what we possess but in our relation to God, not in the goods we have compared with what others have but in the affirming verdict of God upon our lives, is not to say that the things of this world are of no importance. But it does make the issue of trust central.

In *Perelandra*, one of his space fantasies, C. S. Lewis explored this theme—the role played by trust in shaping our attitude toward created things. The protagonist of the story, a man named Ransom, is taken to the planet Perelandra—a newly created world of almost indescribable beauty. He finds himself in "a part of the wood where great globes of yellow fruit hung from the trees."[13] Since the juice of an unknown fruit might not be healthful for a human being, he intends to take just a small experimental sip, but at the first taste he forgets such caution. "It was like the discovery of a totally new *genus* of pleasures, something unheard of among men, out of all reckoning, beyond all covenant. For one draught of this on earth wars would be fought and nations betrayed" (p. 42). Having drained one gourd, Ransom is about to pick another when he suddenly realizes that he is no longer hungry or thirsty. Although he is drawn by the desire to repeat a pleasure so intense, it seems better for him not to eat another at this time.

Shortly thereafter he has a similar experience when he finds a group of "bubble trees." These trees draw up water from the ocean, enrich it in some way, and produce spheres that swell until they burst and emit a delicious fragrance. Before Ransom has discovered the nature of these trees, he puts out his hand to touch one. Instantly (since he has popped it) he gets what seems like a shower with a delicious scent. Now, having discovered the secret, he thinks of new possibilities. He could plunge through the trees, breaking many of the spheres at once, and enjoy the experience "multiplied tenfold." But, as in the case of the fruit, something restrains him.

> He had always disliked the people who encored a favourite air in the opera—"That just spoils it" had been his comment. But this now appeared to him as a principle of far wider application and deeper moment. This itch to have things over again, as if life were a film that could be unrolled twice or even made to work backwards…was it possibly the root of all evil? No: of course the love of money was called that. But money itself—perhaps one valued it chiefly as a defence against chance, a security for being able to have things over again, a means of arresting the unrolling of the film. (p. 48)

Ransom has a similar experience when he finds some bushes that bear oval green berries. These are good to eat, though they do not give "the orgiastic and almost alarming pleasure of the gourds, but rather the specific pleasure of plain food" (p. 49). As he eats, Ransom finds that a few of the berries have a bright red center and are especially tasty. He is tempted to look only for those with the red center but is again strongly restrained from doing so.

> "Now on earth," thought Ransom, "they'd soon discover how to breed these redhearts, and they'd cost a great deal more than the others." Money, in fact, would provide the means of saying *encore* in a voice that could not be disobeyed.
> (p. 50)

This theme is made even clearer in what is perhaps the central image of *Perelandra*. The planet is for the most part a world of floating islands, but it also has a Fixed Land. Its first two inhabitants, the Lady and the King, are permitted to go onto the Fixed Land but not to live or sleep there. And that prohibition becomes the focal point for the tempter—the UnMan sent there to introduce evil into an innocent world. He calls the Lady's attention to the fact that people who live on a fixed land cannot be easily separated, as she and the King have been. They can control their own destinies to some extent and need not—here he borrows her own metaphor—think of themselves as constantly "thrown into the wave." He suggests that the command to live only on the floating islands "stands between you and all settled life, all command of your days" (p. 117). In the end, however, when the UnMan has been defeated, the Lady comes to see the significance of that command.

> The reason for not yet living on the Fixed Land is now so plain. How could I wish to live there except because it was Fixed? And why should I desire the Fixed except to make

sure—to be able on one day to command where I should be
the next and what should happen to me? It was to reject the
wave—to draw my hands out of Maleldil's, to say to Him,
"Not thus, but thus"—to put in our own power what times
should roll toward us...as if you gathered fruits together today for tomorrow's eating instead of taking what came. That
would have been cold love and feeble trust. And out of it how
could we ever have climbed back into love and trust again?
(p. 208)

That is the message of the story—our problem with possessions is
a failure to trust.

The Bible also tells a story—a story of creation corrupted by sin,
redeemed, and finally restored. To think of possessions within that
story is to see how dangerous is our eagerness to fashion our own
security, how intricate is a proper attitude toward the good things of
our world. A life of trust always involves a double movement: affirmation and negation, enjoyment and renunciation of things.

This double movement is grounded first in the fact of creation
itself. Although the things of our world are proper sources of
delight, they always remain *created* things. As gifts of the Creator,
they reflect his goodness and glory. This means that they do more
than offer enjoyment; they convey a message. They call us out of
ourselves, both delighting the heart *and* drawing it beyond created
things to the Creator. The true source of enjoyment is not, finally,
in the things we possess; it comes *through* them. Renunciation—if
not of the thing possessed, at least of the desire to possess—cannot
be separated from enjoyment. That is what the Lady learned on
Perelandra: a receptive enjoyment of Maleldil's gift involved
renunciation of the fruit she had originally intended to eat.

It is because a double movement is required that no single attitude toward possessions can be recommended as the Christian one. Some renunciation must always be present, but renunciation alone cannot be the way all Christians must approach the problem of possessions. Moreover, renunciation is never to be an end in itself. It is part of a total movement intended to honor, esteem, and affirm the good gifts of the Creator. Nevertheless, because the biblical narrative is a story not only of creation but also of sin, renunciation must take on increased importance in the Christian life. We do not only receive our possessions with glad hearts; we grasp after them, want more than we need, take things sometimes at the expense of others, and seek our security in an abundance of possessions. Fallen creatures do that: they want to grasp and retain, to store up rather than to receive daily, to turn from what is given to what is desired—and for such creatures the movement of negation built into the dialectic of creation must often be experienced as painful renunciation.

Since the central problem is the self who does not trust, the renunciation asked is not finally of things or possessions. It is *self-*renunciation, a mortifying and killing of that greedy, grasping, fallen self. Thus, the addition of fallenness to the Christian story necessarily adds a severe, somewhat ascetic note. Christians must always look with suspicion upon luxuries. If we have more than we need, others may have less than they need. If we enjoy considerable luxury, it may be difficult for our hearts to make the other half of the double movement—to renounce as well as enjoy. And the more abstract the form of our luxuries, the more dangerous they may be. Emil Brunner makes the point clearly.

> Money is the abstract form of material goods. This abstrac-
> tion, like all abstraction, includes both great potentialities and
> great dangers.... Where money has become the main material
> good, quantity tends to prevail over quality. The desire for
> wealth becomes infinite. I cannot imagine an infinite number
> of concrete material goods, but I can easily add an indefinite
> number of ciphers to any given figure.[14]

Having noted this, Brunner himself goes on to qualify it. Although
money, as an abstract form of possessions, may give rise to limit-
less craving, it remains true that "within the Christian faith motive
is more important than structure."[15] But perhaps having granted
that structure also shapes spirit, we should be less sanguine. Is it
possible, for example, that delight in our work has become more
difficult in a world in which money (or, a still greater abstraction,
credit) has become the chief material good? Desire is refocused—
and encouraged to become infinite. Without such an infinite scope
for desire, advertising would play a far less important role than it
does in our economic life. And it is, I think, a common observa-
tion—not nearly as paradoxical as it may at first seem—that
advertising, by discouraging renunciation, makes enjoyment of the
goods we possess more difficult. An unfocused and infinite desire
always wants something more.

If the movement from creation to *sinful* creation adds a
severely ascetic note to the Christian story, it is still true that enjoyment is the final goal. To such enjoyment and delight, incarnation
and redemption lead. And however much room there may be for
abstinence and renunciation in our present pilgrim condition,

Christians trust that we are made to enjoy the vision of God. Incarnation is the sign that earthly goods remain objects of delight even in a fallen world. Redemption is the promise that abstinence is not the final word. At the center of Christian piety is a man slowly dying by torture, and it is no surprise that this should be a faith of martyrs and ascetics. But the God whom Christians worship is one who goes the way of self-renunciation in order to redeem the creation. At his right hand, the psalmist says, are pleasures forevermore (16:11).

Christians can, therefore, adopt and recommend no single attitude toward possessions. When they attempt to understand their lives within the world of biblical narrative, they are caught up in the double movement of enjoyment and renunciation. Neither half of the movement, taken by itself, is the Christian way of life. *Trust* is the Christian way of life. In order to trust, renunciation is necessary, lest we immerse ourselves entirely in the things we possess, trying to grasp and keep what we need to be secure. In order to trust, enjoyment is necessary, lest renunciation become a principled rejection of the creation through which God draws our hearts to himself. Indeed, affirmation must, I think, have the final word. Principled renunciation is more dangerous than principled enjoyment because created goods are channels through which the divine glory strikes us, and those who love and delight in any good thing may yet learn to love God. The heart may be drawn from image to reality. But to renounce all enjoyment of created things—to delight in nothing—must *either* be only one part of a movement that, we trust, will end in enjoyment, *or* it must be hell.

PART 4

Books

13

WELCOMING THE HOMAGE OF THE KINGS

Oliver O'Donovan, *The Desire of the Nations: Rediscovering the Roots of Political Theology* (Cambridge University Press, 1996)

G ranting, of course, that there are countless books I have not read, and with apologies in particular to the friends whose books I have read, *The Desire of the Nations* is as significant a work of theology as I can recall reading in the last twenty years. It is also, alas, a very difficult book.

In the preface to the first edition of his *Critique of Pure Reason*, Kant noted that his work, even when set forth in "purely *scholastic* fashion," was already quite large. He therefore deemed it

> inadvisable to enlarge it yet further through examples and illustrations. These are necessary only from a *popular* point of view; and this work can never be made suitable for popular consumption. Such assistance is not required by genuine students of the science, and, though always pleasing, might very well in this case have been self-defeating in its effects.... For the aids to clearness, though they may be of assistance in regard to details, often interfere with our grasp of the whole. The reader is not allowed to arrive sufficiently quickly at a

conspectus of the whole; the bright colouring of the illustrative
material intervenes to cover over and conceal the articulation
and organisation of the system, which, if we are to be able to
judge of its unity and solidity, are what chiefly concern us.

I recalled this passage as I worked my way through *The Desire of
the Nations*, more than once wondering whether to number myself
among the "genuine students of the science" or among those in
need of more "assistance." O'Donovan's style is dense, elliptical,
architectonic—but also enormously learned in ways one hardly
ever encounters in contemporary theological writing. Many books
are worth reading; this book is important.

What makes it important? Chiefly, I believe, two things. It is,
first, a reading of Scripture as a coherent whole and continuous
narrative. This reading is genuinely historical in the sense that it
makes place for change and development within the biblical narrative. It is very far removed from any ahistorical proof-texting;
yet the entire story is told from the standpoint of the church's witness to the resurrection of Jesus. It is the story of God's triumph in
Christ, the desire of the nations. And second, the book is a powerful defense of Christendom—not as a present reality, of course,
since O'Donovan knows that we no longer live in such times, but
as a necessary feature of the church's mission.

Complicated as the book is, its structure is nevertheless carefully plotted. Here I will attempt the following. First, I will very
briefly try to "place" O'Donovan's book in terms of some contemporary theological concerns—and in terms of Augustine and Karl
Barth, on both of whom he draws heavily. Second, and at much
greater length, I aim to summarize the argument of the book—tracing its account of political rule from ancient Israel, through the rev-

elation of the kingdom of God in Jesus and the rule of the exalted Christ in the church, to the church's mission which anticipates the obedience of political authorities and the transformation of societies. And third, having summarized in some detail the course of the argument, I will step back from it and ask what, if anything, it lacks. In particular, I will ponder the fact that it makes power, rather than love, the central theme of biblical narrative.

SITUATING THE PROJECT

If we try to locate O'Donovan's project theologically, we might first recall his description of Barth's political theology as a "magnificent, but incomplete, beckoning movement." Barth, of course, came at political questions from a variety of perspectives at different points in his life, but O'Donovan notes in particular the never completed volume IV/4 of the *Church Dogmatics*, in which Barth approached politics "solely from the point of view of the church's mission." It would not be entirely mistaken to read *The Desire of the Nations* as the completion of that project. It is not only that, however, for it is also a *City of God* for our time, an account of the history of that city of which glorious things are spoken. And O'Donovan calls Barth and Augustine unmistakably to mind when—in a passage that I shall come around to questioning—he writes that "no destiny can possibly be conceived in the world, or even out of it, other than that of a city."

Although I will not be able to do O'Donovan's discussion justice, I intend to summarize it at length, if only in order to encourage other readers to enter into it themselves and probe its complexities. Hans Frei once described Barth's theological writing as having the "peculiar character of being at once accessible and yet so difficult to do justice to in exposition and commentary."

Something similar is true of *The Desire of the Nations*, and Frei's description of Barth's project is not a bad description of what O'Donovan is doing:

> Barth was about the business of conceptual description: He took the classical themes of communal Christian language molded by the Bible, tradition and constant usage in worship, practice, instruction and controversy, and he restated or redescribed them, rather than evolving arguments on their behalf. It was of the utmost importance to him that this communal language...had an integrity of its own: It was irreducible. But in that case its lengthy, even leisurely unfolding was equally indispensable. For he was restating or re-using a language that had once been accustomed talk, both in first-order use in ordinary or real life, and in second-order technical theological reflection, but had now for a long time, perhaps more than 250 years, been receding from natural familiarity, certainly in theological discourse. So Barth had as it were to recreate a universe of discourse, and he had to put the reader in the middle of that world, instructing him in the use of that language by showing him how....

However necessary my attempt at summary, therefore, it cannot be a substitute for the book itself. I can summarize the architectonic but not the reading of the Bible that gives rise to it.

THE STRUCTURE OF THE PROJECT

The first task of political theology is to give an account of what we mean by political authority or rule (the *esse* of politics)—the notion of a political act. A further task will be to unfold the *bene esse* of politics, the proper use of political action. O'Donovan's description of political authority begins with the political vocabulary used in the Bible to describe the reign of Yhwh over Israel. The political tradition of Israel—read as a history that develops over time, in which each development "has to be weighed and interpreted in the light of what preceded and what followed it"—is normative, and its character can be roughly summarized in four affirmations.

The Lord's reign is, first, an exercise of power that gives Israel victory or salvation; it is, second, the execution of judgment or justice within Israel; and it is, third, the establishment of Israel's communal identity as a people that exists over time (which identity is connected at first with the land and, later, with possession of the law). These three affirmations summarize what it means to say that the Lord rules as king in Israel, and, if the features that constitute Israel as a people are normative, what it means to speak of any political authority.

These three—power, execution of right, and perpetuation of communal identity—constitute Yhwh's rule in Israel, but a fourth affirmation must be added. The Lord's rule is acknowledged—though not established—in the praise that Israel, as a worshipping community, offers. "Shall we conclude, then, that within every political society there occurs, implicitly, an act of worship of divine rule? I think we may even venture as far as that." This may strike a contemporary reader as bizarre, but it helps us understand why idolatry always lies near at hand in politics when the divine authority that establishes government is ignored or forgotten. At any rate, we do not create political authority; we acknowledge it and thereby affirm our existence as a political community. "The doctrine that *we* set up political authority, as a device to secure our own essentially private, local, and unpolitical purposes, has left the Western democracies in a state of pervasive moral debilitation, which, from time to time, inevitably throws up idolatrous and authoritarian reactions." Here we see O'Donovan at his most anti-liberal, attacking (on the basis of Israel's normative tradition) the idea that government exists chiefly to foster the pursuit of private aims and interests. That tendency in his thought will, however, be sharply qualified before he finishes.

The story of Israel does not end with the establishment of Yhwh's rule through power, judgment, and establishment of communal identity. This rule must now be mediated to the people, and the nature of that mediation changes over time. Moses is himself a unitary mediator—carrying out all three functions as military deliverer, judge, and one who in the law gives the pattern of communal life. Kings in Israel also claimed to exercise all three functions in an undivided sovereignty that provided a unitary representation of God's rule. Such an arrangement, always controversial in Israel, was a constant temptation to make more of the monarch than he was, to see in the king an image of Israel's God. To avoid such danger, Israel turned not to a notion of "separation of powers" (which notion cannot therefore be quite as politically essential as we sometimes suppose) but, instead, to prophets. The law of the Lord had an independent voice within Israelite society through the prophets, and, therefore, every political authority must understand that it is not the sole mediator of divine authority, that it is itself subject to the community's own independent witness to God's will (which witness could, for example, take the form of a theory of "natural law" that transcends and judges positive law). This independent witness may even become, as it did later in Israel's history when the mediating institutions of government had collapsed, the voice of a single individual (such as Jeremiah) that preserves the community's memory of its own identity and reaches out toward its reconstitution.

This depiction of political rule, drawn from the history of Israel, can also be applied to other nations, for Israel's God was not locally confined. "Out of the self-possession of this people [Israel] in their relation to God springs the possibility of other peoples' possessing themselves in God." To put the point a little differently, but in a way in which its relevance to continuing disputes in the Middle East may be apparent, the God who providentially elects Israel as his chosen people is ready to protect the communal identity of other peoples as well. What Israel's tradition does not authorize, however, is any single *mediator* of divine rule at the international level. There is no single world order or empire. "Yhwh's world order was plurally constituted." He could make his name known to the nations through Israel, and his law could bind the nations universally, but there is no universal mediator of his rule. Hence, in relations among nations the rule of law can be invoked but not the commanding rule of a single government.

> This says something about the limits of our collective identities. To be a human being at all is to participate in one or more collective identities. But there is no collective identity so overarching and all-encompassing that no human beings are left outside it. In that sense it is true that to speak of 'humanity' is to speak of an abstraction. Only in that sense, for in fact 'humanity' has a perfectly conceivable referent, and we should not hesitate to say that 'humanity' is real. But it is not a reality that we can command politically. We do not meet it in any community, however great, of which we could assume

the leadership. We meet it only in the face of Christ, who presents himself as our leader and commander.

Thus far the outline of the essence of political authority as O'Donovan draws it from the history of Yhwh's reign in Israel— without, I hasten to repeat, the rich textual discussion, the gradually developing account of the biblical narrative of Israel's political history, that is the basis for the outline. But what about the *bene esse*, the proper use of political action? To describe that, we must sketch the manner in which the rule of God, which is established in Israel's communal existence, is brought to its completion in the life, death, and resurrection of Jesus. Only then will we have an evangelical political theology.

The very categories that emerge from an examination of God's rule in Israel can be used to set forth the revelation of the kingdom of God in Jesus. He does mighty works of power that bring salvation; he proclaims the judgment of Israel; he reforms the understanding of the law upon which the identity of a restored Israel is based. The praise that acknowledges God's rule corresponds now to faith that recognizes the reign of God in Jesus. Much that passes for political theology (what O'Donovan terms "Jesulogy") might stop here, focusing on Jesus' announcement of the dawning of a new age of liberation. Such an approach "could encourage hope for new acts of divine creativity. But it could not speak meaningfully of the defeat of Jesus' programme, nor of its vindication." A better political theology "must base itself on 'the hidden counsel of God' which worked also through Caiaphas and Pilate." It must, that is, be grounded not in "Jesuology" but in Christology. The starting point for this Christology is the classical "two natures" teaching that turns out to have captured well the manner in which Jesus fills the two roles we have seen within Israel's story—the mediator of God's rule and the representative individual who carries the identity of the people and reaches out toward its reconstitution.

O'Donovan traces the chief "moments" of the Christ event in a fourfold pattern that coheres with the account of political rule derived from Israel's history. These moments are (1) the advent of Christ to save; (2) the passion of Christ in which the judgment of the world is given; (3) the restoration of Christ, which affirms Israel's new identity in its representative; and (4) the exaltation of Christ, the coronation of the one who has triumphed over the powers that oppose God's rule.

Present in his absence until the Parousia, the exalted Christ rules in the church, whose life participates in the four moments of the Christ event. Marked by the sign of baptism, the church now gathers to herself those who acknowledge Jesus as Lord. Marked by the sign of the eucharist, the church now suffers—paradigmatically in her martyrs but in countless other ways as well. Marked by the sign of her keeping of the Lord's day as a little Easter, the church now rejoices in the restoration of the creation. Marked by the sign of the laying on of hands, the church now speaks God's word in prophecy and prayer (which is speech addressed to the God from whom it comes). The churches have often been tempted to understand themselves in terms of one of these "moments" alone—as marked by mission alone, by suffering alone, by triumph alone, or by social responsibility alone. But such truncated understandings cannot recapitulate the narrative coherence of the moments in the story of Christ.

The salvation that Christ brings always remains political in nature. To be sure, the *inward* obedience of faith is given a new and striking centrality, as St. Paul makes clear, but Paul also testifies to the necessity of the continuing existence of Israel (with its public, political tradition). Israel too, of course, must take account of what has happened in the Christ. As it once had moved from conceiving its identity in terms of possession of the land to conceiving that identity in terms of possession of the law, so now Israel is called to see that possession of the law as fulfilled in Christ. But that does not nullify the continuing importance of Israel's normative political tradition. "So until the last reconciliation the two communities must coexist, the one with the witness of its public institutions, the other with a witness founded on and attesting faith...." The structure of public, political life remains an important concern even in the age of the church.

Indeed, the exalted Christ rules not only in the church, but also in political life. After all, the powers have been disarmed by Christ, who has triumphed over them and who is the desire of the nations. Of course, that triumph remains hidden until the end of the age. Hence, we must both assert the rule of Christ and simultaneously acknowledge that it is not yet fully apparent. "Within the framework of those two assertions there opens up an account of secular authority which presumes neither that the Christ-event never occurred nor that the sovereignty of Christ is now transparent and uncontested." It is, I think, fair to say, however, that O'Donovan's discussion emphasizes the disarming and the rule more than the eschatological reservation and the hiddenness.

How, in fact, should political authority survive at all as a bearer of collective identity once membership in the church has emerged as the new center of identity? To be sure, power and communal identity remain aspects of any account of the *esse* of political authority, but the "desacralization" of politics by the Christ-event provides a new understanding of the *bene esse*—the proper use of political action. (It also provides a setting in which the powers of this world might attempt one last desperate act of self-assertion—might, that is, become the Antichrist.) The point of politics must be rethought, for it exists now to serve the advancement of the Gospel. It exists, that is, chiefly to provide the execution of right, the just judgment that preserves the social order toward the further spread of the Christian mission. "The accumulation of power and the maintenance of community identity cease to be self-evident goods; they have to be justified at every point by their contribution to the judicial function. The responsible state is therefore minimally coercive and minimally representative...." This should make clear that, whatever the other tendencies in O'Donovan's thought, he holds that the political doctrine arising from the desacralization of politics can, broadly speaking, be characterized as the classical tradition of political liberalism.

In the time and space provided by secular government the church is in mission, securing the identity of Israel on the one hand, securing for the sake of Israel the obedience of the Gentile nations on the other—until the day when Yhwh gathers both Israel and the nations and Christ delivers the kingdom to his Father. "Nations shall come to your light, and kings to the brightness of your rising," the prophet says, articulating thereby the twofold focus of the church's mission: to society and to political authorities. The aim of the mission is different in the two cases. Society must only be transformed in accord with the purposes of God revealed in Christ. Rulers must disappear, relinquishing their sovereignty now that the stronger one has appeared.

O'Donovan takes up "the obedience of the rulers" in chapter six, perhaps the richest chapter in the book, containing, as it does, his treatment (and, in some respects, defense) of the idea of

Christendom—that is, the idea of a political order that is secular but nonetheless professedly Christian. That this seems to us almost a contradiction in terms demonstrates what has happened to the meaning of "secular" in our world. For Christian political thought, O'Donovan suggests, the alternative to "secular" should be not "religious" but "eternal." Secular government is 'secular' not in the sense that it is irreligious but in the sense that its role is confined only to this aeon (the *saeculum*) that is passing away. It does not and cannot in any way represent the promise of the new age that comes in Christ. "Applied to political authorities, the term 'secular' should tell us that they are not agents of Christ, but are marked for displacement when the rule of God in Christ is finally disclosed. They are Christ's conquered enemies; yet they have an indirect testimony to give…. Like the surface of a planet pocked with craters by the bombardment it receives from space, the governments of the passing age show the impact of Christ's dawning glory." What Christendom attempts, therefore, is to reconceive government in such a way that it bears witness to the triumph of Christ while also recognizing itself as belonging only to the age that is passing away.

O'Donovan is emphatic, however, that the creation of such a political order is not the *project* of the church's mission. That mission is to announce the rule of God in Christ, the desire of the nations. Christendom is simply a result of the church's mission and, here is the crucial claim, "a sign that God has blessed it." Suggesting that we might usefully date the time of Christendom as lying between 313 (the Edict of Milan) and 1791 (the adoption of the first amendment to the U.S. Constitution), O'Donovan traces its history and development in nineteen densely packed and richly learned pages on "the doctrine of the Two." Because the old aeon of the principalities and powers that have been disarmed by Christ overlaps with the coming aeon of God's kingdom, Christians had to explore the meaning of living within two societies. The movement of that exploration was roughly from a struggle between two societies (in the patristic period), to a vision of a single society with two foci of authority (in the medieval period), to a distinction between an inner self and its external roles in society (in the thought of Luther). Recognizing that we no longer live within the time of Christendom, O'Donovan is nonetheless unwilling to brand it a mistaken turn in the road. "The church is not at liberty to withdraw from mission; nor may it undertake its mission without confident hope of success."

The core of the Christendom idea is that each of the two authorities—which we can here call simply the church and the state—is to render service to the other "predicated on the difference and the balance of their roles." The state serves the church by making possible its mission; the church serves the state by instructing it in what it means to be a "humble state." The *esse* of political authority still characterizes the humble state; it exercises power and sustains the identity of a community. But now that the new age has dawned in Christ, we can be clearer about the *bene esse*—the proper action—of political authority. Now the exercise of power and the preservation of communal identity give way somewhat to the execution of right and justice. Power is now exercised *under* law, never as if it were the ultimate source of justice and right. "The responsible state is therefore minimally coercive and minimally representative.... This is not a restraint imposed by the nature of political authority as such, which can thrive on excesses of traditional legitimation and on splendid displays of force; it is imposed by the limits conceded to secular authority by Christ's Kingdom."

Once again, therefore, the anti-liberal strain in O'Donovan's thought is qualified. The "legal-constitutional conception," the limited state, becomes part of the wisdom the church has to recommend to rulers of this world. Indeed, the church may over time have learned a good bit of such worldly wisdom, which has become part of the Christian political tradition and which may be shared with many who do not consider themselves Christian. The temptation in such circumstances is to offer for public consumption the political doctrine "as a substitute for proclaiming Christ." This is, in fact, an apt characterization of much that is currently called "public theology." What public theology has come to mean quite often is that Christian and non-Christian endorse similar political views while (privately) offering different reasons for those views. But that, O'Donovan perceptively suggests, is to withdraw from mission. "Granted, the church may always make the best of any coincidence of political doctrine between Christians and non-Christians that it lights upon; but 'making the best' means making the evangelical content of the doctrine clear, not veiling it in embarrassment."

If the church serves the state by helping it to be the humble state, it in turn serves the church by creating space in which the latter's mission may be carried out. In part it accomplishes this simply by being the responsible state that understands the limits to which the dawning of God's kingdom now makes it subject. It may do this unwittingly, but it may also do it quite consciously, recognizing the church and acknowledging its mission—and a reader should not permit the boldness of that claim to be lost in the complexities of O'Donovan's prose. The most truly Christian state will echo John the Baptist: "He must increase; I must decrease." Not all states are likely to be so humble, of course. And part of the church's mission is to recognize the Antichrist (who claims to unite "earthly political rule and heavenly soteriological mediation" in one agent) when he makes his appearance. In the face of the Antichrist the church will have to be prepared for the possibility of martyrdom, but she should also confidently anticipate that the witness of her martyrs will be powerful. Hence, "the church must be prepared to welcome the homage of the kings when it is offered to the Lord of the martyrs.... No honour is paid to martyrs if they are presented as mere dissidents, whose sole glory was to refuse the cultural order that was on offer to them. Martyrdom is, as the word itself indicates, witness, pointing to an alternative offer." And that alternative offer is Christendom—the humble state that knows it is destined to pass away and that, in the meantime, helps to make the church's mission possible.

Must not such a state be coercive—at least from the perspective of those not inclined to welcome the church's mission? To the degree that the state seeks to make possible the church's mission, must not some members of the society feel themselves to be "outsiders," in it but not of it? It all depends. If the church's mission has successfully taken root in the lives of many people within a society, it is quite right, O'Donovan suggests, that their deep agreements should be reflected in their government. He argues persuasively that nothing in the classical tradition of political liberalism requires otherwise. That tradition encouraged the shared pursuit of truth, and "one cannot approve the common quest for truth without approving the hope that common persuasions may emerge from it." But what some of our contemporaries have now in fact

begun to believe is that any deep social agreement is itself inherently coercive and potentially oppressive. If we acquiesce in that
claim, however, O'Donovan writes in a passage that may presage
future developments all too accurately, the social agreements that
constitute the church would also be undercut. "If there is no religious test on the right to vote, or to have access to education or
medical care, why should there be one on attending Mass and
receiving communion, which is, after all, a source of satisfaction to
religious temperaments and an important means of social participation?" That is where an unqualified liberal individualism lands
us, and that it should find any societal consensus threatening is
unsurprising. If such a view undergirds the critique of
Christendom, then, O'Donovan is suggesting, one must say a good
word on behalf of Christendom. Of course, the time of
Christendom is for the moment gone, but it was not wrong—and
we would not be wrong—to hope that *kings* might come to the
brightness of Christ's rising.

Nor wrong to hope that *nations* would come to his light. This
directs us to the other focus of the church's mission: not only political authorities, but also societies. If the former must ultimately
disappear, the latter must be transformed. The distinctive features
of liberal society in the West have, in fact, been shaped to some
degree by the four moments that make up the narrative structure
of the dawning of the kingdom in Christ and the narrative structure of the church's life. Hence, O'Donovan thinks of the needed
social transformation as having taken place, at least in part, when
modernity brought to fruition and gave social shape to central
Christian beliefs. But he also suggests that modern society has
taken those beliefs and subverted them by losing the context which
alone enables them to enhance human life. Thus, modern society

both fulfills and subverts Christian teaching. We can briefly sketch this "pair of counter-interpretations" of modernity in terms of the same fourfold structure at work throughout the book.

Christ comes in power to save, the church gathers his disciples through baptism in a manner that transgresses all given communal boundaries—and liberal society has its beginning in this discovery of freedom. "A society founded in conversion and baptism is a society unlike all others." Because no human authority can now be understood as ultimate, space is created for personal freedom. This is not, however, an assertion of individual freedom; rather, it is the freedom that emerges from a new community whose Lord sets it free from all other lords. If, however, individuals become nothing more than freedom, nothing other than abstract will set over against an inert nature, and if consent becomes the only moral language we know, freedom subverts the natural communities and structures of life that are required for us to learn how rightly to exercise that freedom.

Christ endures a suffering in which the judgment of the world is revealed, the church, sharing through the Eucharist in his broken body, shares also in his suffering in the world—and liberal society gradually learns the meaning of sympathy for sufferers, learns that, though judgment remains necessary, mercy in judgment is now essential. But once freedom becomes its own ground, suffering can no longer be accepted. Compassion—basing itself on "the rejection of suffering rather than the acceptance of it"—replaces sympathy. Hesitation to pass judgment upon those who suffer remains, but now it is a hesitation grounded in moral insecurity rather than in religious humility.

Christ is raised to a new life as the representative of Israel's new identity; the church, celebrating on each Lord's Day the joy of that resurrection, rejoices at the restoration of the creation—and liberal society gradually develops a concept of natural right, of a humane social order in which both the equal dignity of every human being and the importance of distinctions that make natural communities possible are affirmed. But when freedom becomes its own ground, natural right becomes simply an interest in self-preservation, and equality can make no room any longer for the nonreciprocal roles that important forms of human community (such as the family) require.

The risen Christ is exalted to rule; the church, empowered through the laying on of hands, raises up its prophetic voice in society and speaks—and liberal society gradually is instructed in an openness to speech. Rulers learn that they must be responsive to the public deliberations of the entire community. But when freedom becomes its own ground, speech becomes mere assertion of self and finally loses its point.

Thus far O'Donovan's rediscovery of the roots of our political theology, making it clear where we now find ourselves—namely, in a society that in some respects fulfills the church's mission and in other respects subverts it. This pair of counter-interpretations of modernity serves "to sharpen our understanding of the decisions we now face; to interpret the two loves which made two cities in a form appropriate to our historical situation, clothing the *amor Dei ad contemptum sui* and the *amor sui ad contemptum Dei* in the dress of those Euro-American truisms and aspirations which we drank in with our mothers' milk." What we are politically and socially bears the unmistakable imprint of Christian thought and action. The inextricable intermingling of the two cities in human history is, by God's providence, directed toward the eternal unveiling of the church as the city for which we hope. But in the meantime, in earthly history, the mission of the church is to disclose to human eyes the true meaning of a city "through the prism of the church." That is the purpose of political theology.

QUESTIONING THE PROJECT

I have indulged myself in this lengthy summary of O'Donovan's argument, not because it can substitute for the book itself, but in order to offer some account of the scope and structure of his undertaking. Moreover, if O'Donovan's project is what I suggested at the outset—conceptual redescription of the world narrated by Scripture—one must first try to live within the world so narrated and see what one makes of it. Nothing is easier than to suggest what an author might have done but did not, and I do not want to engage in that kind of critique. But it may be useful to ask whether anything is missing from O'Donovan's account and, if so, what difference it might make.

One thing that is missing is the primeval history of Genesis 1-11, the backdrop against which the story of Israel, Jesus, and the church is played out. And whatever else we make of that primeval history, it seems to teach us that the work of God in history for our salvation takes place within certain limits, the most fundamental of which is that no return to paradise is possible. The angel with the burning brand is placed east of Eden; Cain, first to found a city, is also author of the first fratricide; the covenant made with Noah recognizes the sad fact that within our history, community will always be sustained through the use of force; the scattering of the peoples at Babel makes clear that we should not hope for a single, harmonious human community. Now, of course, O'Donovan is not wrong to see in the triumph of Christ the restoration of creation, and in the church a community built upon trust into which all peoples are invited. But if we read that story against the back-drop of these opening chapters of the Bible, our reading may be more cautious than O'Donovan's. We will then anticipate that Christ's triumph must remain hidden under the cross, and we will be less certain that we can trace that triumph through history. We will be less eager to have the force of even a humble state joined too closely to the mission of the church.

Is this to take the triumph less seriously? Not really to treat it as a triumph? I think not. It is only to emphasize that the triumph is more evident to faith than to sight. It is only to take seriously the eschatological reservation that St. Paul himself articulates, for example, in Romans 6. The Paul who writes there that "you who were once slaves of sin have become obedient from the heart...and...have become slaves of righteousness" is the same Paul who gives the new creation a decisively future orientation. "For if we have been united with him in a death like his, we shall certainly be united with him in a resurrection like his." To take that eschatological reservation seriously, one need not question the basic contours of the story O'Donovan tells, but one may simply emphasize that the *bene esse* of political action will not replace its *esse* (the use of force).

All that is, however, only a qualification. Something else is missing, though, from O'Donovan's account that may make a still greater difference. "[N]o destiny can possibly be conceived in the world, or even out of it," he writes, "other than that of a city." It is not surprising, therefore, that, in his account, when we gaze upon the face of Christ we look at one who is "our leader and commander." What if we were to think of the God whose face is revealed in Christ not first as one who commands but as one who loves? Perhaps such a move would not be as conducive to political theology, but it might alert us to overlooked possibilities.

Can we really conceive of no destiny in this world or another than that of a city? When in Revelation 21, in a passage that plays an important role in O'Donovan's account, the holy city, the new Jerusalem, comes down from heaven, the seer's metaphor is a decidedly mixed one. For the holy city is described in the non-political imagery of marriage—as "a bride adorned for her husband." And the holy city Jerusalem that is revealed is "the Bride, the wife of the Lamb." We should not readily assume that the holy city is chiefly an image of political rule; perhaps, rather, it is the image of a communion in which each participant is loved personally and intimately. We might try to retell the story O'Donovan has told from this perspective—as the story of Yhwh's wooing of his bride Israel and the marriage of Christ and his church. Not politics, then, but marriage would be the sign of God's ultimate, redeeming intention for the creation. Not command but love would be the dominant motif. The point of politics would be to make possible such private bonds of love. And the promises to Israel would point, not toward a redeemed public realm, but toward a hope that lies, finally, beyond that realm.

But all that is only the sketch of a story someone else might try to tell. O'Donovan has told his in a book that deserves to be widely read and discussed. We shall know the full truth of these matters only in the new Jerusalem, where, we may hope, such discussion will be a part of the praise of God. To work one's way through *The Desire of the Nations* may, therefore, be good preparation for heaven.

14

THE ECLIPSE OF FATHERHOOD

David Blankenhorn, *Fatherless America: Confronting Our Most Urgent Social Problem* (Basic Books, 1995)

S uppose we accept for the moment a widespread depiction of the manner in which our society has systematically oppressed women. It has connected the biological fact that women give birth with the cultural task of childrearing, assigning by far the larger share of that task to women because of the biological "accident" that they are the birthgivers. The woman has already "borne" the child; yet, we have assumed that she must also be chiefly responsible for that child's nurture. Men, by contrast, beget but do not give birth. Biologically, therefore, the link between begetting and nurturing is more attenuated for men than for women. Our culture has—unjustly—allowed that biological fact to shape the way it apportions the tasks of childrearing, thereby depriving women of full and equal participation in the many realms of life outside the home (the professions, the arts, business, politics, etc.).

How should we respond to such a standard depiction? Anyone who has taken the right courses at college is likely to respond that the injustice of this situation can be rectified only if we set our-selves as a culture against biology. We must overcome the male's tendency to opt out of childrearing by emphasizing that those who beget but do not bear are equally responsible for nurturing their children. That task of nurturing, maternal work, is work that men and women are equally obliged to undertake. Men need, in effect, to become more like women, and, however millennia of biological evolution may have shaped us, our culture should set itself against the male as we know him. This will, in effect, free women for ful-fillment outside the home, and, happily, it will be better for men as well—encouraging them to be more nurturing, less aggressive and competitive, less focused on earning a living, less…well, less mas-culine and paternal.

In *Fatherless America*, a work of cultural criticism of a very high order, David Blankenhorn subjects this now deeply entrenched understanding to thoroughgoing scrutiny. His approach is shaped by a distinctive starting point: what is good for children. It turns out that one of the things that is very good indeed for children is to have a father. Not just another human being who provides an additional set of hands with which to carry out what is understood as essentially maternal—or just human—work, but a father. Among other things, this book is a slashing attack on the emphasis upon self-fulfillment exalted by those who propose androgyny as the solution to the standard depiction of the oppres-sion of women. In Blankenhorn's words, the androgynous ideal "constitutes the most radical conception of expressive individual-ism that a society can imagine. It is the belief, quite simply, that human completion is a solo act." Putting the welfare of children first leads Blankenhorn to conclude, in contrast, that the task of childrearing requires "mutual dependency, grounded in the realities of gender complementarity." A society unable to measure up to the requirements of the task is a society whose future is endangered—because its children are endangered.

A profound issue lurks just a little beneath the surface of Blankenhorn's discussion. Though the "realities" that Blankenhorn wants us to take into account, accommodate, and affirm are biological realities about men and women, he himself does not want us simply to take our moral norms directly from biology. Quite in conformity with the standard depiction of our situation, he too sees men's sexuality as much more "hit-and-run" than women's. He too believes—and very helpfully uses the state-of-nature political philosophers to argue—that the socialization of males into fatherhood is a necessary "precondition for the rise of successful human societies." In his analysis, too, there is something a little suspect about the male.

We may therefore legitimately wonder whether he makes his peace too quickly with masculine, paternal tendencies. Since he himself wants to socialize those tendencies and transform the male into a more nurturing fellow, since he wants a "cultural script" for fathers that is not simply a transliteration of biological fact, why not do it more thoroughly? Why not do it in the way the standard depiction recommends? His argument is, I think, systematically ambiguous on this point. At times the androgynous ideal seems simply to be one that fails because it does not reckon with what men are like. Why not, then, just work harder to change what men are like, to make them less masculine and paternal? Because at other times the standard depiction seems to be *normatively* mistaken, an inadequate depiction of our humanity at its highest and best. This problem needs some sorting out, but I set it aside for the moment in order to outline the basic themes of Blankenhorn's case.

Everyone knows, if only because we have heard it repeated regularly, that an increasing number of homes in our society have no father in them. And almost everyone now seems to grant that this situation is bad (even if such an admission came a little too late to help Dan Quayle). But *Fatherless America* would not have to be as big a book as it is, and it would not be as important a book as it is, were that its only point. For Blankenhorn, the problem we face goes far deeper. It is not simply the loss of fathers but the loss of the idea of fatherhood and of our belief in the importance of fathers. We no longer have a distinctive "cultural script" for fatherhood. When I become a father, what have I become? How should it alter my life and habits? A society in which there are no culturally given answers to such questions is one that may experience grave difficulty drawing men into the role of fatherhood and its accompanying tasks and burdens.

In short, our cultural script for fathers is that they are unnecessary. "Today's expert story of fatherhood largely assumes that fatherhood is superfluous." Indeed, since we identify a distinctive paternal role with the "Old Father," who was distant and authoritarian, we may even suppose that fathers are part of our problem. Blankenhorn is quite willing to grant that, in a sense, they are. "Certainly this combustible contradiction inherent within fatherhood—closeness partly through distance, affection partly through coercion—helps explain why fatherhood constitutes such a problematic contrivance in human societies." Given the flaws of the Old Father, and the difficulty we have reconciling ourselves to him, many scholars have concluded that we may be better off without him. They worry less about the absence of a good father than about the presence of a bad one. Blankenhorn is quite convincing in arguing that, while it is true that having a father sometimes fosters anger, having no father at all fosters much greater anger. It leads to "mistrust, violence, nihilism." A violent society results not from the bad example of fathers who abuse their power; it results from fatherlessness.

That many of us have not matured beyond the desire to slay the father is cause for concern, but Blankenhorn is not interested in defending every aspect of the Old Father. What he does seek to accomplish—and what he achieves with devastating effect—is debunking the ideal of the New Father so often offered as a replacement for the Old. The New Father is to be a deeply involved parent and companion, nurturing his children, freely expressing emotion, eager to move beyond gender stereotypes, more interested in being emotionally available than in being a good provider for his family. He is likely to see family and work as conflicting domains. Time spent at work is not time spent in service of his family and its needs; it is time that conflicts with his role in the family. Whereas for the Old Father work was a way of being committed to his family—"proximity through distance"—the New Father sees only competition between the demands of work and family. Precisely such a tension has, of course, led to a good bit of role strain for women in recent decades. "Yet this typically maternal ambivalence and stress about employment are exactly what the New Father model prescribes for men. The New Father's plea is: role strain for me, too."

Blankenhorn is right to note that it is peculiar to find a society downplaying the father's role as "provider" while simultaneously criticizing fathers for failing to support their children. Moreover, he sees the provider role as peculiarly suited to the male.

Paternal attachment to breadwinning is neither arbitrary nor anachronistic. Historically and currently, the breadwinner role matches quite well with core aspects of masculine identity. Especially compared to other paternal activities, breadwinning is objective, rule-oriented, and easily measurable. It is an instrumental, goal-driven activity in which success derives, at least in part, from aggression. Most important, the provider role permits men to serve their families through competition with other men. In this sense, the ideal of paternal breadwinning encultures male aggression by directing it toward a prosocial purpose.

That passage is an instance of Blankenhorn's tendency to read a norm directly off biological and anthropological evidence, and I think more is needed than this to construct a normative argument. But there is more. It flows from Blankenhorn's fundamental commitment to the well-being of children. In attacking distinctive parental roles for husbands and wives, advocates of the New Father may serve the interests of autonomous adults in search of self-fulfillment, but they oppose precisely what children need. Compared to the offspring of other animal species, the human child is dependent on parental care for a comparatively long period of time. During that period, which David Gutmann has termed the "parental emergency," the child's needs, "compel mothers and fathers to specialize in their labor and to adopt gender-based parental roles." That is an argument that takes its start from a certain biological fact but is also based upon a prior normative commitment—the well-being of children as central to human society.

Thus, although Blankenhorn can applaud certain features of the New Father model—its emphasis upon paternal tenderness, for example—he argues that it cannot provide a satisfactory cultural script for fathers. Advocates of the New Father are often also eager to claim that single-parent (usually single mother) families are fine, which means that fathers—as men who fill a distinctive cultural and familial role—are superfluous and unnecessary. Another person, another set of hands, is always helpful. Lacking that extra set of hands can sometimes be harmful. But lacking a father is not in itself harmful.

> At bottom, the New Father idea presupposes the larger thesis that fatherhood is superfluous. In this respect, the New Father is indistinguishable from the Unnecessary Father. In our current cultural discourse, the two are usually understood as opposites; one good, one bad. But in this larger sense, they are interchangeable characters in a single cultural narrative.

These three—the Unnecessary Father, the Old Father, and the New Father—are the central characters in the cultural script for fatherhood currently dominant in our society (or, at least, in its opinion-making wings). There are also five more minor roles into which fathers are placed: Deadbeat Dad, Visiting Father, Sperm Father, Stepfather, and Nearby Guy. These may be minor roles, but Blankenhorn's discussion of them is very perceptive and illuminating. Here I discuss only the first two, leaving the reader some pleasures to discover.

Everyone seems to agree that the Deadbeat Dad is a bad father, a judgment from which Blankenhorn does not dissent. But why is he bad? Blankenhorn's target is the sort of view expressed by Andrew J. Cherlin of The Johns Hopkins University, who told the U.S. House Select Committee on Children, Youth, and Families that "the major problem the children have in a single-parent family is not the lack of a male image, but rather the lack of a male income." The chief problem, in other words, is not that the Deadbeat Dad has abandoned his children; it is that he does not pay. Ironies abound here. The New Father is encouraged to think of himself less as a provider; yet, the Deadbeat Dad is cast in essentially that role. Thus, the Deadbeat Dad also testifies to our belief that fathers—as men playing distinctive roles in families—are superfluous.

One might object, of course, and argue that such criticism is a little unfair. Obviously, one might say, we would prefer that fathers not abandon their children. But common sense suggests that, if they do, it will be better for the children if they pay child support. On Blankenhorn's own principles, that ought to be obvious. It turns out, however, not to be so obvious—and for a reason that is very important to the entire argument of this book. Particularly for the increasingly large number of Deadbeat Dads who were never married to the mothers of their children, our culture sends contradictory signals. We devise social policies that encourage unwed fatherhood, and we become outraged if anyone suggests that a family without a father might be deficient as a family. In short, we send the message that fathers aren't all that important, and then we want to crack down on Deadbeat Dads, insisting that it is very important that they accept responsibility for their children. We cannot articulate a believable moral ideal, for to hold up such an ideal as normative is understood as demeaning those who have failed to achieve it. Toward them we must be understanding, compassionate, and empowering—without ever reflecting on how this undercuts our ability to articulate a moral norm credibly.

This, Blankenhorn suggests, implies a lack of moral seriousness. And he is right. He notes that many of those classified as Deadbeat Dads do not really think of themselves as that, since they have taken seriously what our culture has been telling them about the superfluity of fatherhood. "Their reasoning may be sad, but at least it is consistent. They do not think of themselves as deadbeats precisely because they do not think of themselves as dads. These guys never signed on to do anything. They never agreed to play by any fatherhood code.... By what reasonable principle do they owe anybody anything?"

We should note in passing that this is one place where the powerful cultural criticism of this book suggests more than its author is willing to develop. Throughout, Blankenhorn is careful to focus his attention simply on fatherlessness, which he, perhaps rightly, regards as our most urgent domestic problem. Seeking allies wherever he may find them, he steadfastly avoids being drawn into discussion of related questions. Yet these cultural issues are often of a piece, and Blankenhorn's discussion of Deadbeat Dads cannot be insulated from the issue of abortion, a topic he everywhere avoids. When in *Roe v. Wade* the Supreme Court unearthed a right of privacy broad enough to encompass the right to an abortion, it permitted that right to be limited by only two opposing state interests, if and when they are relevant and compelling: the state's interest in protecting maternal health and life, and the state's interest in protecting potential life. Had the Court added a third possibly compelling state interest for which there is precedent in our jurisprudence—an interest in preserving the family bond—its concept of a right of privacy might have been different. But in *Roe v. Wade* it ratified the idea that bodily acts in themselves do not constitute personal or moral commitments of the self. One becomes a mother only if one explicitly consents to become a mother. Deadbeat Dads think, not altogether unreasonably, that they should benefit from similar logic. This is an issue to which Blankenhorn's argument inevitably drives us, however much he himself may avoid it.

If the Deadbeat Dad is clearly a bad guy in our current discourse, the Visiting Father is not. His is a rather effete role, however—"fatherhood lite" as Blankenhorn so nicely puts it—and it is not surprising that the many men who are cast in that role resent it. The Visiting Father, who maintains some sort of presence in the life of his children after divorce, is finally another example of the Unnecessary Father. He is seen as harmless, perhaps mildly helpful; he "pays child support and does not make trouble." Visiting Fathers try to sustain a certain emotional bond with their children, but, Blankenhorn argues quite persuasively, that bond is not fatherhood. "When it becomes an emotion, detached from daily life and stripped of any empowering context, it is no longer fatherhood. It is an adult sentiment, and it amounts to very little for a child to count on." More strongly still: "Visitation unfathers men. This phenomenon gradually strangles the father-child relationship."

There is much in the book's discussion of the Visiting Father that is worthy of attention; indeed, it may be the single strongest chapter in the book. I focus here only on its astute dissection of our culture's attempt to help the Visiting Father (and the children whom he visits) through the idea of "better divorce." Blankenhorn's analysis of the movie *Mrs. Doubtfire* is itself almost worth the price of the book. The movie's explicitly ideological aim is "to affirm the possibility of better divorce," a possibility whose realization depends on a father who, in order to become a good Visiting Father, must transcend masculinity and become a woman.

Lacking any better idea about how to deal with the prevalence of divorce in our society, we endorse the idea of a better—more amicable, cooperative, and communicative—divorce. Again, it seems at first like an idea that common sense ought to endorse; yet, it proves to be an idea that makes it difficult to sustain a normative understanding of what marriage and family should be. We are exhorted to eliminate the stigma of the broken home, to provide children with positive and empowering images of the unfortunate "family" circumstances in which they find themselves. What we are endorsing, however, is love without structure, feeling without body—as if divorce will be no problem so long as we do it right.

The "better" a divorce looks, Blankenhorn notes, the more it will resemble a marriage. "Living near each other. Cooperating. Communicating. Sharing the joys and responsibilities of parenthood. Making sacrifices and compromises for the sake of family. Reproducing for children what exists in intact families. It all begins to sound like a good-enough marriage, minus the sex." Minus, that is, the body—minus the full meeting of those whose very differences are complementary, but who now run from each other. We deceive ourselves and "indulge in comforting fantasy" if we suppose that we can in this way retain for children the true sense of what it means to belong to a family. Rather, the "solution" of "better divorce" is really "a sign of our unwillingness to confront the problem" that we have become a "divorce culture," unable or unwilling to raise our normative standards—deceived into supposing that we can find even in divorce a good way to seek the well-being of our children.

This book is, I have said, cultural criticism of a very high order. Moreover, in not only the direction but also the directness of its argument, it is a courageous book. But does it go beyond criticism? Does it point us toward any superior "cultural script" for fatherhood? In his concluding two chapters Blankenhorn first depicts an ideal of fatherhood to which we should aspire—what he calls the "good family man"—and then offers twelve proposals as beginning steps toward promoting that ideal.

The Good Family Man wields authority in the home, believes that his fatherhood is necessary and important, seeks to provide for his family. Is this the Old Father redivivus? No, Blankenhorn assures us, for the Good Family Man "knows that his wife also wields authority. He knows that her work in the family, while not identical to his, is equally important and also irreplaceable. He aspires to the ideals of paternal tenderness and companionate marriage. He believes that men who lead are men who serve." I suspect that some Old Fathers might well have affirmed most or all of those tenets, but let us grant that the Good Family Man is different from the Old Father. What are his peculiarly paternal functions? They are to provide, to nurture, and to sponsor.

He seeks to provide for his family, explicitly viewing his work in instrumental terms. Earning a living does not simply take him away from his family. More fundamentally, it unites him with his family as he uses his work to serve the family's welfare. In a world saturated with the idea that work is the sphere of self-fulfillment, it is refreshing to watch Blankenhorn recapture what is in fact an old idea: that work is less a place to realize ourselves than a place to serve the needs of others, among whom are the members of one's family.

Nevertheless, in his understandable polemic against the view that work separates a father from his family, Blankenhorn may underplay the possible conflict between demands of work and family. Even if I understand my work as breadwinning in the service of my family, that work turns out to make its own requirements and have its own demands. It serves the needs of others besides my family and obligates me to those others. I am therefore somewhat reluctant to endorse wholeheartedly the formulation Blankenhorn offers at the outset as a one-sentence distillation of the book: "A good society celebrates the ideal of the man who puts his family first." First? Ahead of his own desire for fulfillment, to be sure, and that is no doubt chiefly what Blankenhorn has in mind. But, first? We need here a little more of the poet's spirit: "I could not love thee, dear, so much, Lov'd I not honour more."

There may, that is, be obligations and callings even more compelling (at certain moments) than that of the Good Family Man. We can, I think, say this without in any way denigrating the immense significance of the ideal Blankenhorn sets forth; for a society of would-be autonomous individuals intent on fulfilling themselves will probably be as deaf to other claims as to those of fatherhood. Even fatherhood itself, as a necessary cultural ideal, may need to be grounded in something that transcends the biological and anthropological "givens" of human development and the social necessities of healthy societies. As a *normative* role that both attracts and compels us, fatherhood may need to mirror something that transcends such givens—a Father whose glory is to serve the child, even if the child would slay him.

In addition to providing, the Good Family Man protects, nurtures, and sponsors. As protector, he seeks to help his children learn how to navigate their way amid the dangers of social life. As nurturer, he spends time, together with his wife, in caring for the children and the household. As sponsor—the "heart of fatherhood"—he seeks to pass on to his children a valued way of life, showing them what sort of persons they are to be and how they are to live. Mothers also provide such sponsorship, of course, but mothers and fathers will do it, Blankenhorn suggests, in ways that are specifically maternal and paternal respectively. A father's sponsorship may be more expectant and demanding, focusing especially on "preparation for the future and on children's success in the larger society." Still more, a father's love will be significantly more conditional than a mother's—dependent on having expectations met. Here again, I question whether this given of the masculine psyche is one with which we must simply make our peace. Should not the norm of fatherhood—instructed once again perhaps by the example of a transcendent Father—be shaped by an *un*conditional love that goes beyond what is given in the natural paternal impulse?

Most readers, I suspect, will be just a little disappointed by the policy proposals of the final chapter. Perhaps that is inevitable, given the scope of the book's critique. Most of the proposals are surely sensible, though I am not much drawn to the request that every man in our society pledge himself to effective fatherhood. Pledges make sense only within ritual contexts surrounded by a shared web of belief, and the largely unanswered question of this book is whether the web in our society has been irreparably torn. Nor am I persuaded that we would be helped much by statements supporting marriage from an interfaith council of religious leaders or by encouragement to clergy from such a council to commit themselves to programs of marital preparation and enrichment. It would be far more effective if clergy simply declined to continue the routine practice of conducting marriage rites—with few or no questions asked—for those who have been previously divorced. But that, of course, may seem less compassionate, and we are once again led to ponder how we can establish practices that are compassionate but do not undercut the norms we seek to uphold.

Much more interesting is Blankenhorn's recommendation that public officials across the nation follow the example of the Hennepin County Board of Commissioners in Minnesota. That Board drafted a vision statement that called upon its citizenry "to move toward a community 'where healthy family structure is nurtured and fewer children are born out of wedlock.'" It should surprise no one that the Commissioners received enormous criticism for their proposal. The moral of the story, in Blankenhorn's words, is that "if you want to say something controversial, say that every child deserves a father and that unwed childbearing is wrong."

David Blankenhorn has said that and more with vigor and grace in this important book. We are all in his debt.

15

A VIEW FROM SOMEWHERE

Michael Walzer, *The Revolution of the Saints*
(Harvard University Press, 1965)

Michael Walzer, *Obligations: Essays on Disobedience,
War, and Citizenship* (Simon & Schuster, 1970)

Michael Walzer, *Just and Unjust Wars: A Moral Argument
with Historical Illustrations* (Basic Books, 1977)

Michael Walzer, *Spheres of Justice: A Defense of Pluralism
and Equality* (Basic Books, 1983)

Michael Walzer, *Exodus and Revolution*
(Basic Books, 1985)

Michael Walzer, *Interpretation and Social Criticism*
(Harvard University Press, 1987)

Michael Walzer, *The Company of Critics: Social Criticism
and Political Commitment* (Basic Books, 1988)

I n a helpful distinction, Michael Oakeshott has written that "philosophy in general knows two styles, the contemplative and the didactic, although there are many writers to whom neither belongs to the complete exclusion of the other. Those who practice the first let us into the secret workings of their minds and are less careful to send us away with a precisely formulated doctrine. Philosophy for them is a conversation, and, whether or not they write it as a dialogue, their style reflects their conception…. [Those who practice the second provide] only a residue, a distillate that is offered to the reader. The defect of such a style is that the reader must either accept or reject; if it inspires to fresh thought, it does so only by opposition."

Oakeshott's first style—if we allow for Walzer's own suggestion that the "conversation" may sometimes have to become an "argument"—seems an apt characterization of the writings of Michael Walzer. They are rich, if sometimes frustrating; thought-provoking, if not always as "precisely formulated" as some might wish; constantly in conversation with the stories of individuals and communities, if sometimes a little too unwilling to distill common meaning from these stories. If Oakeshott is right, it would be silly of us to complain about the defects of a style without appreciating its virtues. In that spirit, my aim here is chiefly to probe the workings of Walzer's mind. If such probing leads to both insight and uncertainty, Oakeshott's contrast suggests that this may be a sign of the success rather than the failure of Walzer's writing.

Many themes intersect in Walzer's work, but I will emphasize the depth of his commitment to particularity: to a pluralistic world of particular communities and, finally, to the individuals who form such communities. This commitment is not without its tensions. For all his emphasis upon communities and shared moral life, his understanding of morality is grounded in something still more particular and arbitrary: the commitments of individuals. Indeed, it may even be that communities become so important in his thinking because they offer the individual a kind of deliverance—an escape from the restricted world of the self and into a larger arena in which to flourish. In any case, we will look first at his case against universal moral claims and his location of moral argument within the life of communities. I will suggest that this case does not fully succeed and that Walzer must be considered a "two-tier" theorist—with some universally shared principles that need considerable enrichment from the particular narratives that form communities. More important, however, I will suggest that Walzer's claims are less epistemological than moral—that his case against universality in morality is essentially a moral one. And finally, in considering the role of religion in his social thought, I will press toward a little more universality than he offers.

WALZER AS NARRATIVE THEORIST

Stories occupy an important place in Walzer's writing. In the two books that are his most ambitious undertakings—*Just and Unjust Wars* and *Spheres of Justice*—the arguments are sprinkled with historical illustrations. These vignettes do far more than provide illustrative material to flesh out the bare bones of a theory. Their presence is important to the kind of theory Walzer himself offers, as he makes clear in *Just and Unjust Wars*.

When we want to argue about warfare, we need not start *de novo*. Instead, Walzer writes, we find near at hand "a more or less systematic moral doctrine." This doesn't mean that we agree about the issues being argued. It means only that we "acknowledge the same problems, talk the same language." The historical illustrations are not, therefore, illustrations of an argument that could, if necessary, get along perfectly well without them. They are the conversation of our culture about war, a conversation and an argument into which Walzer seeks to initiate the reader.

Within the history of this conversation much has been learned, some moves have gradually been ruled out, but the conversation never simply ends. It is important to see this, lest we misunderstand the reasons for beginning here. Indeed, Walzer himself may not always be as clear about this as we might wish. Thus, for example, he writes: "I am not going to expound morality from the ground up. Were I to begin with the foundations, I would probably never get beyond them; in any case, I am by no means sure what the foundations are. The substructure of the ethical world is a matter of deep and apparently unending controversy." But surely this cannot be the reason for beginning with stories that already presume a shared world of moral argument. For *disputes* within this shared world—i.e., the disputes captured in Walzer's historical illustrations—are every bit as unending and frustrating. In fact, it is exactly their frustrating quality that may tempt us to seek what Walzer eschews—a theory comprehending our own and any other moral world, a theory for anyone anywhere.

Indeed, it is hard to know exactly what to make of Walzer's claims in *Just and Unjust Wars* about narrative and a shared moral world. This shared world of conversation can sometimes seem very large indeed—if not so large as to encompass humanity, still rather larger than we might at first have supposed. Thus, for example, in his discussion and rejection of a "realism" that can find no moral limits to the goals sought in war, Walzer writes: "The Athenians shared a moral vocabulary, shared it with the people of Mytilene and Melos; and allowing for cultural differences they share it with us too." Or again, in discussing the Battle of Agincourt, Walzer notes a moral world shared by analysts widely separated in time: Holinshed, Shakespeare, Hume, and "us." It becomes difficult to know who should count as an insider and who as an outsider.

Many of the same ambiguities are present in the more sustained argument of *Interpretation and Social Criticism* (1987), in which Walzer rejects theories of morality that seek a ground or starting point outside a moral world already shared. He turns from such potentially universal moralities (which he terms moralities of discovery or invention) to morality as interpretation of a world within which we stand, a moral world already shared. Why start there? In some moments Walzer seems to suggest that we have no alternative.

> Morality, in other words, is something we have to argue about. The argument implies common possession, but common possession does not imply agreement. There is a body of tradition, a body of moral knowledge, and there is this group of sages arguing. There isn't anything else.

This alone will hardly suffice, however, if only because Walzer himself grants that there *is* something else—a "minimal and universal moral code." Examples include prohibitions of "murder, deception, betrayal, gross cruelty." He grants the existence of such a minimal moral code (a bottom tier in the moral life) but seems to doubt its usefulness. The minimal code is grounded in *nature* rather than *history*. It will serve our needs only to the extent that we can think of ourselves as belonging to no group (or, what comes to pretty much the same thing for him, as belonging simply to humanity). Since Walzer believes it is very difficult indeed to think of ourselves in such a way, he suggests that there can be (almost) no universal moral appeals; for the whole of humanity has only the most minimal shared history and no overarching story of stories.

We may be drawn to his grounding of morality in particular narratives; yet the reasons given by Walzer in *Interpretation and Social Criticism* do not entirely persuade. Sometimes he suggests that appeals to particular shared histories are strategically wiser than more universal appeals to human nature; that is, they are more likely to be persuasive. Yet his own examples from the Hebrew prophets cut the other way: Jonah has more success when making universal appeals to the Ninevites than Amos does when speaking as an Israelite to fellow Israelites. And more generally, intra-family quarrels are notoriously bitter and terrible; the shared story does not seem to make amicable resolution any more likely.

In other places Walzer suggests a second reason. He argues that those who make universal appeals grounded in claims about human nature may be unwilling simply to continue the conversation/argument indefinitely. Instead, like those who step across the line dividing just war from crusade, they may turn to manipulation, compulsion, conversion, and conquest. This is an interesting suggestion, well worth pondering; for Walzer is turning the table on those who argue that people with ethnocentric or parochial viewpoints are unlikely to be able to appreciate or sympathize with the outsider. With considerable insight he notes that this may be untrue. Those who love their own particular history may be most likely to sense the way in which others, in turn, love theirs. By contrast, those who think they see a truth that applies to all human beings past, present, and future are more likely to want to impose that vision through conversation or conquest. Surely there is something to this argument, but perhaps not as much as Walzer supposes. One might surmise that temptations to conquest can arise within either sort of view, although this hunch may be grounded in a belief about what human nature is everywhere like.

Even though Walzer often sounds skeptical about our ability to know much about human nature as such, his description of that "minimal and universal moral code" suggests that we can in fact transcend our historical location to some degree. In a wonderful discussion of John Rawls—even if a discussion that Walzer himself admits to be in part caricature—he imagines a gathering of strangers from different moral cultures meeting in some neutral space. He grants that they could arrive at some minimal principles of cooperation, just as one can design a hotel room suitable for anyone from anywhere to live in for a time. But there is no reason, Walzer argues, for us to suppose that these principles of cooperation, arrived at in the pressure of such a moment, should constitute a "universally valuable arrangement" or "a way of life." Nor is there any reason these strangers should want to bring back to their own culture the principles arrived at there any more than they or we would call a hotel room, however rationally constructed, "home."

The metaphor is a nice one, and I am not inclined to argue with Walzer's claim that almost all people want something more than such a hotel room or minimal principles of cooperation. They do want a home, "a dense moral culture within which they can feel some sense of belonging." They want to be able to locate themselves within a history, a narrative that gives significance to their life. This amounts, though, only to saying that we need to be more than free spirits who transcend every time and place and share a "thin" moral world available to such transcendent spirits. We need also to be bodies with a particular location.

But we are both. The very fact that many who leave a home that provided them with a sense of belonging find it difficult to return suggests they may not want to leave behind everything learned elsewhere. The experience of Camus described by Walzer in *The Company of Critics* is, in fact, only an extreme example of our common problem: to be both "apart and united." That formula points to what must be called a two-tier theory of morality, embracing both the impulse toward universally shared moral understanding and the rich diversity of different ways of life. It is the relation *between* the two tiers that needs more probing than Walzer has thus far given it.

Finally, we should take note that it may not be easy to combine the social emphasis in more recent Walzer writings with his earlier emphasis on consent theory in *Obligations*. If we want to know what are our obligations, we must, he says, look to the commitments we have made. "One does not acquire any real obligations...simply by being born or by submitting to socialization within a particular group." This grounding of obligation in consent gives rise to a tension Walzer never fully escapes. Individuals must be saved from the fate to which consent theory has consigned them, and "belonging" provides the needed salvation. Hence, the importance of public participation in Walzer's thought. The single individual with whom Walzer begins must get beyond that restricted world of self, must become public-spirited rather than self-concerned. Perhaps a philosophy that begins in individual consents must always make a little too much of the narratives these selves tell.

To see this is, however, to begin to discern the real heart of Walzer's critique of universal moralities. The narrative that finally counts is the history of one's consents. This explains why Walzer can make little sense of a "human community" or duties to humanity. For how could we commit ourselves to a group as unorganized as humanity? What would it mean to belong, if belonging is always grounded in our commitment? In *Interpretation and Social Criticism* universal moralities seem to be *epistemologically* deficient. But Walzer's real objection is a *moral* one. Smaller rather than larger groups are to be morally preferred because in them one's consent is less likely to be tacit or presumed and more likely to be explicit. To the moral claim in Walzer's social criticism we now turn.

WALZER AS SOCIAL CRITIC

"There is hardly a word in their letters or tracts to suggest nostalgia or sorrow for England." This sentence, taken from Walzer's first book, a study of the Puritans as revolutionary modernizers, describes the Marian exiles. It also describes, however, what Walzer later terms the disconnected critic. To trace one strand of that early work will indicate the coherence of his thought over time.

The Marian exiles were Protestants, many of them clergymen, who fled England during the reign of the Catholic Queen Mary. Walzer depicts at least some of them as double exiles—first from England and, then, from the less radical of their fellow exiles. Certainly they could speak the language of the England to which they mailed back letters and tracts, but they saw their cause as distinct. In the terms of *Interpretation and Social Criticism*, they thought of themselves as more like Jonah than Amos.

These saints-in-exile no longer thought of themselves as full members of the social order of England. They thought of their prophetic role in Calvinist terms, as a public office to which God had called them. This could, of course, only be the status of an outsider, one no longer "connected" to the old order. "In the old political order, the saint was a stranger. It was appropriate, then, that he be the creation of an intellectual in exile." Along with this new status came a new source of knowledge (grounded in biblical revelation). Walzer notes that Knox appealed to a "special truth." For the saints, "[t]rue knowledge was...identified with religious illumination."

The old world was deeply entrenched in Satan's control. Believing this, these saints-in-exile found themselves having "virtually no social connections or sympathies for it." Ties of personal loyalty or friendship could not be important; what counted was the impersonal loyalty shared by those with similar divine callings. And lacking any real sense of connection with the older England they criticized, they felt little need for "limits" in their criticism of it (or, later, in their war upon it). "In a sense," Walzer writes, "radicalism was the politics of exile, of men who had abandoned 'father and fatherland' to enlist in Calvin's army. This was an army capable of making war ruthlessly, because it had nothing but contempt for the world within which it moved." Thinking of themselves as divine instruments and standing apart from the society they criticized, the saints inaugurated a movement that ended in a (partially successful) conquest and conversion.

Walzer is drawn to the study of these saints because of their public-spiritedness, a quality to which he is deeply committed. But he is also dissatisfied with them as social critics for reasons only fully developed in more recent writings. That Walzer himself sees unifying threads within his thought should be clear from the introductory chapter of *The Company of Critics*, a chapter that explicitly names "the radical divinity students and the dissident divines of the Reformation period" as among the first examples of alienated, unattached social critics. And while it is true that Puritan radicals appealed to a special truth, they still shared a common language and tradition with the old order. Their lack of connection was not, finally, epistemological; it was moral. It was, we might say, a failure to love that which they criticized and sought to change—an inability to be apart *and* united. This is the issue depicted sensitively in the central chapter on Camus in *The Company of Critics*. The difficulty facing Camus was a formidable one: how to direct his social criticism to Europeans who were no longer simply colonizers of Algeria but residents there, people for whom acquiescence to the demands of the Algerian National Liberation Front might well mean destruction.

The problem with universal principles in such circumstances is not that they cannot be understood, nor is it even that they will always fail to prick the consciences of those to whom they are addressed. The problem, rather, is that such principles alone will seem to be all spirit and no body. They will not recognize the absolute centrality of particular ties of love in human life. The critic who can bloodlessly articulate them in such circumstances—who can be apart and not united—has failed morally. "Intimate criticism is a common feature of our private lives; it has its own (implicit) rules. We don't criticize our children, for example, in front of other people, but only when we are alone with them. The social critic has the same impulse, especially when his own people are confronted by hostile forces." Camus was unwilling to violate the implicit rules of intimate criticism, and anyone reading Walzer's chapter must, I think, feel his own sympathy and, indeed, approval. He quotes Camus: "'We could have used moralists less joyfully resigned to their country's misfortunes.'"

Walzer's description of Silone's social criticism seems an apt description of the sort he himself favors:

> The principles of morality are permanent but they are also local. They reflect the needs and hopes of particular people with faces and proper names, occupations, and places of residence, customs and belief. One reaches mankind only through serious engagement with such people—though it seems to me that Silone is in no great hurry to reach mankind.

If my reading of Walzer is correct, a possibility may begin to press itself upon us: For Walzer, the political radical will almost always seem too committed to remaking particular people and communities in the name of some universal—and presumably more rational—ideal. Such criticism fails because it does not embody love for what is given. Is this not, we might wonder, the insight of an essentially conservative thinker?

It is probably fair to say that only in Walzer's more recent writings has the deep influence of Judaism become apparent. The attraction to "interpretation" rather than "discovery" or "invention" as a root metaphor for explaining the nature of morality is very explicitly presented as in continuity with rabbinic thought, and the Hebrew prophets are used to explicate the practice of social criticism. In *Exodus and Revolution* the story of the Exodus provides the narrative from within which revolutionary politics is understood.

But it is Walzer's emphatic defense of particularity that most merits examination here. The impulse toward detachment and a criticism claiming universal applicability is an impulse that Walzer labels Platonic, Stoic, and Christian. Against this Walzer sets the connected criticism of the Hebrew prophets. Other nations might learn from the message of the Hebrew prophets, not by transposing the content of that message to a different social setting, but by reiterating in a way appropriate to their respective societies the kind of criticism the prophets practiced. "Each nation can have its own prophecy, just as it has its own history, its own deliverance, its own quarrel with God." But Walzer has very little interest in any attempt to join these particular stories, to find in them some common narrative thread that might make them a single story. Like Silone, he is in no hurry to reach mankind. And yet one wonders whether he ought to be just a little more interested, if his claim that each nation can have "its own quarrel with God" is to be taken monotheistically, if it is the one God with whom they all quarrel in their particular histories.

In a chapter on Buber in *The Company of Critics*, Walzer discusses the "reiterative" quality of Buber's thought. But then in a footnote Walzer suggests that Buber sometimes goes too far, as, for example, in writing that "'we need...the ability to put ourselves in the place of the other...the stranger, and to make his soul ours.'" This language, Walzer claims, "suggests a good deal more than we need to do (or can do). Morality requires that we recognize, not that we possess, the soul of the stranger." Perhaps "possess" presses Buber's metaphor too far, but surely "recognize" calls for considerably less than Buber had in mind. Walzer will draw back from any suggestion that we should identify our cause with that of a stranger, assuming a shared story. He seems to think, perhaps rightly, that the density of particularity would then be diminished or even endangered.

"The possessive pronoun is a problem." It is indeed, and Walzer is not the first to struggle with it. But perhaps the struggle could make place for a little more common ground if Walzer were to break free of the last vestiges of consent theory that still mark his thought. Or, to put what is the same point in quite a different way, who can say what might happen to Walzer's thought were he to stop bracketing the activity of God as decisively as he does in *Exodus and Revolution* and *Interpretation and Social Criticism*? To say "this is my people" may mean something rather different if it means "the people given me" rather than "the people to whom I have given myself." To say "the people given me" would ground the particular attachment in what always transcends it. Walzer is quite right to reject the notion that, having designed a hotel room useful for certain purposes, we ought to take its design back with us when we return home and use it as a model for transforming that home. But perhaps the movement can be in the other direction—from the old and much beloved home to that same home enlarged and improved in ways that enhance rather than destroy its distinctiveness while, at the same time, making place for others to visit and, perhaps, to stay.

16

THE LIMITS OF TOLERANCE

Michael Walzer, *On Toleration* (Yale University Press, 1997)

I n his very first book, published more than thirty years ago, a study of the "radical politics" of the Puritan revolutionaries, Michael Walzer considered how that radical politics reshaped and, in some respects, dissolved the traditional political world. In particular, by turning the family into something more like a voluntary association, more like a political bond, it lost a certain kind of pluralism that results from divided loyalties. "The child of the patriarchal family, bound within the old kinship system, committed in advance to the family allies and followers, was not so susceptible to political control; a loyal son, he was less likely to become a good citizen."

This concern—how we are to be loyal and involved citizens while recognizing that the political sphere cannot claim us to the whole extent of our being—has been a recurring theme in Walzer's work since then. Thus, he wrote about whether citizens have an obligation, not simply to die for the state, but also to live for it. He considered what it might mean to be a "connected critic"—belonging, yet not fully belonging, to one's community. And such themes

remain prominent in a recent small book, *On Toleration*, published in 1997. Although it begins with a brief typological sketch
of "five regimes of toleration," and although it makes clear that
pluralism has more forms than our own American version, the
book moves toward a consideration of toleration within a democratic politics and the meaning of toleration within our purportedly multicultural society.

Pluralism comes in various forms, and Walzer distinguishes, at
least in the history of the West, five different models of a tolerant
society. In *multinational empires* (e.g., Persia, Rome, the Soviet
Union), different groups exist as semi-autonomous communities,
having their own political, cultural, and religious character, though
governed from afar by imperial power. To "belong" to the empire
need not mean much more than paying taxes and keeping the
peace, but within that overarching peace a number of different
ways of life can be tolerated. "Imperial rule is historically the most
successful way of incorporating difference and facilitating...peace-
ful coexistence. But it isn't, or at least it never has been, a liberal
or democratic way." What imperial authority tolerates is groups—
with their respective group identities—not individuals.

When empires fall, their constituent groups, if they have a ter-
ritorial base, are likely to become sovereign states. And *international society* can be thought of simply as the "very weak regime"
within which quite different sovereign states coexist. Any group of
people with enough territory and strong enough to achieve sovereignty will be tolerated within international society except in the
rarest of circumstances. Multinational empires, when they fade or
collapse, may also give rise to what Walzer terms a *consociation*—
a binational or trinational state. In the consociation, a few
groups—none clearly dominant, none simply a minority—tolerate

one another. "Examples like Belgium, Switzerland, Cyprus, Lebanon, and the stillborn Bosnia suggest both the range of possibility here and the imminence of disaster."

Because the consociation is inherently unstable, a more likely result is the *nation-state*, in which one dominant group essentially shapes the public life while tolerating one or more minorities. "There is less room for difference in nation-states, even liberal nation-states, than in multinational empires or consociations—far less, obviously, than in international society." Less room for difference, that is, in terms of the toleration of groups with distinctive identities. Thus, for example, the nation-state is likely to expect members of its minority groups to learn and use the single dominant language. At the same time, however, the nation-state is itself likely to require its several groups to be more tolerant of individuals than they would if left to themselves. As a result, the nation-state may gradually transform its minority groups into something more like voluntary associations—a transformation that the groups themselves are unlikely to welcome.

In the nation-state, at least as it is characterized within Walzer's typology, the dominant majority is permanent. That makes it different from the *immigrant society*, of which the United States is the preeminent example. Immigrants have arrived in this country in several "waves," but they did not come as organized groups "consciously planning to transplant their native culture to a new place." People join the immigrant society primarily as individuals, and "everyone has to tolerate everyone else." One of the crucial questions for a country such as this one is, therefore, whether groups with distinctive (ethnic, racial, and religious) identities can sustain themselves over time. Can they survive—perhaps even flourish—as purely voluntary associations? Or will a regime that practices "maximal" toleration have the effect of dissolving group differences?

And why should we care? That question moves us beyond Walzer's typology to some of the larger questions that he has in his sights. From his perspective, that of one who is chiefly concerned to think about what will make for a viable democratic politics, we should care because we need to know what conditions create the strongest, most active and involved citizens. Modern democratic politics, in a country such as ours, aimed first and foremost at inclusiveness. No one was to be excluded from an equal share in the common life. But those who were admitted as equal participants were admitted precisely as individuals, not as members of groups. Yet, it may be impossible for the state to have strong individuals unless the character of its citizens has been shaped by membership in strong groups—families, first of all, but also ethnic, racial, and religious groups. If our political culture, emphasizing individual autonomy, acts as a solvent in which group differences gradually disappear, in which all groups become simply voluntary associations in and out of which we can freely move, we may find that we lack the social context necessary to develop responsible citizens. Perhaps free, autonomous, and strong individuals can be shaped only by membership within groups that refuse to regard their members as entirely autonomous. To dissolve such groups might be to lose the soil in which strong individuals grow. That is why we should care.

Walzer sees some reasons for concern. If the project of modern democratic politics—a project Walzer, on the whole, endorses— was inclusiveness, there may also now be a postmodern project about which he is less sanguine. Now people in an immigrant society such as ours have begun to experience "a life without clear boundaries and without secure or singular identities." Eventually, he fears, the result will be "shallow individuals," who may form temporary alliances but who will lack ties that can be characterized by a stronger term such as "loyalties." Moreover, our society is characterized by a variety of "emancipatory processes" that produce "increasingly dissociated individuals." First on his list of such processes—and first, I think, in terms of social importance—are trends that undermine the cohesion of the family as the first group within which we learn what it means to belong and to be loyal: trends such as frequent divorce, rising numbers of children raised by single parents, child abuse and abandonment, an increasing number of people living alone.

Hence, the cultural conflict that most concerns Walzer is not a clash between multiculturalism, on the one hand, and a single dominant American culture, on the other. Instead, it is a clash between what he characterizes as two competing centrifugal forces: the increasingly strong emphasis on group difference, which pulls groups of people away from any dominant center; and the continuing strength of individualism, which pulls persons one by one away from group membership. And in this conflict between the claims of groups and of individuals, "we have no choice except to affirm the value of both sides." For we want to treat all individuals equally, but we want these individuals to be the strong and responsible persons created by group membership. And, hence, we must accept that they will have "multiple partial identities." The loyal son will make a better citizen, one who is more likely to sacrifice his own well-being for the common good, but, at the same time, the loyal son cannot be counted on always to place first the claims of citizenship. The state is only one of the groups to which he belongs. That is the price a nation-state—or, at least, our kind of immigrant society—pays for pluralism.

This makes good sense to me. Moreover, Walzer is clear that no single one among the five regimes of toleration is necessarily superior to the others, and that too seems right. He is also clear that the immigrant society, even while practicing maximal toleration, has the right and duty to sustain itself. Hence, its public schools "ought to provide a sympathetic account of the history and philosophy of our own regime of toleration, which can hardly avoid specifying its particularist (English Protestant) origins. They ought to teach the American civil religion and aim to produce American citizens...."

But why should toleration be quite so important? And, in particular, why should it be so for religious believers among whose "multiple partial identities" there must be one that has even stronger claims on their loyalty than does democratic citizenship? Religious loyalty is, in fact, close to being a test case for any advocate of toleration. If the loyal son was less likely to be a loyal citizen, what of the loyal child of God? How reluctant we often are to reckon with such possibilities became apparent when the now famous *First Things* symposium wondering aloud about "the end of democracy" in this country was published in 1996. Forget for the moment whether the symposiasts were or were not on target about the character of American democracy. Disagreements on that question were not surprising. What was surprising, however, was that many sober people should have seemed amazed to learn that serious religious believers, who were not devotees of anything that could be termed a fringe group, could suppose that the political realm did not claim their highest loyalty. What should be obvious and taken for granted did not, in fact, seem obvious. That may be, in part, for reasons that Walzer's account of toleration clarifies. In a society such as ours, all groups, religious communities included, tend to become understood as voluntary associations. To say that they have claims on our loyalty does not quite get it right. We form them to realize and further our aims, moving in and out of them as they do or do not continue to serve those aims. They cease really to shape us in fundamental ways, it is no longer their truth that claims us, and it is not surprising that they should seem poor contenders for anything like an ultimate loyalty. Under those conditions it is no great trick to be tolerant.

Walzer says too little about such issues for us to be sure about his views, about why, if at all, those who believe themselves to have been grasped by the truth, should think toleration a virtue. In part, of course, as he makes clear, a defense of toleration may simply be an argument from necessity, "a resigned acceptance of difference for the sake of peace." But should it be more than that— what he terms "openness to others" or, even, an "enthusiastic endorsement of difference?" The last description would, as he notes, be a little puzzling, since it is peculiar to talk of tolerating what we endorse. Nevertheless, he does say in his preface: "I write here with a high regard for difference, though not for every instance of it. In social, political, and cultural life, I prefer the many to the one." Noticeably missing from that sentence is "religious life," unless we simply subsume it under culture. If the American civil religion turns out to require a kind of toleration that makes it difficult to press in public for a way of life that is religious, if religious groups are valued chiefly as one more "school" in which citizens learn what it means to argue and deliberate together (and Walzer has some tendencies in that direction), it's not clear that toleration will be important enough to warrant book-length treatment. If nothing lays ultimate claim to our loyalty, we become aesthetes with likes and dislikes, but we no longer encounter others with whom we deeply disagree about the truth of things but whom we must still find reason to tolerate.

To prefer the many to the one, even in social and cultural matters, also remains a little too vague without greater specification. For example, a man might be said to lose his individual identity when he becomes not "Michael" but "just a number" in a large organization that pays no heed to his particular wishes and concerns. He might also be said to lose his individual identity when he becomes not "Michael" but "father." The second loss of individuality is grounded in the community of the family, which also, as Walzer realizes, turns out to enhance and strengthen one's identity. It is not necessarily enough, then, just to support programs that bring people out of their isolation into associations of various sorts, which is what Walzer tends to recommend. These remain voluntary associations, and some important forms of community—the family first of all—cannot be constructed on such a model. It is puzzling, therefore, when Walzer writes that he wants to strengthen family life "not only in its conventional but also in its unconventional versions." We must know what versions he has in mind, and what makes "family" so defined anything more than another lifestyle choice that serves our prior purposes more than it defines and shapes us. Such questions cannot be eliminated from our public life, as if all we wanted or needed was people in groups, learning to be effective democratic citizens. For to eliminate such normative questions would mean, finally, eliminating the need for toleration in any really significant sense—and, hence, the need for so elegant a piece of work as Walzer's own reflections on that subject.

17

BEING MODERN

Charles Taylor, *Sources of the Self: The Making of the Modern Identity*
(Harvard University Press, 1989)

T o describe *Sources of the Self* as a learned book would be
a little like describing Michael Jordan as a skilled basketball player: accurate, but hardly adequate to the phenomenon. And for a reviewer to attempt to capture and explicate
the main lines of Charles Taylor's argument is as difficult as it is to
appreciate the nuances of a Jordan move to the basket. You have
to see it to appreciate it, even as you have to read the 600-page
book about which Taylor says, with no apparent irony or conde-
scension, "All I can do is apologize in advance for the incomplete
nature of this study."

Sources of the Self is in part a work of moral philosophy, and
it might also be said in certain respects to be a work of religious
apologetics; to these aspects I return later. But in the first place this
is a probing piece of intellectual history, tracing what the book's
subtitle calls "the making of the modern identity." Taylor is careful to say that he is not attempting to provide a historical explanation for the rise of this modern self, an account of the causes that
gave rise to it; rather he seeks, by means of a long and complicated
narrative, to elucidate its appeal and its "spiritual power."

In particular, Taylor focuses on what he believes to be three central features of the modern identity: first, its inwardness—its emphasis on and appreciation of the free, rational inner self as a being with inherent dignity, a being disengaged from the natural world around it; second, its affirmation of ordinary life—of the spheres of family and work as the loci of a fulfilled life and the arenas in which our benevolence is to be enacted; and third, its emphasis on the individual feeling and creative imagination of the "expressivist self," for whom personal identity is essentially a work of self-creation.

In Taylor's narrative, Plato stands as the representative of the ancient view of the self, for which being rational meant conforming oneself to an objective order outside the self. And Descartes is the central figure in the modern emphasis on the free inner self, disengaged from nature and able through reason to control the natural world. But "on the way from Plato to Descartes stands Augustine," and the turn inward begins with him. "It is hardly an exaggeration," Taylor writes, "to say that it was Augustine who introduced the inwardness of radical reflexivity and bequeathed it to the Western tradition of thought."

Surely there is truth in such a claim; yet one wonders whether it is sufficient to see Augustine as standing at the beginning of a conveyor belt headed toward the modern expressivist self. He seems in many ways—even when he differs from Plato—much closer to Plato than, say, to Rousseau. And the difference is that Augustine simply could not conceive of personal identity as a work of self-creation, which gives his inwardness its own peculiar character. God is not just the principle of order to be known, but the One who illumines our seeing and empowers our knowing. For that reason the way to God leads inward through the self. But it is always for Augustine the way to the One who is outside the self and other than the self. That is the truth Augustine discovers in his exploration of the longing of the restless heart: such longing should not curve back upon itself but should find its rest in the God who is Absolutely Other.

It seems a much more decisive step in the formation of the modern identity, therefore, when Taylor suggests that in Descartes the turn inward is no longer for the sake of something outside the self. Moreover, the inner self is now thought to be creative in new ways. With ideas gotten from sense experience, the mind constructs scientific knowledge. That is, "ideas" are no longer those substantial, resistant things that Plato thought existed outside the self; they are now within the mind. Something similar happens in morality. As reason should now control and master the mechanism of the natural world, so reason should also control and direct the passions. God remains important, but chiefly as a link in the argument. The existence of God guarantees that, if our minds work correctly, we will gain true knowledge. "The Cartesian proof is no longer a search for an encounter with God within. It is no longer the way to an experience of everything in God. Rather what I now meet is myself...."

Taylor traces this emphasis on inwardness through several permutations in thinkers who follow Descartes. One line, running especially through Locke, accentuates the self's disengagement from any objective, external order. The natural world is controlled when it is objectified and demystified. The real self becomes "extensionless" and can be located only "in this power to fix things as objects." Perhaps paradoxically, then, the turn inward leads to thinking even of human lives as would an external observer. The other line, running especially through Montaigne, emphasizes self-exploration more than self-control. Here there is less tendency toward disengagement or a third-person observer stance. "Thus by the turn of the eighteenth century, something recognizably like the modern self is in process of constitution.... It holds together, sometimes uneasily, two kinds of radical reflexivity and hence inwardness,...forms of self-exploration and forms of self-control."

Hand in hand with increasing inwardness goes a newly developing affirmation of production (work) and reproduction (marriage and family). Taylor locates the genesis of this affirmation chiefly in the Protestant Reformers and, more broadly, in the Judeo-Christian understanding of the world as creation. No longer was there a higher kind of life as there had been for the ancients, a life devoted either to theoretical contemplation or to participation in the public activities of a citizen. Instead, the most ordinary realms of life—what the ancients would have regarded as realms that have "an infrastructural relation" to the good life—can now be sanctified by a God-fearing spirit. In the family and in our labor we enact our benevolence toward others.

Along with this religious emphasis goes an understanding of science not as the leisured activity of a few whose ordinary life is secure but as an activity devoted to serving ordinary life and enhancing it for everyone. As the theoretical matrix for this affirmation of ordinary life gradually fades—as it is seen less as a Calling—the bourgeois ethic's relation to Deism emerges. For a thinker such as Locke, we are to serve our own needs and lead productive bourgeois lives. But by God's providence this also is a way of enacting our benevolence to others. Begin to drop a providentially active God from this picture, and we get a vision of life that makes human happiness central and sees us as beings whose dignity lies chiefly in enacting that benevolence in ordinary life. No thought any longer that some ways of life might be "higher" or more appropriate to our nature. Any such hint, which might call for "asceticism" toward the goods of ordinary life, begins to be rejected. (Taylor does not, I think, give enough attention to the way in which these first two features of the modern identity— inwardness and affirmation of ordinary life—may be in tension with each other. While reading his book, I was also reading *Second Chances*, by Judith Wallerstein and Sandra Blakeslee, a study of the effects of divorce on children. That book's grim findings suggest that the search of many unhappy spouses for personal fulfillment is at war with the needs of children. Inwardness and ordinary life are not easily reconciled.)

At this point in Taylor's narrative we have, then, three possible "moral sources" (as he terms them): one is the traditional theistic view, out of which grew the other two—the emphasis on the free rational self, a being with dignity and fit to master nature; and the emphasis on the natural world as the realm in which our benevolence is enacted. These moral sources are the goods that, when we are drawn and committed to them, empower us to do and be good. But central in the development of the modern identity as Taylor understands it is that the two new moral sources become detached from theism. Human dignity seems free only if we do not submit to God. Wholehearted immersion in natural life seems qualified unless it is freed from the Call of God, which might, after all, ask us to sacrifice some worldly goods. Despite all this, Taylor sees "epistemic gain" in the development of these new moral sources, believing that they have enriched human life with important new possibilities. As I read him, however, he is much less positive about the third element in his picture of the modern identity: namely, the "expressivist self" for whom personal identity is a work of self-creation.

Taylor traces the development of this last feature of modern identity not only through philosophical writings, but also in literature and, especially, the arts. It leads eventually to a kind of "subject-centeredness" that he is willing at one point to term "insidious." Moreover, this third aspect of modern identity carries within it a deep tension that has been present for several centuries. This tension is, essentially, that between the Enlightenment emphasis on disengaged reason exercising control over nature, and the Romantic emphasis on self-expression and creative imagination. Both are present in a thinker like Rousseau—who surely embodies tension if anyone ever did! One way of trying to combine both is to see them as part of a "spiral movement" within history: human disengagement from nature was a necessary prerequisite to development of powers that would make possible reengagement at a new and higher level. Hegel offers such a view at a level of considerable philosophical abstraction; millenarian believers offer another, very different, version of such a view. But, in any case, "a modern who recognizes both these powers is constitutionally in tension."

It is crucial to see that this development moves beyond the notion that we are simply expressing or making manifest something that is within us. To think in that way would still be to countenance the possibility of a given order, discerned within, and then expressed. But there is no longer any such inner order. There is only self-expression, which is now self-creation. We turn inward not because that route offers access to something other than and beyond our personal vision. There isn't anything to which we might get "access" in that sense. There is only the self, actualizing itself. Art comes close to replacing religion. It is no longer mimesis, imitation of nature; instead, the artist becomes the author of (a radically individual) nature. At some point, in fact, this radical turn inward comes to suggest the dissolution of the self. We have not an individual identity, but fragments of experience; not the narrative of a life that is in some sense a whole, but a decentered flow of experience. If that is what Taylor finds insidious, my only quarrel would be that perhaps he needs a still stronger adjective.

This, at any rate, is a rough summary of the story Taylor narrates in lavish detail. But his is also a work of moral philosophy, articulated in the first four chapters of the book. Taylor wants to argue for a certain kind of communitarian vision of the moral life; namely, that human beings cannot live without a moral "framework" that orients them in moral space and that is grounded in or referred to some defining community. Moral questions must be dealt with in "thick" rather than "thin" terms—that is, understood as embedded within frameworks that give them their point. Indeed, the notion of "an agent free from all frameworks rather spells for us a person in the grip of an appalling identity crisis." This philosophical position dovetails nicely with the larger intellectual history Taylor has written. As we have seen, that history tries to demonstrate that for the modern self there is no longer any publicly established moral order to which all can refer; rather, every view "comes indexed to a personal vision."

At the same time, however, Taylor wants to argue, in his opening chapters, that this embeddedness in frameworks is an inescapable element in *human* identity—not just, I think, in *our* identity. He claims to be offering an account of "the limits of the conceivable in human life," an account that shows the embeddedness of our moral claims in frameworks referred to communities.

But, then, what is the particular location in which Taylor the philosopher stands as he provides this account of the limits of the conceivable? He calls his account, in fact, an account of the "transcendental conditions" of human life. It is refreshing in an age when Richard Rorty and his followers have told us that we cannot speak this way to hear a philosopher doing so, but, at the same time, it is hard to know what to make of such talk in the light of Taylor's other claims. An account of the transcendental conditions of human life looks very much like the "deliverances of unsituated reason" which Taylor elsewhere terms an "illusion." It is, of course, a position developed within a community of discourse, and in that (to me, somewhat trivial) sense, it will no doubt always be the case that we can be a self only among other selves. But once one grants, as Taylor does, that this community of other selves may even be a community of the dead, one wonders what the point is. Taylor's account of the transcendental conditions of human life is offered from what he hopes may be a universal, foundational standpoint—or so it seems to me.

Even if the philosophical argument does not entirely persuade, we should not therefore conclude that there is no point to Taylor's insistence that we can be selves only by understanding ourselves in relation to some defining community. It retains a practical edge. The point that is relevant to the larger concerns of this book is that we should not try to draw our purposes, goals, and life-plans simply out of ourselves or seek only those attachments that promise to fulfill us. The true self-creator will be not simply insidious but satanic. That is the stronger adjective Taylor might have tried.

Finally, *Sources of the Self* is also a work of religious apologetics. The features of modern identity described by Taylor took their rise first within a background of religious belief. It may therefore be important to ask whether such features can survive and flourish in ways that are neither destructive nor self-destructive if they are removed from the soil in which they took root. These are questions of the utmost importance, and Taylor is clearly pulled in several directions. A large part of the impulse behind the writing of his book was, he says, the "intuition…that we tend in our culture to stifle the spirit." We forget that morality may require of us considerable sacrifice of our personal fulfillment—and that this may be especially true of a religiously based morality, for which God relativizes all other goods. Our "highest spiritual ideals and aspirations also threaten to lay the most crushing burdens on humankind," and Taylor therefore finds it quite understandable that the modern self might turn from such lofty aspirations to the goods of ordinary life and the satisfactions of creative self-fulfillment. For all his concern, therefore, Taylor is not simply a critic of modern life. He does not call for any simple return to a metaphysic that downplays the goods of worldly life in comparison to theoretical contemplation, religious devotion, or civic participation. In short, critics of modern individualism have, in his view, paid too little heed to those "crushing burdens" that came along with the "hypergoods" of the older order.

Nevertheless, Taylor is not fully persuaded that the moral sources of the modern identity are sufficient to sustain commitment to the notions of benevolence and dignity that have also been a part of that identity. We may, that is, be "living beyond our moral means" in trying to retain such demanding, universal standards of morality without the metaphysical and religious substance that once underlay those standards. Indeed, some of the most wistful pages of this large book—pages that show its author drawn in conflicting directions—are Taylor's pages on Hume. He finds in Hume a thinker for whom no ontological support seems needed as warrant for the significance of our life. The natural ful-fillments that life offers are significant simply on the grounds that they are ours—satisfying to beings like ourselves. Interestingly, Taylor sees Hume drawing such a view in part from classical Epicurean thought, the one school of classical thought that does not fit Taylor's picture of the older order. This suggests, in passing, that the moral stances Taylor is delineating may be permanent pos-sibilities of the human spirit, not quite so tightly built into partic-ular communities of discourse at particular points of historical development. In any case, Hume is attempting to "remove the burden of impossible moral aspirations," to seek in human life not an ideal that calls us to be more than human but a home that is like "a garden, a grateful acceptance of a limited space, with its own irregularities and imperfections, but within which something can flower."

We are here at the center of Taylor's concern, and it is best expressed in religious terms. Is commitment to God finally one of those crushing burdens that, in claiming to make our lives signifi-cant, actually mutilates us? Is the call to holiness, to "a life on God's terms," which has been part of the Judeo-Christian vision, soil in which we ultimately wither or flourish? Does the one who loses his life for the sake of such religious commitment thereby find it?

Taylor makes clear that he is a believer, but he is also certain that such commitment—like any serious moral stance—brings with it pain and cost. There are many worthwhile goods in life, but commitment to the highest among them may exact a considerable price at the level of many of the lesser, but still genuine, goods. To continue on the road that has led to the development of the modern identity may mean, first, the loss of the highest and most ultimate sources of meaning for our lives and, second, the loss of a framework sturdy enough to sustain some of our most cherished commitments, such as universal benevolence. But to turn away from the features of the modern identity would for Taylor amount simply to trying to "invalidate" some genuine goods. In the end, he settles for "a large element of hope." That is, for the hope he finds in the Judeo-Christian tradition's "promise of a divine affirmation of the human, more total than humans can ever attain unaided."

One might wish that Taylor had considered more fully a possibility that emerges only in one rather long footnote—the possibility that a distinction, though not utter separation, of the spheres of politics and ethics might go some way toward addressing the problem that concerns him. In the political realm it may be necessary to permit as many goods as possible to flourish, without seeking to articulate or develop "the good life," one governed by a demanding hypergood. But such political judgment need not be translated into the view that there is no such thing as "the good life," or that we are not ourselves to seek it and seek through a variety of institutional (though nongovernmental) mechanisms to encourage and inculcate that moral and religious vision. Taylor grants that "there is a lot to be said for this," and he writes that "it is quite possible to be strongly in favor of a morality based on a notion of the good but lean to some procedural formula when it comes to the principles of politics."

The fact that he can grant this yet not give such possibility a greater place in his narrative suggests that, with respect to the question of the relation between politics and ethics at least, Taylor is not at all a modern, however much he may believe that the modern identity brings with it some genuine goods. Perhaps the choice he has made is the correct one; yet, a greater distinction between politics and ethics might go well with the hope he affirms in his concluding paragraphs. It would make clear that this hope for a "divine affirmation…more total than humans can ever attain unaided" is truly hope in God, and not in the historical process.

18

JOHN PAUL II MEETS JOHN WESLEY

Michael Novak, *Business as a Calling: Work and the Examined Life*
(The Free Press, 1996)

Only George Gilder rivals Michael Novak in his firm conviction that business is a creative, spiritual undertaking. "The heart of capitalism," Novak writes, "is *caput*: the human mind, human invention, human enterprise." Although the book is subtitled *Work and the Examined Life*, it is not primarily about work in general but about those who found and run businesses.

The book is a small, attractive volume, just the right size for the busy executive to carry on an airplane. If its themes are underdeveloped at certain places, as I think they are, it is nonetheless engagingly and provocatively written. The influence of Pope John Paul II is everywhere apparent—from the dedication to the repeated references to the pope's 1991 encyclical on economic life, *Centesimus Annus*. One wonders, however, whether in retrospect we will judge that *Centesimus Annus*, which was largely positive about Western capitalism, was John Paul's definitive estimation of "advanced" Western societies. In *Evangelium Vitae*, the 1995 encyclical, this same pope discerns (quite accurately) in our society a "culture of death."

To be sure, these several evaluations may not be incompatible. Novak suggests, for example, that people who work in business are more likely to be religious than some of the other "elites" in our society. To the degree that is true, they may be less likely than others to be influenced by the notions of autonomy that underlie a "culture of death." Nevertheless, one would like to see the point argued in a little more detail.

It is, in any case, both fascinating and important that Novak, a Roman Catholic, should have become perhaps the principal advocate of the view that business can be a *calling.* In his classic work *The Protestant Ethic and the Spirit of Capitalism,* Max Weber contrasts the conclusion of Dante's *Divine Comedy*—in which the poet is speechless, lost in contemplation of the vision of God—with the conclusion of Milton's *Paradise Lost,* "the Divine Comedy of Puritanism"—in which Adam and Eve, expelled from the garden, shed a few tears but set out to master the world with Providence as their guide. Weber comments: "One feels at once that this powerful expression of the Puritan's serious attention to this world, his acceptance of his life in the world as a task, could not possibly have come from the pen of a medieval writer." Something new began to happen there, and Novak has both become a carrier of it and learned to express it with Catholic nuance.

There can, at any rate, be little doubt that Novak's vision of business carries what we can only call religious overtones. "Commerce is what people do when they are at peace." I do my work faithfully; you do yours; others do theirs; and many people whom we do not know and may never see are served. Thus Novak reflects upon something as simple as the pipe he is no longer allowed to smoke: the wood of the bowl, the rubber of the stem, the design on the bowl, the metal ring separating stem from bowl, the languages spoken by those who made these separate elements of the pipe, those whose organizational skills brought these elements together into a pipe and marketed it:

> By many invisible paths, with no one knowing or intending all the human relations by which it passed into my hands, and perhaps without any one person in the world having all the knowledge, arts, and skills required in all the steps of its journey to my cabinet, we have nonetheless been brought together in the pleasures my pipe has afforded me. To all these unknown persons I give thanks. In my hands I have held tangible evidence of the world community to which we belong.

Some readers may think the illustration too simple, but I confess that I am not among them. That commerce often makes for peace, that it can bind together quite different people, perhaps even that it is "the most solid, material sign of unmistakable human solidarity"—all that seems on target to me. I have a harder time, I admit, deciding whether I am prepared also to believe what Novak finds in some of the Eastern fathers, especially Chrysostom: that commerce is "the material bond among peoples that exhibits, as if symbolically, the unity of the whole human race—or, as he dared to put it in mystical language, shows forth in a material sign the 'mystical Body of Christ.'" Whatever one says of that, this humble example of the pipe does demonstrate quite aptly that the notion of a "cosmos of callings" need not be a mere abstraction.

There are, however, some complications here that need attention. Charles Williams once wrote a series of Arthurian poems, one of which asks, in effect, whether the development of "coinage" is good or bad. On the one hand, it facilitates greater exchange; on the other, it offers new possibilities for exercising one's autonomy and independence. Commenting on these poems and the ambiguity of money, C. S. Lewis noted that it can encourage a deadly oblivion of the fact that we all live in and on each other, a deadly illusion that the laws of the city permit independence.... The city, by reason of its legitimate complexity, does really need instruments such as coinage that themselves need to be continually redeemed if they are not to become deadly. Civilization is commanded, yet civilization can safely be practiced only by those to whom it is promised that "if they drink any deadly thing it shall not hurt them."

The very same business that testifies to and encourages human solidarity becomes—or can become—a means by which we acquire the wealth that gives us a considerable measure of independence from others.

Novak does recognize such dangers. Even granting, as he gladly does, that the combination of skills needed to manage a large firm is quite rare, he argues that current levels of executive compensation, even if determined by the market, are socially destructive. "For the sake of the moral reputation of business, executive belt-tightening is desperately needed."

One might press some of these worries a little further. There is, for example, big money to be made in advertising. And indeed, having seen beer commercials for years while watching sports on TV, I find it hard to deny that some of the most creative minds around are plying this trade. "The heart of capitalism is *caput*." Indeed, Novak lists "creativity" (not simply the "calculation" that Weber saw as central in capitalism) first among the cardinal virtues of business. The creativity involved in bringing a new business to birth, for example, manifests "the stamp of a distinctive personality all over it. In the pleasure it affords its creator, it rivals, in its way, artistic creativity."

In his own manner, Novak wants to say of the worker what Dorothy Sayers did: "His satisfaction comes, in the god-like manner, from looking upon what he has made and finding it very good." If work were really to become "the full expression of the worker's faculties," Sayers wrote, "we should all find ourselves fighting, as now only artists and the members of certain professions fight, for precious time in which to get on with the job."

Is such creativity in the world of advertising an unmixed blessing? Granting that it may express the stamp of a distinctive personality, does it merit the full expression of our faculties? Granting that advertising may foster exchange and interdependence, do beer commercials or commercials for the latest children's toy truly merit lives of godlike creativity devoted to their service?

These are genuine questions. I do not claim to have answers to them, and I do not want to run afoul of Novak's perceptive critique of those (often academicians) who cannot detect the glories of creativity and solidarity in the cash nexus. But still, they are questions one might ponder. The more we emphasize that the work of business may manifest the *imago dei*, the more we will want to think about what sort of work deserves the investment of minds made in that image.

Moreover, even apart from questions about particular kinds of business, we may sometimes be puzzled about where to place business within the constellation of occupations. Novak regularly refers to it as a "profession." That is understandable, of course; we live in a world in which almost everyone wants to be a "professional." But the traditional professions—theology, law and medicine—were characterized in ways that may or may not apply to managing a business.

For example, professionals did not just have certain acquired skills; they had theoretical knowledge that provided not only know-how, but also understanding. The same may perhaps be true of business executives and managers. Certainly Novak is convincing in suggesting that only a few have the set of abilities needed to manage a large corporation successfully. But to argue this case fully will require coming to grips with the kind of critique offered by Alasdair MacIntyre in *After Virtue*. Basing his claim on a philosophical critique of the very possibility of generalization in the social sciences, MacIntyre argued that the concept of managerial effectiveness is a "contemporary moral fiction." Since the needed theoretical knowledge is lacking, claims to managerial expertise that "purport to be objectively grounded...function in fact as expressions of arbitrary, but disguised, will and preference."

More important still, a professional was one who had something to "profess," who pursued not only goods external to his work (such as wealth or glory) but goods internal to the profession itself. Thus, the clergyman looked up to the sacred and the good of salvation, the lawyer to the law and the good of justice, the physician to human nature and the good of health. To what good—external to the work itself—does the business executive look? Novak does not come at the question in precisely this way, but he does seem to offer some possibilities. Is it the good of human solidarity that commerce makes possible? Is it the good of the creation of wealth? One would like to have greater clarity on this. Thinking through what, if anything, makes business a profession might help us to appreciate better its place in human life.

Among the most interesting features of this book is that Novak seeks to depict the moral responsibilities that are internal to—already inherent in—the practice of business. The woodcarvers of Slovakia, he writes, first study a piece of wood to determine its contours and tendencies before beginning to carve. They must "work with what is natural to it, with the laws and possibilities of its own being." In Novak's view, ethical reflection should do the same when it turns its attentions to business. "Inherent in the practices of any profession are its own laws and possibilities. One ought to study the ideals inherent in those before imposing anything else upon them."

This leads to quite a different approach—and a potentially fruitful approach—to "business ethics." Instead of seeing it as yet another branch of "applied ethics" in which we apply principles drawn from elsewhere to difficult cases, we would seek the norms already inherent in the successful practice of business and distinguish them from other (equally important) norms drawn from outside the world of business itself.

About such an approach one can raise several questions. One line of inquiry has to do with Novak's execution of the project. And here I have to say that, however interesting the project's potential, the execution needs more detail. Some of the internal responsibilities he proposes are important and do seem genuinely to arise from the urgencies of the practice of business itself. For example: "Make a reasonable return on the funds entrusted to the business corporation by its investors." One might try to interpret this as the application of a norm external to business—e.g., fulfill fiduciary responsibilities or keep promises made—but it is not unreasonable to think, as Novak does, that it is inherent in the practice of business itself. But what about the following responsibility, also among Novak's list of internal norms: "To diversify the interests of the republic." I do not doubt that in a democratic regime diverse interests may make tyrannical majorities less likely, and I do not doubt that this is desirable. It is, though, harder to see how such a responsibility grows out of the urgencies of business practice itself rather than out of interests external to the world of business.

Likewise, first among the responsibilities Novak lists as coming from outside business is: "To establish within the firm a sense of community and respect for the dignity of persons, thus shaping within the firm a culture that fosters the three cardinal virtues of business and other virtues." Nevertheless, although a norm of respect for the dignity of persons is known and affirmed outside business, that does not mean that it cannot—or should not—be derived from the requirements of business practice itself. It need not be thought of simply as the application to business of a norm that grows only in other soil, and hence, even if the surrounding society were to cease to respect personal dignity, businesses aiming to suc-ceed might have their own reasons to do so. In short, this very inter-esting and promising attempt to think about ethics as internal to the practice of business needs further development.

A different kind of question arises if we return to the first norm I cited, "Make a responsible return on the funds entrusted to the business corporation by its investors," and ask: What if this norm—internal to the practice of business—should conflict with some other, external norm? Then we face complicated questions about the "social responsibility" of corporations. As far as I can tell, Novak does not offer any method for dealing with such con-flicts. One might, of course, simply deny that such conflict can arise. We could take the Socratic view that the moral life is a seam-less robe and that, since the virtues are one, they will not conflict. I do not think that is Novak's view. He does not, at any rate, say that it is. And if the responsibilities that business itself imposes on us clash on some occasion with responsibilities imposed from outside the world of business, we will face the very old question: Can the good chief executive be a good citizen? Or a good person?

Interestingly, Novak notes favorably the "credo," the company code, of Johnson & Johnson. Quite succinct and simple, it lists five company responsibilities—evidently in an order of priority. First is a responsibility to doctors, nurses, hospitals, and all who use Johnson & Johnson products. Second is a responsibility to those who work in the company's plants and offices. Third is a responsibility to the company's management. Fourth is a responsibility to the communities in which the company lives. And fifth is a responsibility to stockholders. What to make of this order I cannot say for certain. On the face of it there would seem to be possibilities for conflict among such responsibilities.

Novak praises the company's action during the Tylenol tampering incident of 1982, when Johnson & Johnson immediately withdrew all Tylenol capsules from the entire U.S. market—at a cost of $100 million. Perhaps in the long run such action is, in fact, the best way both to be responsible to consumers and the community and to guarantee investors a "reasonable return on the funds entrusted to the business corporation." But it might also be that a responsibility internal to the practice of business has given way to an external responsibility. If so, we would be forced to ask just how crucial these internal responsibilities are to the continued existence of the practice of business.

Finally, there is the matter of charity. Novak's concluding chapter, "Giving It All Away," recounts briefly and appreciatively the story of Andrew Carnegie, who tried in his last years to give away his great wealth. (It happens that, thanks to the wonder of compound interest, he was literally unable to do so, but that is beside the point here—however envious we might be of this predicament.) Carnegie's philanthropy took very controlled and specific forms: it supported libraries, universities, grants for college teachers, pipe organs, schools. What he did not believe in was simple charity to the poor. (And having himself been poor earlier in life, he knew how it looked from the other side.) Novak quotes Carnegie: "Of every one thousand dollars spent in so-called charity today, it is probable that nine hundred and fifty dollars is unwisely spent—so spent, indeed, as to produce the very evils which it hopes to mitigate or cure."

I don't doubt that there is something to this. Nor need we use this as an occasion for considering welfare reform, since government welfare programs, whether they are wise or foolish, are not the same as Christian charity. I simply want to observe, as William F. May has so often perceptively noted, that the philanthropist, for all the good he undeniably does, retains an air of self-sufficiency. That is the one thing he does not give away. Such philanthropy is important in human life, but do we also need something more?

Although not a religious man, Carnegie seems to have been what we might call an "anonymous Wesleyan"—following implicitly John Wesley's famous advice in a sermon on the use of money: Gain all you can; save all you can; give all you can. We need not diminish in the slightest our admiration for Wesley's moral seriousness if we note that a world in which all were like Wesley might not be as desirable as a world in which some were like Wesley and at least a few like St. Francis. Profound, provocative, and engaging as this book is, ready as I personally am to be instructed by it, I am still not sure that Wesley alone should be our patron saint.

19

THE LURE AND DANGER OF FRIENDSHIP

Allan Bloom, *Love and Friendship* (Simon & Schuster, 1993)

Neera Kapur Badhwar (ed.), *Friendship: A Philosophical Reader*
(Cornell University Press, 1993)

The older we get, the more we realize how few original thoughts we ever have. Indeed, all the copyright laws and rules about plagiarism notwithstanding, the notion of intellectual property—of an idea being "mine"—merits a little skepticism. Ideas that, it seemed to me, I alone was thinking turn out to have been "in the air," being thought by quite a few other people for reasons always a little mysterious.

This, at any rate, has been my experience on several occasions, one of them related to friendship, the subject of this chapter. In 1981 I published a small book titled *Friendship: A Study in Theological Ethics*. Very little had been written on the subject of friendship in recent decades, and I thought of myself as pursuing an idiosyncratic interest. It didn't seem to be a topic about which anyone else cared much.

It turned out, though, that I was not nearly as alone in this interest as I had supposed. I may have been riding the crest of one of the first waves to strike the shore, but plenty more were coming. The two books under review bear witness to continued strong interest in the subject of friendship. So strong is this interest that it now worries me. To find my interests—even if not my specific opinions—so much in vogue makes me fear that I may have been misguided. And, in fact, before this essay is completed, I think I shall have jumped ship.

In many respects these two books could not be more dissimilar; indeed, they hardly seem to be about the same subject. The anthology edited by Neera Kapur Badhwar gathers a variety of essays—mostly by philosophers—grouped under three general rubrics: first, the nature of friendship; second, the attempts by different moral theories (Aristotelian, Christian, Kantian, consequentialist) to account for our experience of friendship; and third, friendship as a means for exploring larger social and political issues. Most of the essays have both the virtues and vices characteristic of their genre, the journal article in philosophy. All are worthwhile. Some, in particular, will repay careful study (for example, C. S. Lewis's, "Friendship—the Least Necessary Love"; Nancy Sherman's, "Aristotle on the Shared Life"; Robert Adams, "The Problem of Total Devotion"; Michael Stocker's, "Values and Purposes: The Limits of Teleology and the Ends of Friendship"; Marilyn Friedman's, "Feminism and Modern Friendship"; and John Cooper's, "Political Animals and Civic Friendship"). Badhwar's long introduction is quite helpful in sorting through issues raised by the essays.

Allan Bloom's *Love and Friendship* is less likely to strike the reader as a book about friendship. And for a variety of stylistic reasons, the reader may be uncertain just what it *is* about. Too much of it reads like a long commentary on certain books, especially Rousseau's *Emile* and Plato's *Symposium*. Yet this is a very rich book that requires and deserves a leisured reading. Bloom begins with Rousseau. Having accepted the Hobbesian vision of human beings as naturally isolated, Rousseau must try to forge a way back from isolation into human community. He and the romantic novelists he influenced (Stendhal, Austen, Flaubert, Tolstoy) do this by placing erotic love and marriage at the center of the human quest for "connectedness."

Bloom next turns to five plays of Shakespeare, finding in them "something of a premodern view of man's relations with his fellows"—a view that presumes neither isolation nor connectedness, but simply examines the phenomena. Finally, Bloom discusses at length the speeches in praise of *eros* in Plato's *Symposium*. There he finds an understanding of *eros* and connectedness as natural to humankind and of philosophical friendship as the highest form of love. Thus, if Rousseau, by arranging finally the marriage of Emile and Sophie, had sought to construct a way out of human isolation, a way that exalted romantic love and marriage, if he put "philo-Sophie in the place of philosophy," Bloom wishes "to reopen the quarrel between these two standpoints with respect to what Rousseau and Plato agree to be crucial, love or eros."

Perhaps the most interesting question these books prompt is the obvious one: Why this recent revival of interest in friendship? How can we account for the sudden—and abundant—reappearance of such books? It is true, of course, that people did not cease to have friends or cherish friendship even when the phenomenon of friendship was largely ignored by intellectuals, and in that sense it is misleading to speak of a revival of interest in friendship. Nevertheless, the increased attention to the importance of friendship is noteworthy, not least because it manifests—or so I will argue—our fear of the "universal" and the "given."

Badhwar argues that friendship had to be reconsidered precisely because the standard ethical theories have had difficulty accounting for its importance in moral life. There is surely some truth to this claim. By requiring that we think of ourselves either as agents who must maximize goodness (the consequentialist theory) or as agents who must will the same good as every similarly situated rational agent (Kantian ethics), these standard theories have invited us to treat life as if we were merely observers, not the ones living it. But we are not ideal observers; we are limited creatures with particular loves and loyalties. Because the standard ethical theories ask us to act as if we might be anyone, they seem to make of us no one in particular. Hence the theories are unsuited to beings like ourselves who make and value particular commitments that seem to need no larger justification.

Bloom develops very powerfully a similar theme in his discussion of the speeches of Aristophanes and Socrates—each in praise of Eros—in the *Symposium*. Aristophanes' famous speech offers a mythical explanation of the human longing for wholeness. Human beings in their original condition were split apart by Zeus, and they now go in search of their other half, who may be of the same or the opposite sex. "Aristophanes' tale," Bloom writes in a surprisingly relativist moment, "accounts for the variety of sexual tastes without having to condemn some and approve of others according to some higher standard." And, in fact, Bloom describes Aristophanes' speech as "the truest and most satisfying account of Eros that we find in the *Symposium*." It is truest because it does not destroy our actual experience of friendship by treating it merely as a means to some more universal end. It accepts, that is, the arbitrary particularities of human love and makes no attempts to offer any justification of them in more general or universal terms.

"I think," Bloom writes, that "no healthy person can fail to want Aristophanes' account somehow and in some way to be true.... Nobody really wants to say that there must be some other justification for his connection with his beloved, for that leads to...a certain irresistible movement away from this beloved to some principle that he or she may represent."

And yet Bloom also knows that love as Aristophanes depicts it is not enough. For the loves praised by Aristophanes have no vertical dimension; they point horizontally toward each other but do not call us out toward the transcendent. This does not, Bloom thinks, capture the full truth of *eros*. For, although our particular loves do not stand in need of more universal justification, they do, taken simply as they are, point beyond themselves toward what is universal. "For those who have really plumbed the depth of the erotic experience, there is a haunting awareness that one wants something beyond, something that can poison our embraces."

That "haunting awareness" is the theme of Socrates' speech in praise of love. He says (as he learned from Diotima) that men love not simply their own, their other half, but the wholly other Good. To be sure, they may have particular loves and loyalties, and these may draw them deeply. But in all those particular loves there is hidden also a vertical dimension that draws us out of such particularities toward Goodness itself, in which all true lovers can share. The inner dynamic of *eros*, for those willing to heed it, is toward philosophy, a shared love of wisdom open to all. But this movement toward philosophy may come at great cost to our particular loyalties—as our many attachments are transcended in one shared love.

Bloom offers no solution to this tension, which he regards as the heart of most tragic conflict. He suggests that in order to describe what we need to be whole we would somehow have to combine the arguments of Aristophanes and Socrates, but he himself offers no such resolution. Readers who want to contemplate possible resolutions will be patiently instructed by Robert Adams's essay "The Problem of Total Devotion," in the Badhwar volume. Adams rejects Augustine's teleological (and Platonic) view which sees particular loves as oriented ultimately toward love for God. He turns instead to a more "Protestant" attempt to understand how particular loves such as friendship might grow out of trust in God. He suggests very helpfully that a "continuing relation" to God is "built into the structure of our selfhood and of any relationship between human persons. I do not have to look away from my human partner to see God, and you do not grasp my true selfhood better by abstracting from my relation to God." The horizontal relationship always includes a vertical dimension. What his view may never fully capture, though, is the sense of longing for the One or for God that Bloom so powerfully depicts and that Augustine developed in his *Confessions*. In any case, we ought not—in Bloom's terms—stifle within ourselves the awareness that no finite love can bear the whole weight of the heart's longing. And we ought not—in Adams's terms—abstract the friend from the God-relation. To think of the friend apart from God is to see a mirage.

But ours is an age that lives in fear of the universal. We prefer Aristophanes' celebration of *eros* in its self-justifying particularity to Socrates' sense of being drawn by *eros* to the Good itself. This is at least a part of the explanation for the resurgence of interest in friendship. Friendship is a love especially amenable to our desire for a bond lacking any vertical dimension. C. S. Lewis writes that "every real Friendship is a sort of secession." It is—for better and sometimes for worse—a way of associating chiefly with those who mirror our own character. Friends set themselves against the claims of more universal communities. "The opinion of this little circle...outweighs that of a thousand outsiders.... For we all wish to be judged by our peers, by the men 'after our own heart.'"

Thus, friendship is a love suited to our age. We assert—both politically and epistemologically—the privileged status of our own vision and perspective, our own place and tribe, our own sex and race. We reject whatever would draw us out of ourselves—the generically human, the claims of universal reason, the one God from whom all horizontal bonds are equidistant. Seeking a love that lets us simply be ourselves, we are naturally drawn to friendship.

No doubt it is true in certain respects that the standard ethical theories, by asking us to adopt a universal perspective, risk destroying the particular selves that we are—turning us into everyone and hence no one. But the living God, who has taken humanity into his own life, is not a theory, and all friends must be loved "in God." To do so does not mean justifying our horizontal loves in terms of what is universal. It means, rather, recognizing that our loves already carry within themselves a vertical dimension, and that to think of the friend abstracted from the God-relation is to seek to hang on to a phantasm.

Lacking such a sense of our creatureliness, we are likely always to vacillate between the claims of particular and universal love. This vacillation is evident, for example, in feminist thought, one of the strongest sources for the recrudescence of friendship. The issue is unpacked in Marilyn Friedman's essay in the Badhwar volume. Increased attention to friendship of late has gone hand in hand with a tendency to praise particular communities of belonging. And, of course, "sisterhood" might constitute one such community. From this perspective feminist thinkers could be expected to welcome the rediscovery of friendship as one element in a communitarian emphasis.

Friedman thinks the matter is more complicated, and she wants to praise friendship without becoming "communitarian." She believes that the communitarian emphasis upon "communities of place"—upon the given bonds of life in family and neighborhood—is detrimental to the interests of women and is often oppressive. Rather than emphasizing the importance of communities of place in the constitution of personal identity, women—and men also?—should choose the communities that mean most to them. Freely chosen bonds such as friendship, which have little grounding in the "given," can therefore play a crucial role in resisting the ties imposed by communities of place and in reconstituting individual identity.

Friedman thinks she can manage this without reverting to a Hobbesian notion of the self as isolated from all social relationships. Nevertheless, she surely is extending the politically useful fiction of free, autonomous individuals deep into the private realm. To merge politics and ethics in this manner cannot finally be metaphysically neutral, and to exalt friendship as the highest of the "private" loves, because it has fewer naturally "given" constraints than bonds like marriage or family, may prove destructive of much that is of greatest value in life.

It is not silly to exalt friendship this highly, but it is, I think, mistaken and dangerous. It is not silly, for friendship is—as C. S. Lewis puts it—the least natural and least biological of our loves. "Without Eros none of us would have been begotten and without Affection none of us would have been reared; but we can live and breed without Friendship." Friendship appeals to us because it, more than any other of our loves, expresses that side of us that is spirit, not body. Lewis suggests that the "'nonnatural' quality in Friendship goes far to explain why it was exalted in ancient and medieval times and has come to be made light of in [the modern period].... The deepest and most permanent thought of those ages was ascetic and world-renouncing." It might seem absurd to suggest that such a world-renouncing impulse could, in new guise, account for some of the increased attention to friendship, but I think it may. If the universal seems to constrain our personal vision and freedom, so does the given.

Bloom notes that for Rousseau friendship was secondary to ties of blood or bodily attraction. He made marriage the central form of human connectedness. But, of course, although one may freely decide to marry, the bond itself is sustained by convention, not simply by continued free exercise of the will. And it exists not for its own sake alone but "for the care of the household and the production and education of children." This is a bond that, precisely by committing us to the continuation of life, involves us deeply in the world while at the same time bringing us face to face with our own mortality. We are not free spirits. We must wither that the next generation may flourish, and the marriage vow is, of course, made with one eye on death—until death parts us. In promising fidelity for as long as we live, we seek not to escape the given but to let our earthly commitments take on a vertical dimension and be touched by the eternal. From that perspective, the marriage vow can reasonably be made only if the incarnation, that most world-affirming of beliefs, is true.

Perhaps it is not absurd to see something world-renouncing in our society. We postpone marriage until we have freely formed our character, rather than seeing such formation as a joint venture in time. We have few children and leave the rearing of them largely to others. We even contemplate producing children in ways freed from direct involvement of the body. We regard fidelity to the spouse's mortal flesh as conventional and parochial, and if the one we once chose no longer pleases us, we simply remake our life. New friends, new support group. We are in flight from bodily attachment. The love of friendship, Lewis writes, "ignores not only our physical bodies but that whole embodiment which consists of our family, job, past and connections. At home, besides being Peter or Jane, we also bear a general character; husband or wife, brother or sister, chief, colleague, or subordinate." This is the world we are inclined to renounce in the hope of ourselves creating a better one.

Since the love of friendship so clearly expresses our personal freedom, it is understandable that we are tempted to exalt it above the other loves. But the current interest in friendship expresses in considerable measure our rejection of all that would limit or constrain our own private vision. We flee the universal—the generically human and, ultimately, the one God. We flee the given—the body, with its natural connectedness. We assert our own vision and our own truth, which only a select group of friends can share. We want to be "free to be me," however narrow that self may ultimately be.

We must therefore be wary not so much of friendship as of some ways of regarding friendship. According to Bloom, we are always forced to choose between Rousseau and Plato—between marriage and friendship, one of which must be highest among our loves. In siding with Plato he is (for all his opposition to contemporary culture) giving primacy to the love most at home in our culture.

But the original displacement of friendship by marriage in the West was not the work of Romanticism alone, as Bloom seems to suppose. It was also the result of the slow, gradual development of Christian culture, with its roots in Old Testament faith. And in that culture we find possibilities for an understanding of marriage and family as a bond that does justice to our nature as both free spirit and finite body—a bond that, in its very givenness and in the midst of its constraints, can image God's own faithfulness and permit our lives to be touched by what is eternal. Friendship will—and should—be with us always, a source of great joy. But it is time to recapture and reaffirm the human significance of those loves—of husband and wife; of father, mother, son, and daughter—in which not only the spirit but also the body is centrally involved.

20

STOIC OR CHRISTIAN?

James M. Gustafson, *Ethics from a Theocentric Perspective,*
Volume I: Theology and Ethics (University of Chicago Press, 1981)

James M. Gustafson, *Ethics from a Theocentric Perspective,*
Volume 2: Ethics and Theology (University of Chicago Press, 1984)

I n the last third of the second century A.D. a great Roman
emperor found himself on the northern borders of the empire,
doing battle along the Danube with barbarian invaders who
were beginning to knock insistently at the door to Italy. Much of
the last decade of Marcus Aurelius's life and reign were spent
there; and, while doing battle with the Quadi and Marcomanni,
while administering from afar the affairs of the empire, while suffering private sorrow and ill health, he penned his *Meditations*—
one of the great documents of Stoic thought.[1] Of the Stoics, and of
Marcus Aurelius in particular, H. D. Sedgwick wrote:

> The ancient Stoics were in the same ignorance as seekers
> today who are no longer Christians. They had no authorita-
> tive revelation, no word of God, to teach them the nature of
> the world in which they found themselves, no divine code of
> laws to tell them what to do. They looked about and beheld
> sorrow, disease, old age, maladjustments of all sorts, wars
> between states, civil strife, contention among neighbors,

earthquakes, and tempests. Such was the world then; it is not very different now. In a world of this sort, what shall a man do to persuade himself that it is a world of order and not of chaos, that there is something in it other than vanity, that it has what the human heart, if the human heart had spiritual eyes, would pronounce to be a meaning? The Stoics were honest men and would not go beyond the evidence of the senses, they turned away from Plato's dream that the soul released from the body may behold divine beauty, and created what they called a philosophy, but what we may more properly call a religion, out of the world as their human senses saw it, a religion, austere and cold, but sane, high, and heroic.[2]

This was a religion far too sane and honest to imagine, contrary to the evidence of our senses, that the universe was constructed to achieve our private good. "Accept everything which happens, even if it seem disagreeable, because it leads to this, to the health of the universe" (V, 8). Marcus Aurelius was drawn to the image of the whole and its parts when picturing our place in the universe, "I am a part of the whole which is governed by nature.... Inasmuch as I am a part, I shall be discontented with none of the things which are assigned to me out of the whole; for nothing is injurious to the part, if it is for the advantage of the whole" (X, 6). This maxim was as true of death as of anything else. It too is "one of those things which nature wills" (IX, 3). Therefore, it is not fitting for a human being to long for more than this life, more than reason suggests we can have. "This, then, is consistent with the character of a reflecting man, to be neither careless nor impatient nor contemptuous with respect to death, but to wait for it as one of the operations of nature" (IX, 3). And this truth, that nothing can be injurious to the part which is for the advantage of the whole, was capable of shaping piety. Even in one's prayers one dare not ask too much. Reverence for what nature gives, not persistent petition for what we desire, is most fitting. "Another [prays] thus: How shall I not lose my little son? Thou thus: How shall I not be afraid to lose him?" (IX, 40). "His reason," Sedgwick wrote of Marcus Aurelius, "said that the universe is impersonal, and he turned from the human desire, the human craving, for a Divine Friend, with a renunciation as ready as the welcome with which other men greet the great hopes of life."[3] Small wonder that Matthew Arnold could call this emperor "perhaps the most beautiful figure in history."[4]

We are accustomed to speak of Stoic *resignation*. And yet, at least in certain moments, that term is hardly sufficient to capture the attitude Marcus Aurelius expresses. "Everything harmonizes with me, which is harmonious to thee, O Universe. Nothing for me is too early nor too late, which is in due time for thee. Everything is fruit to me which thy seasons bring. O Nature: from thee are all things, in thee are all things, to thee all things return" (IV, 23). This surely is better described as *consent to being* than as resignation; for it expresses not merely a will to endure but a piety that includes awe, reverence, and gratitude for what is. It is, as Arnold says, a sentiment "which is less than joy and more than resignation."[5]

And yet...to Christian ears this magnificent piety—"sane, high, and heroic"—must seem deficient. Precisely because, as Sedgwick says, it turns from the human craving for a Divine Friend; because, stifling the longing of the restless heart, it settles for an indifferent rather than a loving Father. For this reason the piety of Marcus Aurelius—though it is certainly a marvelous human achievement, and even if it be true—is not Christian. It is more than resignation, but it will not seek joy. Hence Matthew

Arnold, in his famous essay, could speak of "something unat-
tained" by Marcus Aurelius.[6] "We see him," Arnold concludes,
"wise, just, self-governed, tender, thankful, blameless; yet, with all
this, agitated, stretching out his arms for something beyond,—*ten-
dentemque manus ripae ulterioris amore.*"[7]

This has been, no doubt, a rather lengthy introduction. But, as
James Gustafson writes in his preface to the first of the two volumes
here under review, "Theologians are more verbose than analytical
philosophers; their arguments are looser, and their rhetoric freer."
It is a useful introduction, however, because it serves to focus our
attention on the central themes in Gustafson's stoic ethic. This ethic
is developed, as Gustafson indicates at length, from within a kind
of critical attachment to the Reformed tradition in Christian
thought. Calvin, Edwards, and H. Richard Niebuhr are predeces-
sors in that tradition looming large in Gustafson's understanding.
The aspects of the Reformed tradition that Gustafson wishes in particular to appropriate are three: first, the sense of a powerful, sovereign God who stands over against the creation; second, an
emphasis on the centrality of religious affections—dependence,
respect, gratitude, obligation, remorse—within the religious life;
and third, the ethical imperative that we "relate ourselves and all
things in a manner appropriate to their relations to God."

However, Gustafson's attachment to the Reformed tradition
not only appropriates but criticizes, offering criticisms that are
needed, he thinks, if we are to be honest about what science
teaches us. His criticisms are also fundamentally three: first,
Gustafson is unwilling to affirm that the sovereign governance of
God orders events for the sake of human well-being. "It is precisely
at this point that the argument of this book comes to its most critical problem with the Christian theological tradition. Barth says

vividly and categorically: 'God is for man.' I do not say God is against man. But the sense in which God is for man must be spelled out in a carefully qualified way." It must, for example, be made clear that any hope for life after death is unnecessary in Christian theology. Second, the rather strong determinism often present in the Reformed tradition is qualified by an interactional view—a view that sees us as agents always limited by our cultural and natural environments but with a capacity to respond and shape those environments in limited ways. Third, Gustafson prefers impersonal rather than personal images for God, metaphors that suggest that God (like animals!) may have purposes but not intentions. With respect to this point Gustafson writes: "This is to some persons surely an impoverishment of religion; in my assessment it is not." That is, I think, the wrong way to make the point—or, perhaps, the wrong point to make. I, at least, cannot bring myself to find in it exactly an impoverishment of religion. Quite the contrary, I hear in it echoes of Marcus Aurelius, whose piety draws me powerfully because it is so "sane, high, and heroic." The question is not, Is religion impoverished when God is conceived impersonally? The question is rather, Can this be a satisfactory way for *Christian* theology to construe the world, when Christian piety is shaped preeminently by the revelation of God in a person? God's personal being may be more than our own experience of persons can suggest, but should Christian theology conceive of God as less? Can "the powers that bear down on us and sustain us" forgive?

THE THEOCENTRIC TURN

Central to Gustafson's own understanding of his project, however, is the first correction he makes to the tradition within which he seeks to stand. Theology has remained unfortunately "Ptolemaic" in its basic outlook. It has taken as its central concern the welfare of human beings and, thus, used God as a means to further our own human desires. The impulse to correct this tendency is, for Gustafson, twofold. On the one hand, what science teaches us must be taken into account. "The ultimate assurance of the fulfillment of human salvation...cannot be sustained, I believe, in the face of what we know about the probable *finis* of human life and about grave threats to its wellbeing...." The other impulse is religious. God's value should not lie in his usefulness for humanity. A Copernican revolution is needed; we must learn to construe the world from a truly theocentric perspective. But there is some tension between these two impulses. The first impulse—to give the deliverances of science more weight than claims to biblical revelation—does not seem particularly theocentric. Indeed, one might even term it anthropocentric. In any case, it is to the theocentric perspective in its religious dimensions that we must attend.

When, however, we examine more carefully the religious impulse that underlies the theocentric turn, we find that Gustafson's treatment lacks clarity. Consider, for example, his suggestion that *piety* rather than *faith* be understood as the primary religious affection. How does piety, understood primarily as awe and respect, differ from faith as trust? "In my judgment there is a rightly measured confidence in the divine benevolence toward man.... But the benevolence that we know and experience does not warrant the confidence that God's purposes are the fulfillment of my own best interests *as I conceive them*" (italics added). Or again: "Faith as a measured confidence in God is part of piety, but faith in the benevolence of God to fulfill human purposes *as we desire them to be fulfilled in all respects* is not part of piety" (italics added). And once more: "I reject the notion of trust as ultimate confidence that God intends my individual good *as the usually inflated and exaggerated terms portray that good.*"

One way, evidently, to describe the difference between piety and faith is to say that piety refuses to indulge itself in exaggerated hopes (for, we may presume, some form of personal salvation). But what counts as an exaggerated hope? That will depend on the story that nourishes Christian piety, the story on the basis of which theology seeks to construe the world. Nothing in particular makes Gustafson's view more *theocentric* than, say, Calvin's. The difference lies simply in the fact that the *theos* whom Gustafson discerns is not one whose character is definitively seen in Jesus' death and resurrection. Gustafson grants, for example, that "Barth's ethics are as theocentric as any in this century." Wherein, then, are they deficient? Barth's theology gives central place to the "ultimate assurance of…human salvation." He assumes that "the commands of God are primarily in the service of the needs of man." And why does he assume this? "Even the ethics of the neoorthodox theologies…were certain in the end that the Deity, though high and lifted up, was for man. He could not be otherwise for a theology that sought to get its material norms from the biblical materials, and particularly for a theology that centered the knowledge of God in Jesus Christ…." Similarly, Gustafson writes of his critical reclaiming of Calvin's theology: "To be sure, there is a great deal in Calvin's theology that is left out by the process…. Indeed, in the eyes of some I have left out the heart of the matter, the redemptive work of Christ known in the Scriptures."

Thus, we have no reason to regard Gustafson's position as more theocentric than that of Calvin or Barth. The difference is merely that the *theos* central to Gustafson's piety and theology is not Jesus Christ. What looks like *exaggerated* hope to him may, therefore, not be at all exaggerated for one whose piety and theology are more decisively determined by the second article of the creed. If the suggestion that faith, unlike piety, indulges in exaggerated hope will not work, what shall we say of Gustafson's other formulations quoted above? Faith, he implies, anticipates that God will see to my best interests "as I conceive them." Faith anticipates that God will fulfill our purposes "as we desire them to be fulfilled in all respects." Perhaps those sentences are not as carefully crafted as Gustafson would wish, but if any argument ever rested upon a straw man, this one seems to. The Paul who in Romans 8 writes that all things work for good to those who love God scarcely imagines that the good that God brings about will involve no reshaping of our purposes or desires. He is confident that the sufferings of the present will be as nothing compared with the glory God has in store for his children (Rom. 8:18). But he is hardly prepared to stake much on his own "conceptions" of what that glory must be. "For in this hope we were saved. Now hope that is seen is not hope" (Rom. 8:24). Or, if with Gustafson we prefer the synoptic Gospels, we cannot fail to see that resurrection lies on the other side of the cross, that the disciple is not above his master, and that therefore the paradox of the cross applies to every conception and desire that the disciple has: one must lose them before finding what God has in mind.

At an early stage of his argument Gustafson writes: "Certainly the only way in which one can have theocentric ethics which finally sustains and supports the idea that what God wills is what is good for man is to argue that the good for human being coincides with the ultimate divine purpose. Historically, most of Christian ethics has assumed this to be the case." But Gustafson knows better. Christian ethics has not simply "assumed" this. Rather, as he writes of Barth, it "could not be otherwise" for an ethic that affirmed that the Son was the revelation of the Father's purposes toward us.

Anticipating criticisms like those I have offered above, Gustafson often seems to suggest that, like it or not, theologians must come to terms with science, even if that means giving up cherished beliefs. Appeals to revelation cannot be used to rescue beliefs that lack warrant in human experience. Yet, Gustafson usually does little more than assert this; indeed, one of the most disconcerting features of both volumes is their tendency to substitute assertion for argument. We did not need modern science to suggest that humankind might not be the chief focus of God's concern. The psalmist's "anthropocentric" belief that human beings are "little less than God" is set against other possibilities clearly recognized:

> When I look at thy heavens, the work of thy fingers
> the moon and the stars which thou has established;
> what is man that thou art mindful of him,
> and the son of man that thou dost care for him? (Ps. 8:3-4)

The "twilight of the gods" in Norse myth depicts an ending to our world every bit as sober as anything Gustafson has learned from science. Keats wrote of a "fresh perfection" treading on our heels "fated to excel us, as we pass / In glory that old Darkness." And Marcus Aurelius considers with equanimity "the death of the whole race." Nature's book must always be read, experience always interpreted; and it would be a misunderstanding if we were to picture Gustafson valiantly acknowledging the data of our experience against more traditional theologians timidly taking refuge in historical revelation. For that revelation has offered an interpretation of experience, and Gustafson's stance is every bit as much an existential commitment to a story (not "given" in experience but) held to be true. The gradual evolution and growth of our world, the rise to prominence and control of the human being, the slow dying of that universe and its inhabitants—this a powerful story not without its aesthetic attractions, offering a compelling reading of human experience. It may well be true; it happens not to be Christian. That is, it is not the conception of the world nourished in those communities which have made the story of Jesus central in their common life. If Gustafson wished only to offer a theocentric ethic, this would be of little moment. But insofar as he wishes to write within the tradition of Christian theology, these considerations suggest that the burden of proof lies with him—not, as he tends to suggest, with theologians for whom the story of Jesus continues to illumine human experience.

THE ETHICS OF THEOCENTRISM

Gustafson's program is, then, more accurately described as non-Christological than, simply, as theocentric. And when we turn to consider the significance of the theocentric perspective for ethics, we may find cause to wonder whether theocentrism can adequately account for the ethic Gustafson displays. Displacing the human being from the center of God's concern (or, if we like, the center of value) leads, Gustafson suggests, to an increased emphasis on the language of part and whole—and to thinking in terms of ever larger wholes. In a theocentric ethic, "the language of part and whole needs to become more central to our thinking," and this, in turn, will complicate ethics, highlight the ambiguity of all choices, and lead us to give moral priority to the common good. But why should theocentrism lead to an emphasis on larger wholes? Gustafson never really tells us. And sometimes his larger wholes are simply larger human communities. For example, with respect to medical research he writes that there are "risks in restricting research too severely, for other persons and future generations might be deprived of a beneficial therapy." That may be true, but is there anything particularly theocentric about the claim?

One might, for all I can see, argue with equal plausibility that a truly theocentric ethic would focus not on larger wholes but on individual existents—each equidistant from eternity, each particularized and individualized when considered in the God-relation. Unless, of course, what Gustafson means is that individuals somehow really are merged into an undifferentiated whole, thereby losing their individuality. He can write, again in a medical ethics context, that although "the individual patient is a 'whole,' he or she is also interrelated with others in a larger whole, and there can be justification for some risks being taken with the individual for the sake of others." But to be interrelated with others in some larger whole is not simply to be a part of that whole; it need not mean that one is included in that larger community to the full extent of one's being, nor that one can rightly be used as a means only for the good of the whole.

Likewise, at several places in his second volume, Gustafson emphasizes that the physical life of human beings has little value in itself. Its value lies in the fact that it provides "the indispensable condition for the person to realize any proper self-fulfillment and to participate in the human community." Again, we need to know why this follows from a theocentric perspective. One might plausibly assume, especially in an ethic so concerned to make place for biological emphases, that theocentrism would lead to an emphasis on the value of all sentient life. This is not to say that Gustafson's claim is necessarily mistaken. The point is, simply, that it is far from clear why a theocentric turn should issue in this ethical judgment.

These two volumes are permeated with a brooding sense of complexity and uncertainty. This leads quite often to reflection that is cautious, thorough in the considerations to which it pays heed, and soberly judicious. When Gustafson contemplates a moral problem we need not fear that any significant consideration will go unprobed, nor need we doubt that many levels of complexity, tragedy, and anguish will be uncovered. But this sense of complexity is not always beneficial. Sometimes, for example, Gustafson seems to equate persuasiveness with validity. When discussing natural law theories, he writes: "Not all rational persons agree with the basic assumption that the operations of the mind correspond with the moral order of the universe; certainly not all agree with the moral conclusions that are authorized by the adherents to this rational moral theory." This is an argument against natural law theories—that not all are persuaded by them? It is not, of course, but it can be presented as such by one impressed with the complexity of data and the uncertainty of opinions. More serious, though, is the kind of paralyzing effect this disposition can have on our decision-making ability. Indeed, I suspect that many readers of the four chapters in the second volume that discuss particular moral problems will be uncertain how Gustafson's assertions are related to the wealth of descriptive detail he provides.

More important, however, is that this emphasis on complexity serves Gustafson's appropriation of utilitarian "maximalism": an obligation to seek universal wellbeing, an enlargement of the range of probable outcomes that moral reflection must consider. To see this is to understand that, contrary to first appearances, his is *not* at all a modest ethic; for the recurring emphasis on human finitude and limited capacity is embedded in a standpoint that asks the human being to shoulder an almost unlimited moral responsibility, to consider from an almost godlike perspective all the elements involved in moral choice. This anthropocentric inflation of human responsibility needs to be questioned. We might invoke the concluding coda of the second volume and ask that here too we let God be God.

This, in fact, is the real point of the passage from *Paradise Lost* that runs like a refrain through the last chapter of volume two. This passage (from Book IV, 197 ff.) comes at the point in *Paradise Lost* when Satan has journeyed to paradise, leaped its walls, and is sitting on the Tree of Life in the shape of a Cormorant (a symbol of greed). Satan sits on the Tree of Life

> devising Death
> To them who liv'd; nor on the virtue thought
> Of that life-giving Plant, but only us'd
> For prospect, what well us'd had been the pledge
> Of immortality. So little knows
> Any, but God alone, to value right
> The good before him, but perverts the best things
> To worst abuse, or to their meanest use.

Gustafson cites and re-cites "So little knows...," italicizing now one word, now another. But he does not italicize the word *before*. Yet, it is in some ways the key word here. Engaged in a prideful, godlike undertaking, Satan does not see rightly the good *before* him. Genuine discernment is hidden from him—as it can be hidden from us if we fashion a "maximalist" ethic appropriate for gods, not creatures, and if we seek in our moral reflection to bear by ourselves the weight of the world's tragedy.

Gustafson himself suggests at one point that the purpose of ethical reflection is "to reduce, if not resolve, moral ambiguities." This standard is slightly stronger than his later suggestion that the help the ethicist offers others is "to enable them to make informed choices." Judged by the more ambitious standard, his chapters on special moral problems, however informative, seem, strangely, the weakest part of these two volumes. As an example, we may note several features of his discussion of suicide. What makes it such an important moral question? "The seriousness of suicide is basically the same as the seriousness of any other untimely death; the condition sine qua non for a person to experience what is of worth in life and to participate in life is taken away." Can this really be all? Or, in Gustafson's own language learned from Edwards, is there not in the act some failure to consent to being? Gustafson leaves us uncertain, unsure whether in some circumstances despair might enact theocentric piety, just as well as hope. Or again, he writes: "If permitting one's life to be taken for some end is justifiable, that same end would justify taking one's own life. The moral query is about what ends and potential consequences are sufficient to justify the suicide." But this suggests that the enlarging of considerations, which a theocentric perspective forces upon us, extends only to results and, perhaps, motives, but not to aims or intentions.

The sentences I have quoted may make it difficult to distinguish the martyr from the suicide; yet there may be occasions when we will need such a distinction if we seek to reduce, even if not resolve, moral ambiguities. Discussing a problem frequently considered in medical ethics, Gustafson writes: "A special set of cases occurs where patients exercise their legal and moral right to refuse life-sustaining or even life-restoring medical procedures. Their passivity is a factor in their dying; they do, however, intend their deaths." Does such a claim really help to reduce moral ambiguity, ignoring as it does the fact that in at least some of these instances a patient may be choosing and aiming at *living* in a certain manner (free from one or another medical procedure) even while dying? Gustafson also notes that there may be people who have good grounds for despair, whose suicide is, it seems, an appropriate response to what they are enabled (and required?) to do in the patterns and processes of interdependence in which they find themselves. "The powers that bear down upon them are greater than the powers that sustain them. Neither moralists nor God ought to be their judge." Certainly moralists ought not, though, in fear and trembling, they might distinguish between the judgment of a deed, which is within their power, and the judgment of a person, which is not. But on what basis will a truly theocentric ethic say that God—that Almighty whose purposes, as Abraham Lincoln said and Gustafson likes to remind us, are unknown—ought not? God will presumably be God, and it is hard to see how or why a theocentric ethic could say more than that. Can "the powers that bear down on us and sustain us" forgive?

A STOIC SPIRIT

The theocentric turn might ask only that our theology not be sophisticated wish-fulfillment, that we not simply fashion a God who answers felt human needs. This much Gustafson clearly intends, but he means far more than this. More central to his endeavor than the ins and outs of special moral problems is the awful iconoclasm of his God. That God is ever converting and transforming our perspectives, ever smashing the partial loyalties to which we give our hearts. In chapter six of volume one, for me the most finely wrought chapter in either volume, Gustafson discusses the several ways in which sin (the "human fault") has been pictured in Christian thought and, illuminatingly, draws them all together within the metaphor of *contraction*. This is our inevitable tendency; to contract the spirit, to rest in loyalties that are partial. And the sovereign Other that is God must continually judge and shatter those contracted loyalties. But is this all God does? For all Gustafson's emphasis on our place in the universe and on construing the universe theologically, there is little appreciation of what it means to call our world *creation*. All the partial goods we enjoy are *goods*, even if partial. We are not wrong to attach ourselves to them, not wrong to desire more enjoyment of them, not wrong even to say to some moments, "stay a while; you are so lovely."

It is difficult, of course, to experience such enjoyment entirely free from an improper contraction of the human spirit; hence, the smashing of our idols by an iconoclastic God is necessary. But Gustafson—like Marcus Aurelius—has not, and perhaps cannot, picture for us anything of what a proper attachment to partial goods might be. At one point in his criticism of a religious life excessively preoccupied with the self's own good there is a revealing sentence. He writes of "the anthropocentric, indeed egocentric, turn of religion"—an equation of which Nygren would be proud! Our limited, partial loyalties, loves, and commitments are for Gustafson finally egocentric. To wish or to hope—much less to pray fervently—that God should fulfill these loves is too dangerous. It is an unwarranted contraction of the human spirit. And we are led ineluctably to wonder whether all our loves and loyalties should be reconsidered. This is, I think, the reason Gustafson's ethic has a paralyzing effect: everything is considered; but nothing finally matters. That seems, at times, to be the price Gustafson pays for his rejection of an "anthropocentric" ethic.

The tendency of Christian theology and ethics to see God as centrally concerned for the good of the human species is, thus, explained by Gustafson in terms of his metaphor for sin—contraction. We contract our sense of what is desirable to mean our own good rather than the health of the universe. "One may properly ask why some larger, more dramatic, ultimate meaning and perfection is desired. What is so attractive about the assurance given in the New Testament that all things will be made new? From the religious standpoint of this book, part of the explanation is that we do not consent to our finitude properly, that we do not consent to the place of the human species in the universe." Perhaps. But there is another kind of contraction of the human spirit which displays itself in an unwillingness or inability to hope for all things made new. Such hope need not be mere bravado when it has its roots in and is nourished by the Christian story of Jesus' death and resurrection. Gustafson writes: "Theology is the noun. Christian is the modifier." Not so. At least, not so for those who believe what Gustafson also describes as "one of the themes" of his work: "that visions, ways of life, and intellectual activities take place in particular historical and communal contexts." Whatever may be true of other communities, whatever differences there may be among the many Christian communities, they are nurtured by the story of Jesus. And that story is not just—as Gustafson's Christology would have it—that "Jesus incarnates theocentric piety and fidelity." It is also a story, as Barth put it, of a "judge judged in our place" and, as J. R. R. Tolkien put it, of a "eucatastrophe," a story with a happy ending. This story is primary in the shaping of

Christian faith and piety. It is not just a modifier attached to a theocentric perspective already largely in place. That at least is what we must say if we take seriously the location of piety in "particular historical and communal contexts."

SUMMING UP

These two volumes are the fruit of many years' study and reflection. They are also more than that, since many of us could study and reflect for years, yet still lack the learning to write such books. Not only the overall argument, as it emerges slowly and even redundantly, is important. The brief flashes of insight—in which something we know but have not clearly formulated is said—are also here. A few sentences, for example, in which we find summarized the several reasons, motives, and ends of action that have characterized different approaches to theological ethics. The discussion of the four facets of the human fault and its correction—gathered up, then, in the metaphors of contraction and enlargement. The almost liturgical repetition and interplay between "enabling" and "requiring" summed up in the sentence: "Meeting the requirements sustains and nourishes the enabling; the powers of life and caring that enable breathe vitality into the requirements." The acceptance of our rootedness in the created order and a sense of stewardship for it. The insightful commentary on the marriage rite. For all these things we should be grateful.

But it is the turn from a Ptolemaic theology to a theocentric one (as Gustafson understands it) that is really at the heart of these volumes and, one senses, at Gustafson's heart. He cares about this, and so should we. My response, no doubt belabored in these pages, can be summed up in two questions addressed to one of his footnotes:

> On his deathbed my father recited in Swedish the words of I
> John 1:9, "If we confess our sins, he is faithful and just, and
> will forgive our sins and cleanse us from all unrighteousness."
> Without ecclesiastical authorization I was deeply moved to
> respond, also in Swedish, "Father, your sins are forgiven."

In one sense it is unfair to make much of such a footnote, recounting a deeply moving personal experience. Gustafson might have played it safe and left such notes out of the book, though I would not have wanted him to. Rather, we take this simple footnote and these complex books seriously when we address to it two questions. First, is there in the theocentric perspective Gustafson develops sufficient authorization—not ecclesiastical but theological authorization—to warrant his response? Second, what if anything do the words "Father, your sins are forgiven" signify that is not also signified by the sentence with which Marcus Aurelius closed his *Meditations*: "Depart then satisfied, for he also who releases thee is satisfied" (XII, 36)?

21

PSYCHOANALYZING C. S. LEWIS

A. N. Wilson, *C. S. Lewis: A Biography* (W. W. Norton, 1990)

I t was, I believe, Dr. Johnson who told an author that his work was both good and original—but that, alas, what was good was not original and what was original was not good. Something like that is my own evaluation of A. N. Wilson's biography of C. S. Lewis. Wilson does not tell us much that is new about Lewis's life, though he packages what is already known into a lively and readable biography. What is to some degree original is the broadly psychoanalytic narrative thread Wilson uses to unify Lewis's life.

The first biography about Lewis, also titled *C. S. Lewis: A Biography,* was written by Roger Lancelyn Green and Walter Hooper in 1974 (about a decade after Lewis's death). Green had been a close friend of Lewis, and Hooper has edited and overseen the posthumous publication of many of Lewis's essays and letters. But the Green-Hooper biography is not too lively and does not really advance its readers much beyond what Lewis himself had written in his autobiographical works. In 1986 William Griffin published *Clive Staples Lewis: A Dramatic Life.* Griffin deliberately eschews the typical biographer's task: making sense of the unity of a life. Instead, he provides a chronicle of events, for the most part quoting from letters, books and diaries. His over 500-page work is, in a sense, the precise opposite of Wilson's—heavy on information, but with almost no interpretive schema. Certainly the best Lewis biography prior to Wilson's—and quite possibly the best still—is *Jack: C. S. Lewis and His Times* (1988), written by Lewis's pupil and friend George Sayer. Sayer's biography has more detail than Wilson's, disagrees with Wilson's on some points, is not as readable or as witty, and does not attempt to probe Lewis's psyche in the way Wilson does.

Wilson's biography presents an overall interpretation of Lewis's life and also offers critical judgments on Lewis's writings. Some of those judgments are puzzling. For example, of *The Great Divorce*—which has powerful moments but has always seemed to me rather wooden—Wilson says: "[It] shows Lewis at his very best, it is something approaching a masterpiece." *Reflections on the Psalms* is characterized as "notably the scrappiest of all his books"—a judgment I have pondered several times but remain unable to fathom. By far the most peculiar of his critical judgments, however, is the one that is absent. In a book replete with evaluations and magisterial judgments tossed in as throw-away lines, *Till We have Faces*—arguably the most powerful piece of fiction written by Lewis—is mentioned only twice. Wilson offers no extended comment on the book, even though one of the themes in *Faces* is related to his narrative thread: namely, the difficulty of coming to know ourselves as we are and the pain such knowledge involves. Indeed, in one of the best books about Lewis, *Reason and Imagination in C. S. Lewis,* Peter Schakel has offered an interpretation of *Faces* Wilson might have used in partial support of his own thesis. Since he offers at least a few paragraphs, and often a few pages, discussing almost every other Lewis book, the *Faces* omission is genuinely startling. One wonders if this could simply be an oversight; there are some indications that Wilson's biography was hastily written.

Wilson likes best Lewis's literary criticism. "For me," he writes, "the most attractive Lewis is the author of *English Literature in the Sixteenth Century*, a fluent, highly intelligent man talking about books in a manner which is always engaging." Indeed, Wilson's praise of Lewis's literary-critical writings is so lavish one wonders whether Wilson may not have overdone it. But along with his praise, Wilson offers insights about the reasons these books are powerful: Lewis's generosity toward the authors he discusses, the way he finds passages that make them seem interesting; his sense of "wonder and enjoyment" in all he reads; his willingness to take up the great themes that engaged his authors, to put to work in criticism his "creative intelligence." And especially the fact that "the distinction between 'learned' and 'popular' is one which seems in reading Lewis to be quite false. And one feels this even when he is at his most learned." On several occasions Wilson puts his finger on what is surely one of the most striking qualities in all of Lewis's writing: he makes his readers want to read what he has read. Moreover, Wilson sees that—with respect not only to Lewis's literary criticism, but also to all his writing— Lewis's conversion to Christianity "released in him a literary flow which only ceased with death."

Wilson's biography also highlights certain events as crucial in Lewis's personal and literary development, chiefly the death of his mother (when Lewis was nine) and his alienation from his father. Calling the death of Lewis's mother "the catastrophe of his life,"

Wilson writes that "in terms of his emotional life, the quest for his lost mother dominated his relations with women. His companion for over thirty years was a woman not old enough to be his mother, and when she died it was not long before, like a Pavlovian dog trained to lacerate his heart with the same emotional experiences, he married a woman whose circumstances were exactly parallel to those of his own mother in 1908—a woman dying of cancer who had two small sons."

According to Wilson, Lewis and his older brother Warren were driven by a lifelong desire to return to the days of their youth when as young playmates, before the death of their mother, they could give themselves over to the imaginative life of reading and writing that they dearly loved. In the Narnia stories, Wilson thinks, Lewis yielded to this emotional need. Yet Wilson is guilty of some over-interpretation here, as, for example, when he writes: "We hardly need to dwell on the psychological significance of the wardrobe in the first story; we do not need, though some will be tempted to do so, to see in this tale of a world which is reached by a dark hole surrounded by fur coats an unconscious image of the passage through which Lewis first entered the world from his mother's body." Still, the death of his mother must have meant emotional upheaval that may well have marked his entire life. And Wilson quite effectively suggests the way in which the last of the Narnia stories—with its reunion of parents and children in Aslan's world—shows Lewis coming to terms with his past. (Wilson might with equal effectiveness have noted the story of Digory and his mother in *The Magician's Nephew*.) In his children's stories—though also in *Till We Have Faces* and *The Four Loves*—Lewis does come to terms with the pain of emotional attachment and loss.

Moreover, whatever we make of Wilson's discussion of the well-known facts, Lewis's relations with the two women who (after his mother) played important roles in his personal life were, by ordinary standards, quite unusual. In his autobiography, *Surprised by Joy*, Lewis writes that he is omitting one "huge and complex episode." "All I can or need say is that my earlier hostility to the emotions was very fully and variously avenged." This is, it seems, Lewis's reference to his relationship with Janie Moore, the 45-year-old mother of Paddy Moore, the cadet with whom Lewis shared a room when he took his military training in World War I. She befriended Lewis in the weeks before he was sent to France, at a time when his alienation from his father, who did not come to see him before his departure for the front lines, was very great. More important still, she came to London to be near Lewis while he was recovering from wounds (and while she was waiting for news of her own son, who died in the war). "The experience of being mothered, for the first time in his life since he was nine years old, was having a profound effect on Jack," writes Wilson.

Moore was married, though separated from her husband—and would remain in that state throughout the years she lived with Lewis. An interesting, albeit unanswerable, question has been the precise nature of their relationship. In later years, when they shared a home, they referred to each other as adopted mother and son. Sayer doubts that they were lovers. Hooper concurs and even holds—contrary, I think, to the best evidence—that Lewis's later marriage was never consummated. Wilson is quite confident that Lewis and Moore were lovers and suggests that "the burden of proof is on those who believe that Lewis and Mrs. Moore were *not* lovers—probably from the summer of 1918 onwards." Less persuasive, to me at least, is the claim that this probably continued until 1931, the year in which Lewis converted to Christianity (and would now think a relation with a married woman to be wrong). Wilson's way of making this point is, however, an instance of a very undesirable trait in his writing: the tendency to assert indirectly and to be glib while seeming to eschew it: "It would be far too glib to suggest that he consciously made the second change, to adopt Christianity, merely to give himself an excuse to abandon sexual relations with Mrs. Moore, whatever the nature of those relations had been."

Late in his life, a few years after Moore's death, Lewis married Joy Davidman Gresham, an American who, while still married, went to England with the intention of meeting Lewis. She returned again to England with her two sons and eventually divorced her husband. Lewis married her first in a purely civil ceremony in 1956—an act of kindness, he said, since the British Home Office was refusing her a permit to remain there. In the fall of 1956, Joy learned that she had cancer and only a short time to live. With some difficulty Lewis found an Anglican priest who would solemnize an ecclesiastical marriage between himself and a divorced woman. Shortly thereafter, Gresham's cancer went into remission and she and Lewis enjoyed three deeply satisfying years of marriage until the cancer returned and took her life.

The bare bones of such a story do not capture the searing intensity that Lewis recorded in *A Grief Observed*, the short diary-like jottings that he wrote and published after Gresham's death. Wilson's prose captures both the strangeness and the poignancy of the marriage, but there are aspects of his discussion about which a reader should be warned. Wilson suggests that Lewis and Gresham engaged in sexual relations prior to marriage (whether civil or ecclesiastical) and before she was divorced from her first husband.

This is evidently part of Wilson's effort to recapture Lewis from those who would turn him into a "plaster saint." "According to an oral memory of Joy's son Douglas [who would have been eight years old at the time], transcribed in the Marion E. Wade Collection at Wheaton College, Illinois, the two of them were already lovers in 1955. Douglas on one occasion came into his mother's bedroom at 10 High Street and found it occupied by Jack and Joy in a compromising position." Readers should be aware that Lyle Dorsett, curator of the Wade Collection and the person who videotaped the approximately seven-and-a-half-hour oral history interview with Douglas, has said that the comment to which Wilson is evidently alluding here actually refers to a time after their (ecclesiastical) marriage, when Gresham had come to live in Lewis's home. Dorsett has also noted that Wilson made only one visit of less than three hours to the Wade Collection.

Wilson emphasizes the importance of both women for understanding Lewis; unfortunately he is facile in discussing these two relationships. When he describes Lewis as having had "two liaisons with married women," the reader will certainly presume that "liaison" means "illicit sexual relationship." Yet the only evidence Wilson even offers in the case of Gresham is his disputed claim about her son's interview. In the case of Moore, where the circumstantial evidence is much stronger and to me relatively persuasive that the relationship was sexually illicit, Wilson himself writes: "Nobody would ever quite know, truly know, what he had shared with [Moore] in those early days." And in another context, asserting that it would be surprising if the relationship had been asexual, he also writes that "no evidence is forthcoming either way."

The story of Lewis's relationships with these two women is one very important element in Wilson's interpretation of his life:

having lost his mother as a young boy, Lewis spent his life searching for a substitute. The second time around, after Moore's death,
Lewis found himself at a point where he could finally unwind and
open up emotionally. He "found a woman with whom he felt able
to be completely open about himself"—and this not long after the
Narnia stories, in which Lewis finally made his peace with the loss
of his mother and his alienation from his father. But there is
another thread in Wilson's interpretation—namely, the debate with
Elizabeth Anscombe in 1948 at the Socratic Club in Oxford. Lewis
was the president of that society from its founding in 1941 until he
went to Cambridge in 1954. (It is worth noting that he continued
to participate after the Anscombe debate.) In this context, Lewis
was known as a sturdy and polemical defender of the faith. The
dispute with Anscombe centered on Lewis's argument against naturalism in *Miracles*. I doubt that most readers of Wilson's pages
are likely to get a very clear idea of what the dispute was. Indeed,
they are likely to conclude that we hardly need a philosopher of
Anscombe's status to disprove Lewis, for Wilson writes that "any
dispassionate reader can at once see many flaws in Lewis's arguments here." Lewis had argued that the deliverances of reason
could not be trusted if they were ultimately produced by something
less than rational. Anscombe had responded that, however our
rational nature came into existence, reasoned argument might be
valid even if our reason was the product of nonrational causes.

The debate was a sharp one and many, including Lewis, felt
that Anscombe had the better of it. This confrontation, writes
Wilson, "had a profound effect on his career as a writer. It was the
greatest single factor which drove him into the form of literature
for which he is today most popular: children's stories." This may
be difficult to reconcile with Wilson's statement that Lewis had

already begun trying to write the first of the Narnia stories in 1939, but, in any case, Wilson regards its psychological impact as crucial. The encounter "awakened all sorts of deeply seated fears in Lewis, not least his fear of women.... [H]e became a child, a little boy who was being degraded and shaken by a figure who, in his imagination, took on witch-like dimensions." As a result, Wilson concludes, "Lewis never attempted to write another work of Christian apologetics after *Miracles*." He came to feel that the "method and manner" of his apologetic works were "spurious," and he turned to "make-believe" as "another way of talking about the reality of things."

It is, to begin with, not fully accurate to say that Lewis wrote no more Christian apologetics after *Miracles*. *The Four Loves*—with its argument that the natural loves cannot flourish if isolated from supernatural love—is, among other things, an apologetic work. Looked at from a different perspective, *Miracles* is by no means simply a piece of apologetics. The second half of the book is as deeply infused with Lewis's imaginative power as almost anything he ever wrote. And Wilson's theory will have considerable difficulty explaining the fact that when, as late as 1960, Fontana Books published a new edition of *Miracles*, it included a revised version of the crucial third chapter to which Anscombe had objected. Lewis does not seem to have given up on the argument. We do not, in fact, need Wilson's theory about the effects of the Anscombe debate in order to explain the shifts in Lewis's writing. The kind of philosophy that was coming to prominence—logical positivism and then ordinary language analysis—was bound to seem less engaging to one with Lewis's longstanding metaphysical interests.

Thus, what is original in Wilson's biography—the exploration of Lewis's psyche in search of a unified understanding of the man and the location of that center in his relationships with women—can't carry the interpretive load Wilson places upon it. The threads form an informative and witty narrative, but the facts do not fully persuade.

In 1955 Lewis published *Surprised by Joy*, omitting, as mentioned above, any discussion of his relationship with Moore. Even were he free to speak of it, he wrote, he doubts that "it has much to do with the subject of this book." Likewise he passes over his father's death with the comment that it "does not really come into the story I am telling." At several points Wilson flags these omissions as indications of Lewis's repressed emotional life. Wilson describes the claim that his father's death does not come into the story as a "preposterous assertion," and Wilson may be right. Yet Wilson's own story line cannot account for Lewis's reticence in 1955. Wilson claims that the great emotional reawakening had already occurred after Moore's death when the Narnia stories were written. "The children's books...were a sort of sluicing of the system which...represented a conversion every bit as deep as the conversion to a belief in the supernatural and the divinity of Jesus Christ which occurred in 1929–1931." These years (when the Narnia stories were written) are years in which, according to Wilson, "the self-disclosure in what he wrote became still more marked and more relaxed." Yet they are also the years in which Lewis wrote *Surprised by Joy*—over which Wilson pauses on several occasions to emphasize its reticence about the self. The longer one ponders Wilson's narrative the more difficult it becomes to grasp its logic.

Two other features of this biography deserve some mention, since they are, for me at least, troubling. One is a matter of tone. I have already said several times that Wilson's writing is lively, readable, witty and enjoyable. It is also snide and condescending. Very few people are mentioned without that tone of voice creeping through. Hooper is "one of nature's devotees." Green is "a rich man who had cultivated Lewis ever since he had heard his lectures before the war." J. B. Phillips thought that Lewis's spirit had twice appeared to him after Lewis's death. "It would be churlish to point out that in a subsequent volume of autobiography Canon Phillips explained to his readers the nature of these 'difficult circumstances' through which he was passing: depressions and nervous breakdowns so severe as to constitute periodic bouts of lunacy; churlish because irrelevant. However we explain the experience, it was an experience." Now this is all rather funny, and I admit to smiling. But I ought not. Letter XI of *The Screwtape Letters*, in which Screwtape distinguishes between the "Joke Proper" and "Flippancy," is relevant here: "Among flippant people the Joke is always assumed to have been made. No one actually makes it; but every serious subject is discussed in a manner which implies that they have already found a ridiculous side to it.... It is a thousand miles away from joy: it deadens, instead of sharpening the intellect; and it excites no affection between those who practice it."

Similarly, Wilson very quickly dismisses the questions raised recently by Kathryn Lindskoog in *The C. S. Lewis Hoax*, asserting incorrectly that her central thesis "has been disproved." In brief, Lindskoog argues that Hooper systematically misrepresented his relationship with Lewis, making it appear much closer than it could possibly have been, and she claims that "The Dark Tower" (a posthumously published fragment of a story) is a forgery not actually written by Lewis. There are other elements in Lindskoog's web of arguments, some more persuasive than others, some eccentric. But there is nothing there to warrant Wilson's description of it as "one of the most vitriolic personal attacks on a fellow-scholar...that I have ever read in print"—especially not for a man as widely read as Wilson. Moreover, he clearly accepts several of Lindskoog's claims: that Hooper could only have known Lewis for a few weeks before Lewis's death and that he has changed his handwriting over the years so that it closely resembles Lewis's own.

More disturbing than Wilson's tone is his attitude toward religion, revealed chiefly in asides that seem to need no argument. Wilson observes that it is not the "rational Lewis" that has continuing appeal; rather, "it is the Lewis who plumbed the irrational depths of childhood and religion who speaks to the present generation." But why should religion (or, for that matter, childhood) be irrational at its depths? Wilson's assumption, so glibly stated, almost steals by us. Again: over their Christmas vacation in 1910, the Lewis brothers went to see *Peter Pan.* According to Warren Lewis, it was a momentous experience for them, and Wilson therefore finds it surprising that the experience is not mentioned in *Surprised by Joy.* He terms it "one of the Grand Conspicuous Omissions" in that book. "For there was no children's story more apposite to his life than that of the little boy who *could* not grow up, and who had to win his immortality by an assertion of metaphysical improbabilities." Speaking of what he regards as "unedifying" disputes among the several camps of Lewis scholarship, Wilson writes that it shows us "in microcosm something which is perhaps symptomatic of the religious temperament as a whole, the need to erect images and worship them." As a theory of religion, this statement can use a little work, and one wonders why it is only the religious temperament that displays this touching need.

Near the end of his book Wilson mentions the eight-foot-high stained-glass window of Lewis in an Episcopal Church in

California. It might, he notes, seem to be the "ultimate idolatry"; yet, he says, the matter is more complex. "Many perfectly sane religious believers have received insight and help from Lewis's writings, and it seems a natural progression from here to commemorate him in a window.... If people have found it so, it is so." Now my own taste in stained-glass windows runs more to triangles, circles, and lambs carrying banners. Nonetheless, like Wilson, I can think of some good reasons for a Lewis window. But the way Wilson rests the matter—"If people have found it so, it is so"—again fails to take the issue seriously. Wilson's manner does not take us much further than the words of the song in *The Music Man*: "How can there be any sin in sincere?" No sin, Wilson seems to be saying with a wink—but plenty of occasion for gently mocking laughter. Screwtape would, I fear, have approved.

22

C. S. LEWIS RECONSIDERED

John Beversluis, C. S. *Lewis and the Search for Rational Religion*
(Eerdmans, 1985)

I n the rite of baptism the sign of the cross is placed "upon the forehead and the breast" of the baptized one. That is to say, both the mind and heart are claimed by and offered to the God who has revealed himself as the Crucified One. But the task of offering mind and heart to God—and offering them in concert—is lifelong. Perhaps some day reason and imagination, intellect and passion, will be reconciled, but even in the experience of believers the cleavage between them is often deep and some conflict inevitable.

Few Christian writers in this century have managed to speak as effectively to both mind and heart as did C. S. Lewis. Some readers have been attracted by the persuasive force of the reasoned argument he provides; other have been drawn in through his metaphors, analogies, and stories, and have had their imaginations baptized by his writings, even as he said his had been by the books of George MacDonald. In C. S. *Lewis and the Search for Rational Religion*, John Beversluis examines Lewis's arguments on behalf of religious belief and finds them sorely wanting. On Beversluis's

reading, Lewis displayed toward the end of his life a "divided mentality, a mentality at odds with itself"—no longer able to find persuasive arguments for what he still desperately wanted to believe.
It must be said at the outset that Beversluis's book is not very good.
Still, Beversluis does focus on some of Lewis's central arguments,
and we can use his book to reconsider Lewis's case for Christianity.
First, though, at least a few of the book's defects call for notice.

AN INDICTMENT INDICTED

One of the problems with Beversluis's work is that he pays little
attention to Lewis's imaginative writings and, in particular, to *Till
We Have Faces*—this despite the fact that he has surely read them
and must know them well. Beversluis says that he will focus on
Lewis's apologetic writings. But with Lewis the imaginative works
are part of the apology, and to ignore them is to skew one's reading considerably. The author who, in recounting his own conversion, focused on the baptism of his imagination through reading a
fantasy; who claimed (only partly with tongue in cheek) that
anyone who did not wish to become a believer had better be careful what authors he read; who at the conclusion of one of his own
fantasies suggested that what moderns need is not new beliefs but
new images; who forthrightly stated that in writing his children's
stories he was trying to steal past the "watchful dragons" that keep
us from believing—such an author's "apology" for Christianity
cannot be found only in books with titles like *Miracles* or *The
Problem of Pain*.

Lewis once wrote that while reason is the organ of truth, imagination is the organ of meaning. And since Beversluis is interested
not only in the truth, but also in the meaningfulness of religion (he
treats us to a short discussion of the verification/falsification

debate in twentieth-century philosophy), he cannot capture the full force of Lewis's views apart from the imaginative writings.

Beversluis writes, he tells us, to rescue Lewis from the "excessive hostility" of his fierce critics as well as from the "excessive loyalty" of his uncritical admirers. Not that Lewis's admirers are entirely to be blamed, according to Beversluis. Lewis's crisp, no-nonsense prose has perhaps seduced them, and they lack the training and sophistication needed to see through Lewis's glibness. "The people to whom he primarily addresses himself are not trained in philosophy; they are on the whole simply not in a position to recognize his distortions, omissions, and oversimplifications." This despite the evidence that can be found in Beversluis's own citations to show that most of the arguments Lewis put forward in his books aimed at "popular" audiences were also in essays delivered at places like the Socratic Club in Oxford, where the famous exchange between Lewis and the philosopher G. E. M. Anscombe about Lewis's refutation of naturalism took place.

Beversluis tells us that Lewis often wrote irresponsibly, not taking the pains necessary to understand the views he was rejecting. This is a strange criticism from an author who himself has a disconcerting tendency to tell his readers in no uncertain terms what a biblical or orthodox view is. He tells us—concerning Lewis's "lord-or-lunatic" dilemma—that the Jews of Jesus' day may have regarded Jesus as a blasphemer but certainly not a madman. Perhaps he should consider Mark 3:21. For Beversluis, the view that God is the One whom all truly desire has "not a shred of evidence in the Bible" to support it. Perhaps he should become acquainted with the Gospel of John. Beversluis writes, citing I Corinthians 1:21ff., that Christianity and Hellenistic philosophy are irreconcilably opposed; yet, we might wonder whether the *Logos* of John's Gospel can be entirely alien to "his own" creation to which he came.

An author who holds that "in the Bible" human beings and God do not share "a common moral world," and that to be a Christian one must simply "bow the head and bend the knee" but never raise a question, needs to be asked once again what St. John means in saying that the *Logos* came to "his own," what the significance of the incarnation is. Beversluis is in no position to damn Lewis for oversimplifying; one senses in his theological excursions the remains of some Calvinistic Sunday School lessons imperfectly nuanced. These remains could lead to a rejection of God—or as easily to some form of "revelational positivism."

Beversluis tells the reader that among Lewis's most serious weaknesses as an apologist was "his fondness for the false dilemma." Yet his own book fairly bristles with one dilemma after another that supposedly confronts Lewis. He is surprised that Lewis should describe God both as the One for whom our hearts long *and* as One from whom we shrink. In thus describing our relation to God, Lewis may or may not be correct, but he is simply reworking a common Christian understanding of what it means to be both a creature made by and for God *and* a fallen creature living a lie by seeking to be independent of God. To need and long for God, while in pride denying our neediness, is a relatively common description of the state of the sinful creature, at least in the Augustinian strand of Christian thought. On this view, our sinfulness is displayed precisely in the fact that we are thus torn and divided and cannot love God with a whole heart. To be sure, there are difficult issues here, and much of the literature about the relation of *agape* and *eros* probes these issues both historically and philosophically. But Beversluis, in the grip of an understanding of sin that imagines that depravity could not possibly leave any place for desire for God, can find here only a dilemma: "Either God is the ultimate Object of desire or he is not. If he is, then it makes no sense to talk about shrinking from him the moment he is found. If he is not, then we will not find our heart's desire by following Joy any more than mice will find theirs by pursuing the cat." A writer who thinks this theologically sophisticated must simply be left to his own devices.

A THREEFOLD CASE

Still, though, a bad book may treat important issues, and Beversluis's does. He focuses on three sorts of arguments Lewis offers for belief in God. Two of them—arguments from the nature of reason and the nature of morality—are quite similar; a third—an argument based on what Lewis called longing for joy—is rather different. Each is worth thinking through as Beversluis has tried to do.

Lewis attempts—in *Mere Christianity* and several of his essays—to argue from the nature of our moral experience to the existence of a divine being, what in *Mere Christianity* he calls "a Something which is directing the universe, and which appears in me as a law urging me to do right and making me feel responsible and uncomfortable when I do wrong." Beversluis correctly notes that Lewis's version of the moral argument depends upon two claims: that morality itself is objective and that an objective moral law must be grounded in a supernatural reality. Lewis begins by noting that almost all our moral arguments presuppose certain principles. Quarreling, as opposed to fighting, loses its point unless we have some shared standard in the light of which to conduct our argument. These standards—what Lewis calls the law of nature in *Mere Christianity*—cannot be subjective; that is, they cannot be grounded ultimately in our tastes, preferences, attitudes, or decisions. Not if moral argument is to be meaningful.

Thus far so good, I think—though Beversluis does not. He contends that, when Lewis argues that subjectivist moral theories cannot account for our sense of moral obligation or the possibility of moral argument, he is guilty of "irresponsible writing." "To give vent to so ill-considered an opinion is to betray either that one knows next to nothing about ethical theory or that one simply chooses to ignore inconvenient points of view."

Lewis is mistaken, Beversluis contends, because he overlooks *objectivist* moral theories (from Aristotle to the utilitarians) which have gotten along quite well without any grounding in the supernatural. One suspects, however, that Beversluis has missed an important point. The long list of such objectivist but possibly naturalistic moral theories that he offers is, for the most part, a list of *normative* ethical theories. Almost all of them could be held, as a normative position, by either a subjectivist or an objectivist. Lewis's point in this argument is not normative but *metaethical*. It is that, whatever our normative ethic may be, we will not do justice to our moral experience if we hold it as a matter of taste or preference, attitude or decision of principle. Naturally, this claim is arguable and has often been argued, but it is neither silly nor naive. I suspect, indeed, that it is correct.

But a moral argument for that Something directing the universe needs more than the case for an objective moral law; it needs a Lawgiver. And Lewis does not, I think, satisfactorily bridge this gap. Contrary, however, to what Beversluis and some other readers have thought, I am not certain that Lewis really thought he had bridged it. How get from the objective moral law to the divine Lawgiver? In *Miracles* Lewis suggests that if our conscience were itself a product of nature (which is nonmoral), we could have no confidence in the objectivity of its judgments. What he means, I think, is clearer in *Mere Christianity*, and it is essentially a claim about what best makes sense of our moral experience. Knowing ourselves to be under a moral law, we have learned something about ourselves that we know only as "insiders." An external observer studying human behavior could only chart what we do; for an understanding of our sense that we act in accord with a sense of obligation he would have to rely on our own reports.

That is to say, studying human beings in the way we might study cabbages, trees, earthquakes, tides, glaciers, or (probably) wolves will not account for human moral experience. We cannot explain it in terms of natural phenomena or the methods by which we examine those phenomena. We can account for it only if we assume that there is more to human nature than can be found in the rest of the natural world. And therefore—and here is the gap that is not, I think, really bridged—we cannot account for human nature if we understand it as the product of the rest of nature. We can account for our moral experience—a surd in the rest of the natural world—only if we assume that Something beyond the natural world directs and communicates with us through our sense of moral obligation.

I agree with Beversluis that this final move, at least as I have described it, is not rationally conclusive. But there is more than that to be said about it. For one thing, if as an argument it is not conclusive, as a "consideration sufficient to determine the intellect" (to use John Stuart Mill's phrase), it may still be weighty. What is worth noting is the way in which Lewis here appeals to an impulse that is very basic to religious belief. If he is not giving us an argument that admits of no disagreement, he *is* providing some sense of why believers of many stripes have felt that the "lower" cannot explain the "higher," however much the great evolutionary myth (whose funeral oration Lewis composed in one of his essays) may claim that it can.

It is not logically impossible that the lower should ground the higher, but Lewis has offered one sort of consideration that may help us explain our uneasiness with the idea that it does. He is asking us to imagine the universe in two quite different ways and consider, then, which most plausibly accounts for our experience—and, in particular here, our moral experience. Notice that this is in many ways not simply an argument but an exercise of the imaginative powers something like that suggested by Lewis in *The Discarded Image* when he described the medieval model of the universe.

> If the reader will suspend his disbelief and exercise his imagination ...even for a few minutes, I think he will become aware of the vast readjustment involved in a perceptive reading of the old poets. He will find his whole attitude to the universe inverted. In modern, that is, in evolutionary, thought Man stands at the top of a stair whose foot is lost in obscurity; in this, he stands at the bottom of a stair whose top is invisible with light.

It is possible that Lewis never really decided whether he was offering only an argument that appealed to logic or whether he was offering something more like a consideration that might incline the intellect to a certain view. At certain places—chiefly in *Miracles* and *Mere Christianity*—it seems to be the former. But in *The Problem of Pain*, he clearly states that coming to think of morality in the way he does is not required by logical reasoning alone. Someone may refuse, he says, "if not without violence to his own nature, yet without absurdity." We may miss the truth to which our moral experience points, but there is no logical argument that can compel us to see it. Similarly, in his essay "Transposition," he suggests that we may deliberately refuse "to understand things from above" and continue to inhabit a natural world that is "all fact and no meaning." It is imagination that is the organ of meaning, and we can refuse to image the world in certain ways.

Most important of all, in *The Abolition of Man*—a book sadly underrated and in some ways misunderstood by Beversluis—Lewis, having put forward an argument for the objectivity of moral norms, writes: "I may add that though I myself am a Theist, and indeed a Christian, I am not here attempting any indirect argument for Theism." If this contradicts, as it may, the thrust of his argument in *Mere Christianity*, it is nevertheless more likely to be his considered position. In an essay, "The Poison of Subjectivism," he likewise declines to move from the existence of the moral law to the existence of God (for the very good theological reason that this might seem to make God bound by the moral law), and he contents himself with laying down "two negations: that God neither *obeys* nor *creates* the moral law." And, of course, if God does not create the moral law, logic cannot require that we move from the existence of that law to the existence of God.

Lewis's argument from reason is very much like his argument from morality. He argues—in many of his essays, and, especially, in chapter three of *Miracles*—that we could never trust the conclusions our rational powers reach if reason itself could be fully accounted for as the result of irrational causes—which, according to Lewis, means that reason could not be explained if it were the product of nature. To account for reason we must suppose that there is a realm other than the natural. It is this argument that triggered the famous exchange between Lewis and Elizabeth Anscombe, an exchange that Beversluis recounts.

Anscombe targeted two points at which Lewis's argument was particularly vulnerable. She noted that to say that reason was the product of nature might be to say that it had *non*rational causes, but that was quite different from holding that it was *ir*rationally caused. This objection, though on target, is easily dealt with. One simply changes the argument to read non- rather than irrational. But that leaves us with the more crucial issue: is it plausible that our rational faculty should have grown out of or been produced by a "lower," *non*rational world? Anscombe argued that there was no logical reason why this should not happen. For Lewis to claim, as he had, that the validity of our reasoning (and the naturalist's reasoning) would be undercut if reason were the product of nonrational nature was, Anscombe correctly noted, to confuse *reasons* and *causes*. Whatever the cause of our reasoned conclusions, their validity cannot be determined simply by tracing the causes that moved us to think this way.

The old joke about the man whose car got a flat tire in front of a mental institution makes Anscombe's point: changing the tire, the man had the misfortune to have all four lugs roll off the road and into a ditch where he could not find them. Cursing his misfortune, the man was helped by the timely suggestion of a resident who had been watching. Why not, the resident of the institution suggested, take one lug from each of the other three wheels and secure each tire with three lugs until he could get to the nearest town. The obvious sanity of this solution impressed the man, and he thanked the resident while quite obviously failing to keep from his face a look of surprise that such a rational solution should have come from this source. "Well look," responded the resident, "I may be mad, but I'm not crazy." Who knows why he offered the suggestion, what delusion may have led him to intervene? Whatever the cause, the rationality of his suggestion did not depend on it.

Lewis realized that Anscombe had fingered a serious weakness in the argument, which he revised in a later edition of *Miracles*. But he continued to believe that the argument had a point. An argument's validity, he granted, is a function solely of the structure of the argument itself. That validity cannot be determined by investigating the causes that led the arguer to think in this way. Nevertheless, Lewis noted, when I think a valid thought, the event of my thinking (though not the thought's validity) is subject to explanation in terms of nonrational causes. Suppose my thinking this (valid) thought can be *fully* accounted for in terms of nonrational causes, is this ground for worry? Lewis thought so; for in that case it would be a felicitous but accidental circumstance if I happened to be caused to think what (on other grounds having to do with the structure of the argument) we know to be true.

That Lewis has a point seems clear, though here, as in the argument from morality, I think it is not so much a conclusive argument as a consideration that may help to determine the intellect. Beversluis, on the other hand, thinks it largely worthless. He notes that events can be explained in many different ways and from many points of view. They can even, he says, be "fully" explained from any given point of view without invalidating other perspectives.

> Take the string quartets of Beethoven. There is a sense in which one would be on perfectly safe ground in claiming that they can be fully accounted for in purely casual terms.

Beethoven, one might say, composed them because of an irresistible creative urge that allowed him to do nothing else even
to the point of neglecting his health and business affairs. He
was "driven" to compose music. In this sense, his string quar-
tets are, in principle, fully explicable in terms of his psychological and temperamental makeup. *Fully* but not *merely*.

"*Fully* means 'exhaustively' *only from a particular point of view*."
Other explanations, almost without limit, are also possible:

> He needed extra money, he was bent on convincing his critics
> that his deafness had not deprived him of his creative talent, he
> was trying to catch up with Haydn, he was obsessed with com-
> posing for string instruments, and so on. All these explanations
> "fully explicate" the composition of the quartets. But they are
> not mutually exclusive. They are not even in competition.

Beversluis's view is possible, but hardly as obvious as he suggests.
Not everyone will be satisfied to understand "fully" to mean
"exhaustively, but only from a particular point of view." For this
leads to the possible but puzzling circumstance that continued to
worry Lewis: that the event of my thinking a true thought (true
according to the canons of rational argument) might be fully
explained as the product of nonrational causes. Possible—and
therefore Lewis can offer no conclusive argument to the contrary.
Possible, but a felicitous happenstance—and therefore Lewis does
offer a consideration that might again lead one to wonder whether
anything less than Reason could explain reason, whether the
"higher" could be adequately explained in terms of the "lower."
Lewis would never have denied that our thinking was conditioned

by many nonrational causes, but he continued—with good reason—to puzzle over a view that tried to "fully explain" thought in such terms.

Lewis's third argument is quite a different one, and it grows out of the Augustinian and Romantic elements in his thought; it is the argument from desire. Here again, Beversluis sees that the argument is not a conclusive proof, but he is largely blinded to its significance. The theme of "longing for joy" is present in many of Lewis's writings and is developed most systematically in *The Pilgrim's Regress*, *Surprised by Joy*, and "The Weight of Glory." It is, in large part, St. Augustine's theme: "You have made us for yourself, and our hearts are restless until they can find peace in you."

Beversluis creates distinctions that are, for the most part, artificial between Lewis's development of this theme in different writings. The nature of the argument itself is reasonably clear: human beings, if they will investigate honestly the longing of their hearts, will find within themselves a desire that no finite object can satisfy. They may try various possible satisfactions—pleasure, power, knowledge, fame—but these will all, finally, fail to satisfy. They will then, if they are honest to their experience, be led to conclude that the human heart must be made for a joy greater than any finite object.

Now it is no very powerful philosophic achievement to see the weakness in this argument, stated as baldly as I have put it. Lewis himself sees, as Beversluis notes, that the argument will work only if we add the premise that Lewis several times quotes from Aristotle: "Nature makes nothing in vain." If we find ourselves with a longing that no finite object can satisfy, and if such a longing natural to human nature cannot be in vain and must have its fulfillment, then it is reasonable to conclude that there must be something beyond the natural world that will satisfy this longing. This is a reasonable conclusion but not the only possible one. We might also conclude—as has been the modern fashion—that the world is absurd and the human being a vain and futile creature, driven by a longing that cannot be satisfied. We might picture the human being not as St. Augustine did but as the Faustian man who could never find a moment in which to rest the heart, a moment so lovely that he would say to it, "stay a while." Lewis recognizes this possibility but thinks there is good reason (even if not conclusive reason) to side with Augustine. He raises the question and offers his answer in a paragraph in "The Weight of Glory."

> Do what they will, then, we remain conscious of a desire which no happiness will satisfy. But is there any reason to suppose that reality offers any satisfaction to it? "Nor does the being hungry prove that we have bread." But I think it may be urged that this misses the point. A man's physical hunger does not prove that that man will get any bread; he may die of starvation on a raft in the Atlantic. But surely a man's hunger does prove that he comes of a race which repairs its body by eating and inhabits a world where eatable substances exist. In the same way, though I do not believe (I wish I did) that my desire for Paradise proves that I shall enjoy it, I think it a pretty good indication that such a thing exists and that some men will. A man may love a woman and not win her; but it would be very odd if the phenomenon called "falling in love" occurred in a sexless world.

Beversluis, commenting on just this paragraph, insists—rightly, no doubt—that the fact of hunger does not prove that there is food. But would we be entirely foolish and unreasonable to think, with Lewis, that it offers "a pretty good indication" that there is something like food? We would not. Though, to be sure, we would, from the start, be presupposing that our universe was *not* a vain and futile place—presupposing, that is, something like the end we hoped to demonstrate.

The argument is really an invitation, and it is no accident that "The Weight of Glory" is a sermon in which Lewis admits that he is trying "to weave a spell." But, as he tells his listeners, "remember your fairy tales. Spells are used for breaking enchantments as well as for inducing them. And you and I have need of the strongest spell that can be found to wake us from the evil enchantment of worldliness which has been laid upon us for nearly a hundred years." For Beversluis, however, the argument is "simply adolescent disenchantment elevated to cosmic status." Well, that is possible. But if the argument is an invitation, we will have to consider it and see what we think. Lewis does not suppose that he is exploring an experience that is solely his own or just having an attack of adolescent nostalgia. He supposes that if we examine our heart we will find there—manifested no doubt in quite different ways—the longing he writes of and seeks to evoke.

At a lesser level we could say of his argument here what Dorothy Sayers wrote of Dante: "The *Commedia* is at the same time intensely personal and magnificently public.... Dante's experience is personal, but it is not in the least private; it is universal, and he intends it to be thus understood." Dante's love for Beatrice leads him to God, but, of course—and this is part of Beversluis's criticism—some loves might lead away from rather than to God. How shall we distinguish that desire which is truly part of our created nature, the desire for the fulfillment proper to creatures such as we are, the desire for God—how to distinguish this from desires that, because they finally lead away from God, must be termed profoundly *un*natural? Sayers offers a clue: "There is no more insidious enemy of the true Beatrice than the false Beatrice who bears to her so deceptive a superficial likeness. The two are distinguished most readily and surely by their effects—the false images turning for ever inwards in narrowing circles of egotism; the true working for ever outwards to embrace the Creator and all creation." There again, in effect, is the invitation: to see whether any object other than God can truly satisfy the desire of our heart and, in satisfying it, enrich, broaden, and purify our love.

SUFFERING AND THE JOURNEY TOWARD GOD

As an apologist for the faith, Lewis does more than offer these three arguments for believing in God's existence; he also considers—and is troubled by—one of the strongest arguments *against* God's existence: the fact of evil and pain in our world. We are tempted to think that a God both wholly good and all-powerful should have been able to do better. One of Lewis's first apologetic works, *The Problem of Pain*, was devoted to this question, and he continued to probe it in some of his later writings, especially *Till We Have Faces* and *A Grief Observed*.

Beversluis, ever given to simplifying matters for his nonphilosophical readers, divides the possibilities into two positions, which he terms Platonist and Ockhamist. The Platonist, in his sense, "holds that the term *good* when applied to God cannot mean something radically different from what it means when applied to men." If God is to be called good, it will have to be in our ordinary sense, and there can be no special pleading that permits God to do what we ordinarily call evil. For the Ockhamist in Beversluis's sense, the word "*good* when applied to God *does* mean something radically different from what it means when applied to human beings." Beversluis is persuaded that an orthodox Christian must be an Ockhamist. "Orthodox Christians unhesitatingly affirm that obedience to God is absolute and unconditional. He is to be obeyed because he is God, not because we have judged him good by some human standard." (Again, we should keep reminding ourselves that, according to our author, it is Lewis who is guilty of oversimplification.)

Indeed, the Platonist and Ockhamist positions, thus described, so fully circumscribe the boundaries of possible positions that Beversluis can quickly confront Lewis with a dilemma: "either Lewis is a Platonist or he is not. If he is, then he should insist upon the ordinary meanings of ethical terms and draw whatever conclusions about God's goodness they require. If he is not, then he is of course free to redefine ethical terms in any way he sees fit. But in redefining them, he is no longer operating within our shared moral vocabulary...."

Beversluis contends that late in his life Lewis tried to switch from his earlier Platonist view. Overcome by grief at the loss of his wife, Lewis struggled to believe that God was good in the face of such loss—and finally, and somewhat pathetically, held on to faith by declining to judge God according to our ordinary standards of goodness. This, at any rate, is Beversluis's claim. The shift in Lewis's thinking comes in *A Grief Observed* or, more precisely pinpointed, half way through the book. In the first half of the book Lewis is still the same old Platonist; in the second half "everything changes" and he switches to an Ockhamist view. True, even in the last half of the book his acceptance of Ockhamism is "half-hearted"; of course, he still casts "wistful backward glances at the Platonic view"; indeed, he himself "was apparently not aware of the decisive reversal of his thought in the second half of this book."

What shall we say of this thesis? That Beversluis's credentials as a serious expositor are more than ever in doubt. Lewis may or may not have managed to deal effectively with the problem of evil, but Beversluis's argument can hardly be accepted. It is important to remember that for Lewis there is no problem of pain except for the believer. We do not come to faith only if we solve this problem; rather, having been driven to believe on other grounds, we then have two awkward facts—pain and God—with which to come to terms. We must say that faith "creates, rather than solves, the problem of pain, for pain would be no problem unless side by side with our daily experience of this painful world, we had received what we think a good assurance that ultimate reality is righteous and loving."

If, then, we come to believe in a God of goodness, love, and mercy, how shall we deal with the fact of pain? Lewis was never either Platonist or Ockhamist in the simple senses used by Beversluis. In *The Problem of Pain*, Lewis set forth a position that, though he deepened, he never gave up. God's goodness cannot be utterly different from our understanding of goodness, for then we could mean little by calling him good. Yet, at the same time, any believer will admit that what seems to us good may often not really be good in the eyes of a holy and wise God. This means that the believer, having experienced not only pain but also the goodness and beauty of his Lord, is committed to a journey, a pilgrimage: gradually coming to know better the God whose goodness he trusts. The image of growth was present already in *The Problem of Pain*, where Lewis uses an analogy from human experience. Suppose that a "man of inferior moral standards enters the society of those who are better and wiser than he and gradually learns to accept *their* standards," how shall we describe his journey into self-understanding? He does not think that he has simply been asked to give up his own views about goodness; rather, he sees that he is gradually moving in the direction of greater goodness. His standards are gradually transformed and, sometimes, even reversed, but he himself recognizes that he is moving toward the good.

> It is in the light of such experiences that we must consider the goodness of God. Beyond all doubt, His idea of "goodness" differs from ours; but you need have no fear that, as you approach it, you will be asked simply to reverse your moral standards. When the relevant difference between the Divine ethics and our own appears to you, you will not, in fact, be in any doubt that the change demanded of you is in the direction you already call "better." The Divine "goodness" differs from ours, but it is not sheerly different: it differs from ours not as white from black but as a perfect circle from a child's first attempt to draw a wheel. But when the child has learned to draw, it will know that the circle it then makes is what it was trying to make from the very beginning.

One could devote a lifetime to learning to draw that perfect circle, and, similarly, the believer devotes an entire life to coming to know better the goodness—indeed, the strange goodness—of God. The believer is not likely to—and certainly need not—live out this journey in the way Beversluis says an "orthodox Christian" must: "Good soldiers do not raise searching questions about their orders; they obey them." The believer may prefer familial imagery: loving the parent, and being assured on other grounds that the parent wishes nothing but good for him, he may nevertheless often struggle to trust the parent whose goodness is not mere kindness and is not, therefore, always readily apparent.

Lewis's later writings powerfully depict such a struggle. If God intends that we should reach the fulfillment for which we are created, that we should delight fully in and give ourselves wholly to him, our swollen egos are often reluctant to see this journey through. For Lewis our reluctance is usually grounded in possessiveness. To put it simply, we love other things and people more than we love God, and we struggle with all our might to hang on to them and find a sense in which to call them "ours." They are created goods, gifts of God, and it is not bad to love them; indeed, not to feel "the tether and pang of the particular" would be less than human. But because, in St. Augustine's terms, we love them inordinately, we suffer when we lose them—even if that loss is part of our journey toward fulfillment in God.

In *The Four Loves*, Lewis powerfully depicts the necessary but painful transformation of our natural loves as they are taken up into a life of love for God. This process, the conversion of our natural loves and transformation of them into modes of charity, "will always involve a kind of death." But here again, painful as this "kind of death" may be, Lewis sees it as part of the believer's pilgrimage toward God, part of the journey by which we come to know better the goodness of God. The image of the perfect circle and the child's first attempt to draw, used by Lewis in *The Problem of Pain*, is given a human face in *The Four Loves*.

> We were made for God. Only by being in some respect like Him, only by being a manifestation of His beauty, loving kindness, wisdom, or goodness, has any earthly Beloved excited our love. It is not that we have loved them too much, but that we did not quite understand what we were loving. It is not that we shall be asked to turn from them, so dearly familiar, to a Stranger. When we see the face of God we shall know that we have always known it.

First, though, we ourselves must get a *human* face. Lewis's most haunting depiction of the movement toward God is in *Till We Have Faces*. Orual, overcome by the cruelty of the gods who seem to take from us all whom we love, writes her book and makes her case against the gods. Our misery, she writes, is that there should be gods at all, for there's not room in the same world for them and us. (Notice that this is simply a powerful way of phrasing what Beversluis regards as the "orthodox Christian" view: that God and human beings do not share a common moral world.) But the gods have the last word, and good for Orual that they do. She comes— most painfully—to learn that the problem lay in the possessive quality of her loves. Because her loves were swollen and bloated, because she was struggling to live independently and fashion life solely according to her own conception of goodness, the process of transformation could only be painful. She could not come to know the gods and see their beauty fully until she herself, having given up the falsifying illusion of independence, was truly able to see. "How can they meet us face to face till we have faces?" Orual has been stripped naked before the gods, and the carefully crafted speech that had lain at the center of her soul for years has been revealed for the sham it is, when she finally meets the god. And then, nothing remains to be said.

> I ended my first book with the words *no answer*. I know now, Lord, why you utter no answer. You are yourself the answer. Before your face questions die away. What other answer would suffice? Only words, words; to be led out to battle against other words.

One might picture this as Beversluis's Ockhamist capitulating before God, but it would be an insensitive reader who ended *Till We Have Faces* thinking that. Sacrifice indeed—that Orual must make. But she sees that the god is beautiful (though dreadful), and she sees that she too has become beautiful. She has become, that is, what she had always wanted to be—every bit as much a fruition of her desire as the perfect circle completes the child's first attempt at drawing. Her knowledge of the gods has been deepened and transformed until she sees what readers of Narnia learn about the great lion Aslan: that though he's no tame lion and could hardly be called safe, he is good.

If any reader of *The Four Loves* and *Till We Have Faces* is still able to believe that a crucial shift in Lewis's thinking takes place at the midpoint of *A Grief Observed* …well, we must consign such a reader to Beversluis. Powerful as it is, *A Grief Observed* continues and develops the line of thought already set forth decades earlier in *The Problem of Pain*: only because we believe on other grounds in a good God does pain seem such a problem. A good God, who is more than a kindly fellow and who truly desires for us the fulfillment of our nature, will be neither tame nor safe. But the process of coming to know that God ever more fully, if we persevere on our journey even in the face of great temptation to lose heart, will find its completion when we see the face on which we have always longed to look—not the face of a stranger but the face that we ourselves know to be both good and beautiful. Even then, though, a face terrible in its goodness. For, as Lewis wrote more than a decade before Aslan came bounding into the Narnia stories,

> I think the lion, when he has ceased to be dangerous, will still be awful: indeed, that we shall then first see that of which the present fangs and claws are a clumsy, and satanically perverted, imitation. There will still be something like the shaking of a golden mane: and often the good Duke will say, "Let him roar again."

To set the Christian life into the context of a journey toward a Goodness that is alien yet recognizable as good is to be relieved of Beversluis's false dilemma between Platonist and Ockhamist.

But it is not, of course, to be relieved of the perils of the journey itself. Throughout, the struggle to offer in concert both mind and heart to God will be just that—a struggle. And despite the weaknesses, inadequacies, even faults in Lewis's writings and person, those who come to the writings for guidance along the way will not, I think, be seriously misled and will often be helped immeasurably. The truth about the journey, and the truth about the relation of mind and heart in the Christian life, must finally be lived. Lewis's own formulation suggests as much: "In relation to the philosophical premises, a Christian's faith is of course excessive: in relation to what is sometimes shown him, it is perhaps just as often defective." That was written by a man who believed what the children in Narnia learn about Aslan: that the longer you know him, the bigger he gets.

23

(RE)READING AUGUSTINE'S *CONFESSIONS*

"And in all these things over which I range as I am consulting you I find no secure place for my soul except in you, and in you I pray that what is scattered in me may be brought together so that nothing of me may depart from you."

To reach a certain point in life, the point we describe as "middle age," is quite often to feel "scattered." One's energies are dispersed in countless different directions—work, whether paid or unpaid; children, whether relatively grown or still at home; parents, whose continuing claim on us is not diminished; friends, who may themselves be scattered hither and yon.

That sense of being "scattered" St. Augustine knew well, as the passage above from his *Confessions* demonstrates. He knew also what it means to have achieved a good deal but not to have found in such achievements the "sweetness" we seek. "I panted for honors, for money, for marriage, and you were laughing at me. I found bitterness and difficulty in following these desires, and your graciousness to me was shown in the way you would not allow me to find anything sweet which was not you." And he knew what it means to have come a long way, and, yet, to see a long road stretching out ahead. "It is one thing to see from a mountaintop in the forests the land of peace in the distance…, and it is another thing to hold to the way that leads there.…"

In his wonderful biography, *Augustine of Hippo*, Peter Brown notes that at the time Augustine wrote the *Confessions*, a time when he had only begun his work as a bishop of the church in North Africa, he had good reason to introduce himself to his fellow Christians. But, Brown writes, "only a very profound, inner reason would have led him to write a book such as the *Confessions*; he was entering middle-age." This alone might be reason enough for one who has never read the *Confessions*, or has read only as far as the conversion in Book VIII and missed the magnificent Book X, or has read the whole but cannot recall being either instructed or moved by it, to have another go at it. Perhaps one can even learn to say of this great work what Augustine says of God: "Late it was that I loved you, beauty so ancient and so new, late I loved you!"

Whatever reasons move us to take up the *Confessions*, there is much to be learned from the book that some regard as the first autobiography in our culture's history. Augustine asks of us a crucial decision: We must decide whether he is right to claim that the human heart—our heart—is driven by a longing to which only God answers. For if that is true, if we long to rest in One who is not an object of ordinary human experience, then we are given a sobering vision of life. Robert Meagher has described succinctly the choice with which Augustine presents us. Happiness requires that we, first, love the good rightly—which means, love God, who is the highest and unchanging good, above all else; and that we, second, "possess" the good we love. The pathos of our life is that—within human history—these two requirements are incompatible. Therefore we must choose either to love rightly but not possess the good we love, or to love a good that can be possessed but that cannot finally satisfy the heart's longing. "Here I have the power but not the wish to stay; there I wish to be but cannot: both ways, miserable."

Augustine, of course, made his decision, and the *Confessions* invites us to do likewise. Deferring "possession" of the good, Augustine comes to understand himself as a pilgrim. This man who, as Peter Brown puts it, "always resented travelling" and "associated it with a sense of protracted labour and of the infinite postponement of his dearest wishes" will now come to use it as "the most characteristic image of the spiritual life in his middle age." For those who suppose themselves to have graduated beyond the sentiment of the hymn, "I'm but a stranger here; heav'n is my home," a dose of the *Confessions*, reminding us that we are pilgrims and foreigners, may be salutary. Not that Augustine himself has mastered the art of loving this world without clinging to it. He knows that he is deeply drawn to the delights of our world, and he often has a hard time knowing whether to enjoy these delights or to "pass on" from them to the One who gives them and to whom they point. He knows the many occasions when he is "sitting at home and…[his] attention is attracted by a lizard catching flies or by a spider entangling them in his web," and he worries lest he delight too much in these curiosities and forget God. Augustine does not resolve the problem of how to love all else in relation to God, but he invites us unforgettably into reflecting on this central problem for human life and love.

And he manages to do all this while ultimately directing our attention away from ourselves, away from the narcissism that is natural to the young and pitiable in the middle-aged. Few readers find the long interpretation of Genesis in books XII and XIII of the *Confessions* to be the high point of the work; indeed, most readers simply skip these last two books. Such a choice is understandable;

certainly they could never be as gripping as the story Augustine tells in the earlier books. And, indeed, interpreters have often been puzzled, wondering what Augustine can possibly be doing. Some have even been drawn to the view that Augustine is simply "clearing his desk," seizing the opportunity to answer questions that have been directed to him.

Perhaps so. We cannot say for certain. But I suspect that we do him an injustice if we do not see more than this. Having drawn his readers into pondering their own deepest longings, Augustine also sets them free of such endless introspection. They are travelers—on the way toward God. Hence, their attention—our attention—is directed to what is outside the self: from the mystery of the single individual ("man who is only a small portion of what you have created") to the entire creation, all part of a vast movement back to the Creator. To be delivered from constant attention to one's self, to have one's gaze redirected toward God, toward that "beauty so ancient and so new," is a great gift to be given at any age.

NOTES

1

1 Xenophon, *The Oeconomicus*, in *Memorabilia and Oeconomicus*, trans. by E. C. Marchant (London: William Heinemann, 1923), III, 12.

2 Mary Hunt, *Fierce Tenderness: A Feminist Theology of Friendship* (New York: Crossroad, 92).

3 Aristotle, *Nicomachean Ethics*, trans. Martin Ostwald (Indianapolis: Bobbs-Merrill Library of Liberal Arts, 1962), VIII, 7. Future citations will be given by book and chapter number in parentheses within the body of the text.

4 C. S. Lewis, *The Four Loves* (New York: Harcourt Brace Jovanovich, Inc., 1960), p. 99ff.

5 Cited in Ronald A. Sharp, *Friendship and Literature* (Durham, NC: Duke University Press, 1986), p. 73.

6 J. B. Priestley, *Talking: An Essay* (New York and London: Harper & Brothers, 1926), p. 59.

7 Lillian B. Rubin, "Women, Men, and Intimacy," in *Eros, Agape, and Philia*, ed. Alan Soble (New York: Paragon House, 1989), p. 22.

8 Deborah Tannen, *You Just Don't Understand: Women and Men in Conversation* (New York: William Morrow, 1990), p. 25.

9   *Arizona Star*, June 8, 1992, p. 3B.

10   Katherine Paterson, *Bridge to Terabithia* (New York: Avon Books, 1972).

2

1   St. Augustine *City of God*, XII, 22.

2   Perhaps the classic treatment of this theme in the twentieth century has been volume 1 of Reinhold Niebuhr's *The Nature and the Destiny of Man* (New York: Charles Scribner's Sons, 1941).

3   Dorothy Sayers, "The Dogma is the Drama," in *The Whimsical Christian* (New York: Macmillan, 1978), p. 23–28.

4   The classic works that set the terms of discussion about *eros* and *agape* were Anders Nygren's *Agape and Eros* (London: SPCK, 1953) and John Burnaby's *Amor Dei* (London: Hodder & Stoughton, 1938). A careful summary of the issues involved is Gene Outka's *Agape* (New Haven and London: Yale University Press, 1972). Equally influential works focusing on structures and institutions were Ernst Troeltsch's *The Social Teachings of the Christian Churches* (New York: Macmillan, 1931) and H. Richard Niebuhr's *Christ and Culture* (New York: Harper & Brothers, 1951). A work that captures both personal and institutional concerns is James Gustafson's *Christ and the Moral Life* (New York: Harper & Row, 1968).

5   John Updike, *Too Far To Go: The Maples Stories* (New York: Fawcett Crest, 1979). Most of the stories in this collection were first published separately in *The New Yorker*. A few were originally published elsewhere. The stories, taken as a whole, however, form a coherent narrative.

6   Margaret A. Farley, *Personal Commitments* (New York: Harper Collins, 1986), p. 40.

7   Ibid.

8   Denis de Rougemont, *Love in the Western World* (New York: Harper Colophon Books, 1974), p. 306. Few have, I think, been persuaded by de Rougemont's historical thesis about the myth of Tristan and romantic love, but the concluding chapters, in which de Rougemont turns to what might be called moral theology, are a probing analysis of the place of love and commitment in Christian marriage.

9   Niebuhr, *Nature and Destiny*, I, p. 175.

10 de Rougemont, *Love*, p. 309.

11 C. S. Lewis, *The Four Loves* (New York: Harcourt Brace Jovanovich, 1960), pp. 158–99.

12 de Rougemont, *Love*, p. 314.

13 Josef Pieper, *About Love* (Chicago: Franciscan Herald Press, 1974), pp. 121–122.

14 de Rougemont, *Love*, p. 308. It is important to note, lest we underestimate the mystery here, that de Rougemont adds: "And it may also be that nothing rewards our loss: we are among dimensions where ordinary worldly measures no longer avail."

15 de Rougemont, *Love*, p. 304.

16 Ibid.

17 Farley, *Personal Commitments*, p. 134.

3

1   Robert W. Jenson, "Faithfulness," *DIALOG*, 14 (Winter, 1975), p. 39.

2   Karl Barth, *Church Dogmatics*, Vol. III/4 (Edinburgh: T. & T. Clark, 1961), p. 116.

3   Eph. 5:32. Cf. Barth, p. 123: "Humanity as fellow-humanity, here actualised in the encounter between male and female, and supremely in marriage, is the real witness (apprehended or otherwise) to the Alpha and Omega of the will and counsel of God, of His covenant with man. This is what we are told by Eph. 5:32."

4   Cf. Eph. 5:21–23.

5   Barth holds that this differentiation is to be observed throughout the whole of life (in which, after all, our fellow-humanity is enacted) and not only in marriage (the central expression of that fellow-humanity). I am not persuaded. Some of the New Testament passages speaking of male "headship" do seem to have in mind a range wider than marriage alone (e.g., I Tim. 2:11–15, I Cor. 14:33–36). But one can make

sense of such an extension of "headship" beyond marriage only, perhaps, within a society understood in organic, familial images. To the
degree that we genuinely manage to conceive of the church in such
terms—as a "body" in which membership means something quite different than it does in an association formed by social contract—the
concept of "headship" may still find applicability there. From that
question—with its implications for ordination—I prescind here, however. To imagine, though, that the man's "headship" must be enacted
throughout a society that is—quite properly and for good political
reasons—organized on a basis that is not organic or familial is to fail
to distinguish the different spheres of life in which our faithfulness
should be enacted in different ways. Krister Stendahl is therefore very
wide of the mark in arguing that commitment to any form of emancipation of women (e.g., in the political sphere) requires giving up the
concept of "headship" in all contexts (cf. *The Bible and the Role of
Women* [Philadelphia: Fortress Press, 1966], e.g., p. 40). This kind of
thinking is characteristic of those who attempt to proceed directly
from biblical texts to ethical reflection without passing their thought
through the alembic of ethical reflection.

6   Dorothy L. Sayers, *Gaudy Night* (New York: Avon Books, 1968).

7   Ibid., p. 323.

8   Ibid., p. 382.

9   Cf. the interesting appearance of this metaphor on p. 1 of Carol
Gilligan's *In A Different Voice: Psychological Theory and Women's
Development* (Cambridge, Mass. and London: Harvard University
Press, 1982): "Over the past ten years, I have been listening to people
talk about morality and about themselves. Halfway through that
time, I began to hear a distinction in these voices, two ways of speaking about moral problems, two modes of describing the relationship
between other and self. Differences represented in the psychological
literature as steps in a developmental progression suddenly appeared
instead as a contrapuntal theme, woven into the cycle of life and
recurring in varying forms in people's judgments, fantasies, and
thoughts."

10 Janice G. Raymond, *A Passion for Friends: Toward a Philosophy of
Female Affection* (Boston: Beacon Press, 1986), p. 13.

11   Mary Midgley and Judith Hughes, *Women's Choices: Philosophical Problems Facing Feminism* (New York: St. Martin's Press, 1983), p. 115.

12   Ibid., p. 185f.

13   C. S. Lewis, *Mere Christianity* (New York: Macmillan, 1960), p. 87f.

14   Helmut Thielicke, *The Ethics of Sex* (New York: Harper & Row, 1964), pp. 154–59 passim.

15   Gilligan, p. 2.

16   Ibid., p. 18.

17   But only at her best. Gilligan has a certain tendency to regard contextual thinking (characteristic of women) as superior, and her attitude toward "absolutes" (never very precisely characterized) suggests a lack of appreciation for their possible importance in an ethic of justice.

18   Gilligan, p. 165.

19   Carol McMillan, *Women, Reason and Nature: Some Philosophical Problems With Feminism* (Princeton: Princeton University Press, 1982).

20   Ibid., p. 41.

21   Ibid., p. 53. McMillan continues: "Disastrously, however, these ways of thinking and acting are being continually eroded by the wholesale emphasis in our society on methods and procedures appropriate to spheres of activities dominated by scientific method, technology and productivity goals."

22   Benjamin R. Barber, "Beyond the Feminist Mystique," *The New Republic* (July 11, 1983), p. 32.

23   Barth, p. 169.

24   Ibid., p. 175.

25   Ibid., p. 152.

26   Cf. Barth, p. 153: "The specific differentiation[s] particularly of male and female which are at issue in the divine command and its requirement of fidelity lie somewhere above and beyond the sphere in which such typologies are relatively possible and practicable."

27 Ibid., p. 154f.

28 G. K. Chesterton, *The Collected Works*, Vol. 1. Ed. David Dooley (San Francisco: Ignatius Press, 1986), pp. 186ff.

29 Barth, p. 172ff.

30 C. S. Lewis, *A Grief Observed* (London: Faber & Faber, 1966), p. 40ff.

4

1 Martin Luther, *Large Catechism*, I, p. 207.

2 "Revelation & Homosexual Experience: What Wolfhart Pannenberg says about this debate in the church," *Christianity Today*, 40 (November 11, 1996), p. 37.

3 Oliver O'Donovan, *The Desire of Nations: Rediscovering the Roots of Political Theology* (Cambridge University Press, 1996), p. 177.

4 C. S. Lewis, "Preface to the Paperback Edition," *The Screwtape Letters* (New York: Macmillan, 1973), p. x.

5 C. S. Lewis, *Surprised by Joy* (New York: Harcourt, Brace & World, Inc., 1955), p. 110. Cf. Plato's *Phaedrus*.

6 "The St. Andrew's Day Statement: An examination of the Theological Principles affecting the Homosexuality Debate." Published by a theological work group in response to the request of the Church of England Evangelical Council. (November 30, 1995), p. 6.

7 Victor Paul Furnish, *The Moral Teaching of Paul* (Nashville: Abingdon, 1979), p. 53.

8 Richard B. Hays, *The Moral Vision of the New Testament* (Harper San Francisco, 1996), p. 368f.

9 Thomas E. Schmidt, *Straight & Narrow?* (Downers Grove, IL: InterVarsity Press, 1995), p. 48.

10 C. S. Lewis, *Miracles* (New York: Macmillan, 1947), p. 166.

11 For a fuller discussion of this passage in its context, a discussion upon which I rely here, see Richard B. Hays, *The Moral Vision of the New Testament* (Harper San Francisco, 1996), pp. 383-389.

12 Ibid., p. 385.

13 Ibid., p. 382.

14 Mark D. Smith, "Ancient Bisexuality and the Interpretation of Romans 1:26-27," *Journal of the American Academy of Religion*, 64 (Summer, 1996), pp. 223–256.

15 Ibid., p. 243.

16 Ibid., p. 246.

17 Mary Stewart Van Leeuwen, "To Ask a Better Question: The Heterosexuality-Homosexuality Debate Revisted," *Interpretation*, 51 (April 1997), p. 144.

18 Smith, p. 248.

19 Van Leeuwen, p. 144.

20 Hays, p. 388.

21 Smith, p. 249.

22 Hays, p. 399.

6

1 P. D. James, *The Children of Men* (New York: Knopf, 1993).

2 Ibid., p. 153f.

3 Gabriel Marcel, "The Mystery of the Family," in *Homo Viator: Introduction to a Metaphysic of Hope* (New York: Harper Torchbooks, 1962), p. 88.

4 Ibid., p. 90.

5 Ibid., p. 88.

6 Ibid., p. 87. There is, of course, also a difference between a *brood* and a *large family*. And for those who take seriously the idea that the truest fidelity is to be creative—the idea that our own creativity participates in and mirrors the divine creative power—there is something to be said, at least in principle, for the large family. Marcel himself makes the point nicely in another essay, "The Creative Vow as the Essence of Fatherhood," also collected in *Homo Viator:* "[I]t would

be impossible to exaggerate the extent of the difference which separates a large family from a family of one or two children: a difference
comparable to that which in the philosophy of Bergson separates the
Enclosed from the Open. It is a difference of atmosphere in the first
place: that which exists between fresh air and the air in a confined
space. We must, however, go much further. By the multiplicity, the
unpredictable variety of the relationships which it embraces, the large
family really presents the character of a creation..." [p. 113].

7   Ibid., p. 91.

8   Ibid., p. 88.

9   *Washington Post*, August 7, 1975.

10   Gen. 1:24; 5:3.

11   Ps. 127:3.

12   Ps. 78:2–7.

13   Luke 11:27–28.

14   Eph. 6:4.

15   Aristotle, *Politics*, II:iii, 1261*b*. Cf. A.W. Price, *Love and Friendship in Plato and Aristotle* (Oxford: Clarendon Press, 1980), p. 188.

16   Michael Walzer, *Spheres of Justice* (New York: Basic Books, 1983), p. 238f.

17   Augustine, *City of God*, I, 29.

18   G. K. Chesterton, *What's Wrong with the World*, vol. 4 of *Collected Works* (San Francisco: Ignatius Press, 1987), p. 212.

19   Ibid., p. 65.

20   Ibid., p. 217f.

7

1   A version of this essay was first presented to the National Bioethics Advisory Commission in March of 1997. The Commission had specifically requested me to address the topic of cloning from a Protestant theological perspective, and other speakers were invited to address the topic from other perspectives.

2 In what follows I draw upon the argument of Oliver O'Donovan, *Begotten or Made?* (Oxford: Clarendon Press, 1984), p. 16f.

3 Ibid., p. 17.

4 Paul Ramsey, *Fabricated Man* (New Haven and London: Yale University Press, 1970), p. 72.

5 C. S. Lewis, *That Hideous Strength* (New York: Macmillan, 1965), p. 174.

6 O'Donovan, p. 1ff.

7 William F. May, *The Physician's Covenant* (Philadelphia: Westminster Press, 1983), p. 32.

8 Hans Jonas, "Philosophical Reflections on Experimenting with Human Subjects," in *Readings on Ethical and Social Issues in Biomedicine*, ed. Richard W. Wertz (Englewood Cliffs, NJ: Prentice Hall, 1973), p. 35.

8

1 Barbara Katz Rothman, *The Tentative Pregnancy: Prenatal Diagnosis and the Future of Motherhood* (New York: Penguin Books, 1987). Page references are given in parentheses within the body of the text.

9

1 C. S. Lewis, *Reflections on the Psalms* (New York: Harcourt, Brace & World, 1958), p. 57.

2 C. S. Lewis, *Christian Reflections*, ed. Walter Hooper (Grand Rapids, MI: Eerdmans, 1967), pp. 129–41. The essay is incomplete because several pages in the middle of the text were missing from the manuscript edited by Walter Hooper after Lewis's death.

3 Austin Farrer, "In His Image," in *C. S. Lewis at the Breakfast Table and Other Reminiscences*, ed. James T. Como (New York: Macmillan Collier Books, 1979), p. 243.

4 Cf. C. S. Lewis, *Letters to Malcolm: Chiefly on Prayer* (New York: Harcouort, Brace & World, 1963), p. 89: "*pleasures* are shafts of the glory as it strikes our sensibility."

5   To be technically correct, we must note that *Fear and Trembling* is one of Kierkegaard's pseudonymous works, published under the name of "Johannes de Silentio." On the significance of the pseudonyms hang some important questions in Kierkegaard scholarship. For my purposes here, however, it will be sufficient to think of Kierkegaard himself as the author.

6   Søren Kierkegaard, *Fear and Trembling*. Translated by Alastair Hannay (New York: Penguin Books, 1985), p. 68f.

7   Ibid., 70.

8   C. S. Lewis, *Miracles: A Preliminary Study* (New York: Macmillan, 1947), 67.

9   C. S. Lewis, "A Note on Jane Austen," *Selected Literary Essays*, ed. Walter Hooper (Cambridge University Press, 1969), p. 185f.

10   C. S. Lewis, "Addison," *Selected Literary Essays*, ed. Walter Hooper (Cambridge University Press, 1969), p. 167.

11   C. S. Lewis, *Surprised by Joy* (New York: Harcourt, Brace & World, Inc., 1955), p. 141–3.

12   Ibid., 143.

13   Ibid., 143f.

14   C. S. Lewis, *Poems*, ed. Walter Hooper (New York: Harcourt, Brace & World, 1964), p. 134.

15   C. S. Lewis, "Learning in War-Time," in *The Weight of Glory and Other Addresses* (Grand Rapids, MI: Eerdmans, 1965), p. 44.

16   C. S. Lewis, *The Screwtape Letters* (New York: Macmillan, 1961), p. 60.

17   Ibid., p. 58.

18   Ibid., p. 56.

19   C. S. Lewis, *Till We Have Faces: A Myth Retold* (New York and London: Harcourt Brace Jovanovich, 1956), p. 284.

20   C. S. Lewis, *The Pilgrim's Regress* (Grand Rapids, MI: Eerdmans, 1958), p. 198.

21 C. S. Lewis, "Preface to the Paperback Edition," *The Screwtape Letters*, ix.

22 C. S. Lewis, *The Last Battle* (New York: Macmillan, 1956), 149f.

23 C. S. Lewis, *A Grief Observed* (London: Faber & Faber, 1961), p. 44.

24 Ibid., 24.

25 C. S. Lewis, *The Four Loves* (New York: Harcourt Brace Jovanovich, 1960), p. 158.

26 Josef Pieper, *About Love*, trans. Richard and Clara Winston (Chicago: Franciscan Herald Press, 1974), p. 122.

27 *The Four Loves*, p. 191.

28 *Till We Have Faces*, p. 276.

29 *Letters of C. S. Lewis*, ed. W. H. Lewis (New York and London: Harcourt Brace Jovanovich, 1966), p. 274.

30 *Till We Have Faces*, p. 291.

31 *The Four Loves*, p. 169.

32 *Miracles*, p. 135.

11

1 Stephen Crites, "The Narrative Quality of Experience," *Journal of the American Academy of Religion*, 39 (1971).

2 C. S. Lewis, *The Problem of Pain* (New York: Macmillan, 1962), p. 115.

3 St. Augustine, *City of God*, XV, 1.

4 Langdon Gilkey, *Shantung Compound* (San Francisco: Harper & Row, 1975), p. 80.

5 Eph. 4:13.

6 Ps. 84:1–4.

7 Thomas Hobbes, *Man and Citizen*, ed. Bernard Gert (Garden City, NY: Doubleday Anchor, 1972), VIII, 1.

8   Thomas Hobbes, *The Elements of Law*, Part I, chap. 9, para. 21. Cited in Michael Walzer, *Radical Principles* (New York: Basic Books, 1980), p. 292.

9   Thomas Hobbes, *Leviathan*, ed. Michael Oakeshott (New York: Collier Books, 1962), chap. 11, p. 80.

10 Ps. 4:8.

11 C. S. Lewis, *The Pilgrim's Regress* (Grand Rapids, MI: Eerdmans, 1958), p. 198.

12 Josef Pieper, *About Love*, trans. Richard and Clara Winston (Chicago: Franciscan Herald Press, 1974), p. 122.

13 John Calvin, *Institutes of the Christian Religion*, Library of Christian Classics, vol. XX, ed. John T. McNeill, trans. Ford Lewis Battles (Philadelphia: Westminster Press, 1960), III, x, 6 (p. 725).

14 St. Augustine, *Confessions*, trans. Rex Warner (New York: New American Library, 1963), IV, 16 (p. 88).

15 Einar Billing, *Our Calling*, trans. Conrad Bergendoff (Philadelphia: Fortress Press, 1964), p. 24f.

16 Ibid., p. 34.

12

1   Philip Turner, *Sex, Money and Power* (Cambridge: Cowley Publications, 1985), p. 90.

2   See Martin Hengel, *Property and Riches in the Early Church* (Philadelphia: Fortress Press, 1974), p. 12ff.

3   Reinhold Niebuhr, *The Nature and Destiny of Man*, vol. 1 (New York: Scribner's, 1964), p. 219ff.

4   Turner, p. 92.

5   Luke Timothy Johnson, *Sharing Possessions* (Philadelphia: Fortress Press, 1981), p. 31.

6   *Ibid.*, p. 32.

7   *Ibid.*, pp. 36–37.

8   Clement of Alexandria, "The Rich Man's Salvation," in *Christian Ethics: Sources of the Living Tradition*, ed. Waldo Beach and H. Richard Niebuhr (New York: Ronald Press, 1973), p. 94. Subsequent references to this work will be cited parenthetically in the text.

9   Turner, pp. 88–90.

10 C. S. Lewis, "Williams and the Arthuriad," in *Arthurian Torso* (London: Oxford University Press, 1948), p. 134.

11 C. S. Lewis, *Mere Christianity* (New York: Macmillan, 1960), p. 62.

12 For a more detailed argument, see my essay "Is What Is Right for Me Right for All Persons Similarly Situated?" *Journal of Religious Ethics* 8 (1980): pp. 125–34.

13 C. S. Lewis, *Perelandra* (New York: Macmillan, 1965), p. 42. Subsequent references to this work will be made parenthetically in the text.

14 Emil Brunner, *Christianity and Civilisation*, Part 2: *Specific Problems* (London: Nisbet, 1949), pp. 8788.

15 Ibid., p. 93.

20

1   Marcus Aurelius, *Meditations*. trans. George Long (South Bend: Regnery/Gateway, 1965). All references to the *Meditations* will be given by book and paragraph number in parentheses within the body of the text.

2   Henry Dwight Sedgwick, *Marcus Aurelius* (Yale University Press, 1922), p. 12f.

3   Ibid., p. 256.

4   Matthew Arnold, *Essays in Criticism, First Series*. A Critical Edition ed. by Thomas Marion Hoctor (University of Chicago Press, 1964), p. 210.

5   Ibid., p. 217.

6   Ibid., p. 223.

7   Ibid., p. 224.

INDEX

143; female relationships of, 321–23, 326; friendship and, 11, 286, 290–91, 292–94; God and, 134–38, 163, 346–54; headship and, 47, 48, 51; human life and, 133–34; imaginative writings of, 332–33; Joy and, 136; literary criticism of, 319; longing for joy and, 335, 343–46; marriage and, 57; monotony and, 160; moral life and, 157–58; natural loves and love for God and, 138–41; as "popular" religious thinker, 123–24; psalms and, 151; psyche of, 325–26; religious belief and arguments of, 331–32; religious writings of, 123–24, 126–29; simplicity and generosity and, 192, 193; success of writings of, 132, 143; thought of, 2; trust and possessions and, 194–97; truth and, 156; vulnerability and, 173–74; Wilson's interpretation of life of, 323–25

Lewis, Warren, 320

liberal education, 177

liberal individualism, 218

life: affirmation of beauties of, 2; elements of everyday, 2; embeddedness of, 160–64, 166, 174; family bond and, 149; finitude of, 32; goal of, 25; goods in, 272; Jesus Christ and drama of, 26–27; ordinary decisions of, 131; ordinary pleasures of, 127, 134; paradox of, 31; possessions and, 185; religious,

300, 312; sources of, 25; suffering in, 2; ultimate truth of, 170; *See also* moral life; ordinary life

Lincoln, Abraham, 311

Lindskoog, Kathryn, 327–28

"Listen up, jerks! Share innermost feelings with her", 16

Locke, John, 265, 266

Logos, 334

longing for joy (Sehnsucht), 132–33, 335, 343–46

Lord's day, 211

love: Aristophanes' depiction of, 289; as central theme of biblical narrative, 205; commitment and, 30–31, 35; community and, 90–91; courtly, 32; divine, 32–33, 136; erotic, 9; fidelity and, 33; forms of, 9; friendship and, 138–39, 290–91; God's, 35, 38; meaning of, 61; mutual, 38, 62–63; parent-child bond and, 96; perfection of, 33–34; procreation and, 104–5; self-, 14; self-giving, 94–95; sexual, 61–62; sufferings and, 154–55; *See also* eros

Love and Friendship (Bloom), 285; difficulty with, 286

Luke, 172, 183

Luther, Martin, 59, 66; moral life and, 155; O'Donovan's use of, 215; problem of possessions and, 193; vocation and, 176, 179

Lutheranism, 178

moderation, 190

modern identity, 263–74; central
features of, 264; development
of, 272–73; features of,
267–68; goods of, 273–74;
inwardness and, 267, 269;
moral sources of, 271

modes of charity, 140, 141, 350

Montaigne, Michel de, 265–66

Moore, Janie, 321, 322, 323, 324,
326

Moore, Paddy, 321

morality, 253; commitments of
individuals and, 242; fulfillment and, 271; God's existence
and nature of, 335, 338–42;
two-tier theory of, 247; universality in, 242–43, 243–48

moral life: communitarian vision
of, 269; Jesus Christ and, 27;
meaning of, 153–55; place of
everyday experience in, 2;
requirements of, 157–58; See
also life; ordinary life

The Moral Teaching of Paul
(Furnish), 64

Moses, 208

mothers: freedom of, 113–14; relation of fetus to, 113; relationship between children and, 15,
50; sponsorship provided by,
238; See also wives; women

moving, 160, 164–65, 170,
172–75

Mrs. Doubtfire, 234–35

multiculturalism, 259

multinational empires, 256

The Music Man, 329

Narnia stories, 131–32, 320, 324,
325, 352, 353

National Institute of Coordinated
Experiments (NICE), 106

"natural", 73

naturalism, 333

natural law, 208, 308

natural loves: conversion of, 350;
love for God and, 138–41

natural right, 219–20

Nearby Guy, 231

Neuhaus, Richard, 177–78

New Father, 229, 230–31, 232

Newsweek, 145

New Testament, 46, 73, 75, 152,
176, 187, 313

NICE. See National Institute of
Coordinated Experiments

Nicene Creed, 107

Nicomachean Ethics (Aristotle), 8

Niebuhr, H. Richard, 300

Niebuhr, Reinhold, 31, 184

Nietzsche, Friedrich, 11

Ninevites, 245

Noah, 221

Norse myth, 305

Novak, Michael: capitalism and,
275; problems with argument
of, 281–82; review of Business
as a Calling: Work and the
Examined Life of, 275–84